AUCTION QUOTAS AND UNITED STATES
TRADE POLICY

POLICY ANALYSES IN INTERNATIONAL ECONOMICS 19

AUCTION QUOTAS AND UNITED STATES TRADE POLICY

C. Fred Bergsten
Kimberly Ann Elliott
Jeffrey J. Schott
Wendy E. Takacs

INSTITUTE FOR INTERNATIONAL ECONOMICS
WASHINGTON, DC
SEPTEMBER 1987

C. Fred Bergsten is Director of the Institute for International Economics. He was formerly Assistant Secretary of the Treasury for International Affairs; Assistant for International Economic Affairs to the National Security Council; and a Senior Fellow at The Brookings Institution.

Kimberly Ann Elliott, a Research Associate at the Institute, is a coauthor of Trade Protection in the United States *(1986), and* Economic Sanctions Reconsidered *(1985).*

Jeffrey J. Schott is a Research Fellow at the Institute. He was formerly a Senior Associate at the Carnegie Endowment for International Peace and an international economist at the US Treasury Department.

Wendy E. Takacs, a Visiting Fellow at the Institute, is Associate Professor of Economics at the University of Maryland.

INSTITUTE FOR INTERNATIONAL ECONOMICS
11 Dupont Circle, NW
Washington, DC 20036
(202) 328–9000 Telex: 248329 CEIP Fax: (202) 328–5432

C. Fred Bergsten, *Director*
Kathleen A. Lynch, *Director of Publications*
Ann L. Beasley, *Production Manager*

The Institute for International Economics was created, and is principally funded, by the German Marshall Fund of the United States.

The views expressed in this publication are those of the authors. This publication is part of the overall program of the Institute, as endorsed by its Board of Directors, but does not necessarily reflect the views of individual members of the Board or the Advisory Committee.

Library of Congress Cataloging–in–Publication Data

Auction quotas and United States trade policy.
  (Policy analyses in international economics ; 19) September 1987.
  Includes bibliographical references.
    1. United States—Commercial policy. 2. Import quotas—States. I. Bergsten, C. Fred, 1941–
. II. Institute for International Economics (U.S.) III. Series.
HF1455.A83 1987   382′.52′0973   87–12948

ISBN 0–88132–050–1

ACKNOWLEDGMENTS

The authors thank Harvey Bale, Carl Hamilton, John Jackson, Jules Katz, Peter Lloyd, Patrick Messerlin, Janet Nuzum, Gardner Patterson, and Richard Snape for providing thoughtful comments. Ian Forsyth and Ross Tanner provided ongoing assistance and input on behalf of the governments of Australia and New Zealand. Deepest appreciation goes to Lisa Salaz, Alda Seubert, and Renae Sledge who typed the many drafts of the manuscript.

C.F.B.   K.A.E.   J.J.S.   W.E.T.

Preface

Trade policy is a focal point of international economic attention in 1987 and will be for the foreseeable future, with new legislation under consideration in the United States Congress and the launching of the Uruguay Round of multilateral negotiations in the GATT. In an effort to contribute significantly to the debate, the Institute is simultaneously releasing studies on four major trade policy issues: agriculture, auction quotas, the politics of antiprotection and textiles.

This study on auction quotas addresses a topic which has received far too little attention: the methods by which the United States (and other major trading countries) implement their quantitative import controls. The distribution of billions of dollars' worth of windfall profits, and major trade policy effects, are determined by whether such controls are administered by the importing or exporting countries (usually via so-called "voluntary" restraint agreements) and whether they are allocated administratively or sold (including by auction). The Institute's extensive work on trade policy has concluded that trade controls should be avoided, in most cases, but has also recognized that such controls will inevitably be applied from time to time in the real world, and recently have been applied more and more frequently. Hence it is essential to analyze the alternative means by which import restraints can be administered, and this study attempts to do so—with a focus on auction quotas, which appear to offer a number of substantial advantages over other techniques which are in vogue today.

The Institute for International Economics is a private nonprofit research institution for the study and discussion of international economic policy. Its purpose is to analyze important issues in that area, and to develop and communicate practical new approaches for dealing with them. The Institute is completely nonpartisan.

The Institute was created by a generous commitment of funds from the German Marshall Fund of the United States in 1981, and continues to receive substantial support from that source. In addition, major institutional grants

vii

are now being received from the Ford Foundation, the William and Flora Hewlett Foundation, and the Alfred P. Sloan Foundation. The Dayton Hudson Foundation provides partial support for the Institute's program of studies on trade policy. A number of other foundations and private corporations are contributing to the increasing diversification of the Institute's financial resources.

The Board of Directors bears overall responsibility for the Institute and gives general guidance and approval to its research program—including identification of topics that are likely to become important to international economic policymakers over the medium run (generally, one to three years) and which thus should be addressed by the Institute. The Director, working closely with the staff and outside Advisory Committee, is responsible for the development of particular projects and makes the final decision to publish an individual study.

The Institute hopes that its studies and other activites will contribute to building a stronger foundation for international economic policy around the world. Comments as to how it can best do so are invited from readers of these publications.

C. FRED BERGSTEN
Director
July 1987

Contents

ix

1 Introduction

Debates over the desirability of "protection" or "free trade" have raged for more than a century. A key issue—both in the United States and abroad—has been whether to increase or reduce barriers to imports of particular products. The outcome of those debates has differed substantially over time: toward freer trade in the mid-nineteenth century; extensive use of restrictions during the early 1930s; and steady liberalization for the first two or three decades after the Second World War. In recent years, the outcome has been ambiguous: continued reduction of barriers by some countries in some sectors and erection of new restraints in other sectors and by other countries.[1]

Within the context of this broader debate, there has also been considerable discussion of different types of import controls. In the postwar period, nontariff barriers (NTBs) have been used extensively, particularly as traditional tariffs have been reduced in successive rounds of trade negotiations under the auspices of the General Agreement on Tariffs and Trade (GATT). The Tokyo Round of multilateral trade negotiations in the 1970s addressed a number of those "new" devices. The most extensive discussion has probably concerned the relative merits of tariffs and quantitative restrictions (QRs) when decisions are made to limit trade flows.

There has been relatively little discussion, however, except to a limited extent in the technical economic literature, of the different methods for implementing QRs. This is surprising for several reasons. First, the use of QRs has been rising sharply, not just in relative terms—to "replace" tariffs

---

1. Problems of trade *imbalances*, the focus of much current policy discussion in the United States and abroad, are conceptually distinct from problems of trade *policy*. Trade deficits and surpluses are caused primarily by macroeconomic forces: changes in exchange rates, divergent growth rates among countries, changes in national fiscal and monetary policies, and the like. Trade controls in individual sectors generally have quite modest effects on overall balances, although sizable imbalances clearly intensify the political pressure to adopt additional trade controls. For details, see Destler (1986, ch. 9).

1

as their levels have steadily declined—but in absolute terms. In the United States, for example, 18.3 percent of all imports were covered by QRs in 1986, whereas only 5.1 percent were covered as recently as 1980. Eight major American industries are now protected by QRs: automobiles, carbon steel, dairy products, machine tools, meat, specialty steel, sugar, and textiles and apparel.[2]

Second, QRs imposed under the "escape clause" or other provisions of national law to provide "safeguards" (temporary and degressive import protection) for domestic industries are increasingly rare. Instead, the United States has resorted more and more to "gray area" negotiated trade restraints. Such protection has become a major focus of international negotiation and discord. Efforts to negotiate a GATT Safeguards Code in the Tokyo Round failed totally despite the success in reaching agreements in many other difficult areas (including export subsidies and government procurement). The United States and the European Community are periodically at loggerheads over steel quotas. The Multi-Fiber Arrangement (MFA), which sanctions QRs on a large part of world trade in textiles and apparel, is one of the most contentious economic issues between industrial and developing countries.

Third, substantial amounts of money are involved. Estimates presented in this study will suggest that as much as $9 billion annually was transferred from the United States to other countries as recently as 1984–85 because of the techniques the United States has used in applying QRs.[3] Within countries, the impact of QRs will be distributed very differently as a result of different methods of implementing import controls.

The purpose of this study is to assess the case, positive and negative, for a potentially new approach to implementing US quantitative trade controls: auction quotas. Under this approach, import quota licenses—which convey the right to import a certain amount of a product under quota—would be sold at auction to the highest bidders. At present, such quota rights are given away in all cases.

---

2. The increased share of US imports affected by QRs results primarily from new restrictions imposed during this period and not simply from the expansion of existing restraints to new suppliers. These products are also subject to tariffs, although at relatively low rates on average except on textiles and apparel. For details on these import regimes, see Hufbauer, Berliner, and Elliott (1986).

3. This figure includes windfall profits that go to uncovered suppliers of products covered by voluntary export restraints. Thus, not all the estimated rents are actual quota rents that could be captured by an auction. Estimates of the "capturable" rents are described in ch. 4.

The Congress authorized auctioning of import licenses in the Trade Agreements Act of 1979, with certain exceptions, but to date the auction quota option has not been used. A good deal of interest in it developed during the trade debate in the Congress in 1986 and early 1987 and in the congressional budget deliberations as well (since auction quotas could become a new source of revenue for the federal government). This analysis assesses the advantages and disadvantages of auction quotas to determine whether their utilization could improve the conduct of trade policy for both the United States and the world trading system as a whole.

Quantitative Trade Restrictions: Techniques for Implementation

There are four basic ways to implement QRs. The initial decision is whether they will be administered by the importing or exporting countries. Although the initiative to restrain trade almost always comes from the importing country, most "American" QRs are, in fact, applied by the exporting countries under headings such as "voluntary" export restraints (VERs), "voluntary" restraint agreements (VRAs), and orderly marketing arrangements (OMAs).[4]

The countries that administer the QRs in a particular sector must then make the second key decision: whether to *give* the quotas away or to *sell* them instead. Techniques vary for carrying out each approach: free allocation of the quotas can be based on historical market shares or simply on a first-come-first-served basis, while their sale could occur at some fixed price or via auction. In practice, most QRs are given away by both exporting and importing countries even though, as shown in chapter 5, most other economic assets transferred by the US government to its private sector are sold.

Thus, the alternatives for implementing QRs can be conceptualized as a simple two-by-two matrix, as shown in table 1.1. All QRs must be administered by either the exporting or importing countries, and they must be either allocated or sold. Perhaps surprisingly on both counts, almost all "American" QRs are implemented abroad, and all are allocated rather than

---

4. There are legal and some technical differences among these restraints, but they are not central to the purpose of this study. We will use the abbreviation VERs throughout the study as shorthand for this set of measures.

TABLE 1.1 **Administering "American" quotas**

Country	Method	
	Administrative allocation	*Sale*
Exporting	Automobiles (Japan) Carbon steel (EC, Japan, others) Machine tools (Japan, Taiwan) Meat (Australia, New Zealand, others) Specialty steel (8 major suppliers) Sugar (39 countries) Textiles and apparel (43 LDCs and Japan)	none
Importing (US)	Dairy products	none

sold—whether by the exporting countries or, in the one applicable case, by the United States itself. The central issue in this study is whether it might be desirable, in at least some instances where the United States (and other importing countries) employ QRs, to reverse both key components of the current approach—for the United States to implement the QRs itself and to do so by auctioning them rather than giving them away.

The Auction Quota Alternative

Like virtually all economists, we believe that import controls of any type are usually undesirable. When such restrictions are required, tariffs are generally the preferred instrument (for reasons described in chapter 2). However, QRs are frequently employed in the real world; the problem is to implement them in ways that will do the least damage and that will facilitate the most rapid return to free market conditions. As such, the "case for auction quotas" does not suggest that they are desirable in absolute terms, but only that they are less bad than the alternative administrative techniques.

This limited case for auction quotas, which will be elaborated in the subsequent chapters along with the case against such a device, derives from five basic considerations. First, auction quotas provide far greater transparency than do VERs—the practical alternative in most cases—because the restriction itself is more evident and the price paid for the auctioned tickets indicates the protective effect of the quotas. All interested parties thus have a better foundation for deciding whether to maintain the basic quantitative import restraint. We will also suggest that VERs have pernicious effects on the trading system as a whole and that their replacement by auction quotas would carry considerable systemic benefits.

Second, the information on the protective level of quotas generated by the auctions (and by prices of quota tickets in the resulting secondary market) could provide a sound basis for substituting tariffs for quantitative restraints (thus moving to a less distortive means of protection) by indicating the magnitude of the tariff needed to provide equivalent import relief. This motive was a major factor in the decisions of Australia and New Zealand to adopt auction quota systems over the past few years, as discussed in chapter 7.

Third, auction quotas appear to be largely consistent with the international trading rules of the GATT, whereas VERs, at best, are gray area measures outside both their spirit and their legal framework. A shift from VERs to auction quotas thus could enhance the general effectiveness of the GATT and facilitate the adoption of a meaningful safeguards code in the Uruguay Round of multilateral trade negotiations, as explained in chapter 9.

Fourth, substitution of auction quotas (or tariffs) for VERs could shift a substantial part of the excess profits generated by protection (''quota rents'') from the exporting to the importing country. This would halt the perverse practice, prevalent under VERs, of augmenting the profits of companies in the exporting countries—which, by definition, are already extremely competitive—by enabling them to capture a large part of those rents. This practice creates, in effect, a ''coalition for protection'' among established exporters and import-competing industries that both discriminates against competitive new suppliers and makes it harder to disengage from trade controls (as indicated by the lengthy duration of quotas in sectors such as dairy, steel, sugar, and textiles and apparel).

Furthermore, the revenues generated by auction quotas could be used to finance programs of trade adjustment for the protected industry and workers in the importing country, permitting earlier liberalization (including elimination) of the import restraints. Such revenues could also be used to reduce aggregate budget deficits, which would also inter alia facilitate trade adjustment in deficit countries. In addition, a shift to auction quotas from QRs already allocated by the importing country could provide new revenues for both purposes by transferring rents from the private sector to the government.

Fifth, as described in chapter 5, it appears that most transfers of economic benefits by the US government to the private sector in this country—offshore oil leases, logging rights, and the like—are conveyed at a market price rather than given away. An equity question thus arises: Why should the rights to import quotas, economically valuable as they are, be transferred free of charge to a few lucky individuals? This represents a final possible consideration in favor of auction quotas.

A number of concerns have been raised about the auction quota approach. First, some argue that it could increase the protective effect of QRs and thereby increase their costs to consumers. According to this view, the auctions themselves would represent an additional trade barrier, so that the adverse impact of protection would be increased by their adoption.

A second analytical concern is that exporting countries could effectively counter the use of auction quotas by an importing country and keep it from capturing the revenues generated by protection. To the extent that auction quotas were motivated by an effort to seize those revenues, for adjustment or budgetary purposes, they could be frustrated and the basic purpose nullified.

A third argument against auction quotas is that they would violate the GATT. Auction quotas are seen by some as an import fee adopted for fiscal purposes, an impairment of tariff bindings, and in conflict with the GATT Code on Import Licensing—each of which would contradict the international obligations of the United States. A related concern is that a US effort to convert some existing restraint agreements from VERs to auction quotas, notably for steel and for textiles and apparel, would violate the terms of international agreements already negotiated for those sectors.

A fourth source of opposition to auction quotas is that any congressional mandating of their use, especially to supplant VERs, could reduce the flexibility of American trade negotiators and thus render trade policy more difficult to carry out. US trade negotiators can frequently induce exporting countries to limit the volume of their sales to the United States and to agree not to retaliate in return for letting those countries administer the quotas and thus capture for themselves much of the resulting price increase for the products in question. Any abolition of the VER option in favor of auction quotas would obviate these possibilities and increase the likelihood that the United States would have to provide compensation in other sectors or accept retaliation against US exports.

A fifth concern about auction quotas centers on their administrative feasibility and practical operation. Some importers and retailers fear that auctions would greatly disrupt trade patterns, generating uncertainty in the marketplace and thereby raising the costs of the QRs to consumers and others. Some take the view that auction quotas would represent an administrative nightmare for governments to implement and would require substantial personnel and budgetary costs.

A sixth consideration against auction quotas comes from free traders who fear that the ability of the auctions to generate revenues for the US government would significantly increase the pressures to adopt new import controls and retain those already in existence. The government, and beneficiary private groups, would become "hooked on the revenues"—particularly at a time of acute budgetary pressure. Hence, auction quotas would intensify, rather than relieve, the increased use of trade restraints.

A related and final concern, which we call the "Chinese menu" problem, is that any adoption of auction quotas through the American political process could tend to emphasize their narrow benefits to the United States—notably the capture of revenues—but ignore the corollary steps needed to obviate, or at least limit, their potential costs. For example, it could be tempting for Congress—given budgetary constraints—to dismiss the risks of violating US international agreements in favor of revenue-generating auction quotas. Such considerations could override the positive contributions auction quotas could make to trade policy by providing a way station to retariffication and eventual elimination of quotas, devoting the new revenues to constructive industry adjustment, eliminating VERs, and thereby strengthening the GATT trading system.

The State of the Debate

The preceding considerations were debated by the Congress in 1986 and early 1987. The House Ways and Means Committee discussed auction quotas during its Florida retreat in March 1986 to plan for new trade legislation and again during the public hearings of the Trade Subcommittee in April 1986 and February 1987.[5] After the hearings in 1986, Subcommittee Chairman Sam Gibbons (D-Fla.) instructed his staff to include, in the "discussion draft" to be considered in markup, a provision requiring that all future quantitative restraints be implemented via auction quotas and that all existing quantitative restraints be rapidly converted to the auction method.

A primary source of congressional interest in the proposal stemmed from the desire to enhance government revenues, thereby providing a source of funds both for trade adjustment assistance (via a new Supplemental Adjustment Assistance Trust Fund in Chairman Gibbon's proposal) and to reduce the overall budget deficit. In early 1987, Chairman William H. Gray, III (D-Pa.) of the House Budget Committee repeatedly suggested auction quotas as one potential source of additional funds. At his request, the Congressional Budget Office (CBO) developed an analysis of the budgetary effects of such an approach.[6]

The omnibus trade bill (HR 3), adopted by the House in April 1987, included a requirement that any new quantitative restrictions recommended by the US International Trade Commission (USITC) be administered "by means of public auction of import licenses, unless the ITC finds that such auction system would lead to undesirable economic results." As such, the bill "establishes a presumption in favor of auctioned quotas." Undesirable economic results are defined as monopolization of market power, where one entity would be likely to purchase all the tickets and then exert undue power over market prices, or when auctioning might "seriously disrupt the market." HR 3 listed orderly marketing agreements as an alternative device for implementing import relief, however, and it gave the administration discretion to implement relief in any way it chooses—whatever the recommendation of the USITC (US Congress, House, Committee on Ways and Means 1987b, p. 104). If it were to become law in this form, HR 3 would increase the attention paid to auction quotas, but would fall far short of mandating their use.

In early 1987, several members of the Senate Finance Committee also expressed interest in auction quotas. In May, the committee adopted an amendment by Senator Max Baucus (D-Mont.) calling for a pilot program

---

5. Invited testimony was presented by C. Fred Bergsten, and Robert E. Litan of the Brookings Institution before the Subcommittee on Trade, House Committee on Ways and Means, 15 April 1986, and by C. Fred Bergsten, Peter Mangione of the Footwear Retailers of America, and Doug Tompkins of Esprit de Corps before the same subcommittee on 27 February 1987.

6. See ch. 4 for a comparison of our own and CBO estimates of auction revenues. See also Congressional Budget Office (1987).

under which the next three cases of import relief administered via quantitative restrictions under section 201 of the Trade Act (the escape clause) would be implemented via auction quotas. Unlike the House bill, which specifies OMAs as an alternative to auctioned import quotas, the Baucus amendment retains presidential authority to negotiate OMAs under section 201 but requires that they be administered by auctioning import licenses. The Senate Finance Committee report on S 490 expressed concern that "quota premiums too often go to foreign producers under current quota systems." The committee also noted the positive effects of using the revenues from auction quotas to "help [the affected domestic] industry adjust and decrease the likelihood that the industry would need further trade protection in the future" (US Congress, Senate, Committee on Finance 1987, pp. 62–64).

The General Accounting Office (GAO) has similarly called for "experiment(ing) with auctions in selected Section 201 cases." It concluded that "the potential advantages of auctioned quotas, relative to the known disadvantages of...allocated quotas, could be significant" (Comptroller General 1986, p. 18).

The Plan of the Study

The purpose of this study is to provide a comprehensive analysis of auction quotas, taking fully into account the various considerations raised in the public debate. The following eight chapters provide the analyses of both auction theory and practical experience with auctions that underpin our conclusions and policy recommendations in the final chapter.

Chapter 2 presents a basic analysis of quantitative trade restraints (including tariff quotas as well as different types of "pure" QRs). It describes their economic effects, the different methods of implementing them, the key issues that must be considered in designing and administering any QR system, and how they compare with tariffs. The chapter attempts to develop a methodology for determining the distribution of benefits under the different quota techniques and identifies the factors (such as the relative degree of industry concentration on the export and import sides of the market) that influence that division. Readers not interested in the theoretical aspects of this issue may want to skip over this chapter.

Chapter 3 traces a brief history of the use of QRs by the United States. For the major industries cited earlier, it describes the domestic legal authority for imposing QRs, how quota rights have been allocated, and the distribution of quota rents.

Chapter 4 analyzes in detail the economic and practical impact of auction quotas compared with other techniques of import restraint. It also addresses some of the analytical objections to auction quotas.

Chapter 5 assesses the American experience with auctions in other areas in which the government conveys the rights to economic assets to private parties. The list includes inter alia offshore oil leases, coal and other mineral resources on public lands, stumpage rights in national forests, sales of commodities from the national defense stockpile, and sales of Treasury securities in financial markets. Virtually all such rights are auctioned and generally have been in the past. The free allocation of import quotas appears to be an anomaly. The chapter seeks to draw lessons for auctioning import quotas from the previous experiences with auctions in these other contexts, particularly in response to the practical concerns raised about them by market participants.

Chapter 6 reviews the surprisingly active debate over auction quotas in the United States during the past 25 years. The idea was considered for oil imports as early as the 1960s and again in the 1970s. It has been recommended by the US International Trade Commission in two cases (sugar in 1977, footwear in 1985) and by the Federal Trade Commission (steel in 1984). As noted earlier, Congress authorized auctions in 1979 and has renewed consideration of the issue in 1986–87.

Chapter 7 describes and analyzes the auction quota systems now used extensively by Australia and New Zealand. Both countries decided to shift from allocated to auction quotas in the early 1980s, and have moved in that direction to a considerable extent. The concepts developed in earlier chapters, and the advantages and disadvantages of auction quotas cited thus far, are tested against actual experience and implications are drawn for the United States. We recognize, however, that the extent to which the Australia–New Zealand experience can be applied to the United States is limited by institutional and other differences between the United States and those two countries.

Chapter 8 develops in some detail the possible techniques for conducting quota auctions, partly to assess the validity of the practical objections to the approach raised earlier. Based on the experience cited in the previous chapters, it sets out our proposal for the design of a US auction system.

Chapter 9 elaborates on the international implications of auction quotas.

Do they conform to the GATT? How would they affect existing bilateral agreements (and the MFA)? Would US adoption of auction quotas require payment of additional compensation to other countries? Would it risk retaliation? What would be the effect on negotiations for a safeguards code and perhaps other components of the Uruguay Round?

Finally, chapter 10 attempts to draw together the previous analyses and to offer proposals for US trade policy. What is the balance between the advantages and disadvantages of the approach? What specific variant would be most likely to maximize the advantages and minimize the drawbacks: the comprehensive adoption of auction quotas à la Chairman Gibbons in May 1986 to include existing as well as new restraint arrangements, a modest "pilot project" à la Senator Baucus that applied only to new cases, or something in between?

How could the United States achieve the largest possible transfer of rents? Should the resulting revenues be used to fund trade adjustment assistance or for general budget relief? How could the proposal be integrated into the US negotiating approach in the Uruguay Round, and what leverage (if any) might its inclusion afford? To provide a firm foundation for any new policy initiatives in the area of auction quotas, this concluding chapter will attempt to devise specific proposals that would promote US and global trade objectives.

2 Quantitative Trade Restrictions: A Theoretical Overview

Before turning to the specifics of auction quotas, we will review the properties of quantitative trade restrictions (QRs) in general and the various options for administering them. QRs can take the form of import quotas, export quotas (including "voluntary" export restraints or VERs), or tariff quotas. Unlike tariffs, which simply tax imports, QRs set an upper limit on the amount of a good that can be traded. An import quota usually imposes an upper limit on all imports, while VERs limit shipments only from the exporting countries that impose them. A tariff quota combines elements of both tariffs and quotas: a lower tariff rate applies to imports up to the quota level, and any imports above that amount enter at a higher rate of duty. Tariff quotas have the same impact as quotas if the overquota rate is high enough to be prohibitive.

This chapter analyzes the economic effects of quantitative restraints, including the impact on prices in the domestic and world markets, the severing of the linkages between those markets, the protective effects, the creation of quota rents, and the costs to consumers. It also examines the distribution of quota rents under different methods of administration and the effect of different types of quotas: volume-based versus value-based and global versus discriminatory, including VERs. It concludes with a comparison of tariffs and quotas.

Economic Impact of Quantitative Trade Restrictions

To keep the analysis as simple as possible at the outset, assume the following conditions: the imported product is standardized, so there is no appreciable difference between imports and domestic products; the industries producing the product abroad and in the importing country are competitive, so supply curves can be used to depict the reactions of these industries to price changes; and the importing country is not a significant buyer of the restricted good on

13

FIGURE 2.1   **Effect of an import quota in the domestic market**

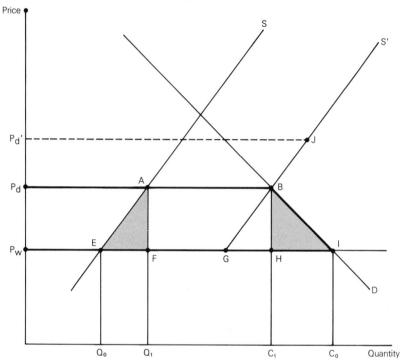

the world market, so the price at which the product can be imported from abroad does not change when imports are restricted by quota.[1]

The expected impact of an import quota under these assumed conditions is illustrated in figure 2.1. Without any trade restrictions, the good can be purchased in the world market, imported and sold at the price P_w. Because the imported and domestically produced products are assumed identical, both will sell for P_w. The equilibrium price is not at the point at which the

---

1. What actually happens to production costs in the exporting country depends upon the effect of decreased sales on costs, which depends on the importance of the importing country to the market. Unless there are economies of scale in production of the restricted good, production costs could remain the same or even decrease if the importing country is so large that its decreased demand lowers the world price.

domestic supply and demand curves S and D in the figure intersect because those curves reflect only supply and demand in the home market, not in the world market. P_w is the equilibrium given the interaction between the two markets. At the price P_w, consumers of the product will purchase C_0 along their demand curve D, and producers of the product within the importing country will produce and sell Q_0 along their supply curve S. The difference between the amount consumed and the amount produced domestically, represented in the diagram by the distance Q_0C_0, will be imported. Suppose a quota is imposed on imports of this product. If the import quota is binding (that is, if it reduces imports below what they would be without the quota), P_w could no longer be an equilibrium price. With imports limited to less than Q_0C_0, demand would exceed supply, and the price of the imported product and its domestically produced import-competing substitutes would be driven up. Market forces would establish a new equilibrium price where the amount supplied by domestic producers along the supply curve plus the amount allowed in by the import quota equals the amount demanded by consumers along their demand curve.

Suppose an import quota limits imports to half their original volume, shown by the distance EG in figure 2.1. The new equilibrium price after the quota becomes effective can be located by finding the price (in this case P_d) at which the horizontal distance between the S and D curves equals the quota limit. Alternatively, the new equilibrium with the quota can be found by identifying a "total" supply curve to the market, S', which lies to the right of the domestic supply curve S by the amount allowed in under quota. The total supply curve and the demand curve intersect at B, identifying P_d as the equilibrium price once the specified quota is imposed. Just as would be expected of any supply restriction, the import quota drives up the price of both the restricted good and domestically produced substitutes.

It is important to emphasize at the outset that, given the domestic demand and supply conditions (depicted in this case by the supply and demand curves), and provided the quota is filled, the equilibrium price after the quota is imposed depends only on the volume of imports allowed. The size of the price increase depends upon the severity of the import quota (that is, the amount by which imports are reduced) and not upon the method of administering the quota. The size of the price increase would be affected by the method of administering the quota only if administrative details resulted in an actual volume of imports below the quota ceiling, thus creating an additional barrier to imports.

The severity of the quota also determines the degree of protection for the domestic industry, the costs to consumers and to the economy as a whole, and the size of the quota rents. Because a quantitative restraint severs the linkages between prices in international and domestic markets, the negative impact may be exacerbated if economic conditions change and the quota is not adjusted accordingly.

SEVERING OF MARKET LINKAGES

If there were no quantitative restrictions on trade, markets for products throughout the world would be interconnected. If demand for a product were to increase in one country, the resulting higher prices in that country would create an incentive for other countries to ship the product there. The increased supply would tend to bring the price down to the same level as in the rest of the world. Thus, prices for goods in different markets would not diverge by more than the costs of transportation and tariff charges, if any.

Quantitative restrictions sever these linkages. Once the quota limit is reached, no more of the good can be imported no matter how large the price difference between countries. The certainty that imports will be limited to a set amount regardless of changes in underlying economic conditions is one of the major reasons why industries seeking protection prefer quotas to increased tariffs. Domestic producers do not have to worry about increased import penetration if their international competitive position erodes because of increased home production costs, exchange rate changes, new entrants into the world market, or improved technology abroad.

Quantitative restrictions also will be more inflationary than tariffs if domestic demand for a restricted good increases. Because imports cannot increase to help satisfy increased domestic demand, prices for the protected product will rise.[2] To illustrate, if demand for the product under quota were to increase, so that the demand curve in figure 2.1 crosses the total supply curve S' at point J, the price of the restricted good and domestic substitutes would be driven up to P_d'. The inflationary impact of increased demand will be particularly acute if inherently cyclical industries such as steel and autos

---

2. The effect of this sectoral inflation on overall inflation will depend upon the importance of the product to the economy; for example, price increases on steel will have a much broader impact than will similar price increases for sugar.

are protected during downturns by quotas that are not removed immediately after the economy begins to recover.

The severing of market linkages under quantitative restrictions can also have serious implications if the domestic import-competing industry is concentrated in the hands of a few firms. Unlike tariffs, which allow increased imports as long as the duty is paid, a quota allows producers in concentrated industries to exploit their market power by reducing the supply of goods in the domestic market and increasing prices beyond the quota-induced level without a threat of competition from increased imports.[3]

PROTECTIVE EFFECTS

The higher price after a quota has been imposed encourages increased output, profits, and employment in the import-competing industry. The quota increases the domestic industry's production level from Q_0 to Q_1. This increase in output would be expected to draw more resources, including more labor, into the protected industry. Industry profits will increase by area P_dAEP_w. This area equals the price increase on the units Q_0 originally sold at P_w, plus the difference between extra revenue and extra cost (shown by the height of the supply curve) for all additional units produced Q_0Q_1. Given domestic demand and supply conditions, the more restrictive the quota, the greater the protective effect.

QUOTA RENTS

The quota creates a gap between the price consumers pay in the protected market and the cost of production abroad. In figure 2.1, the import quota increased the price of the imported good in the domestic market to P_d, but the country was assumed to be such a small buyer of the product that the world market price remained at P_w. Whoever is able to buy the product in the world market at P_w, import it, and sell it internally at P_d will earn a profit per unit equal to the difference between the two prices. The total profits from importing under the quota, called "windfall profits" or "quota rents," will equal area ABHF.

---

3. For a comparison of tariffs and quotas when domestic production is monopolized, see Bhagwati (1965).

These windfall profits can go to anyone along the chain of supply that links producers abroad at one end and consumers in the protected market on the other: producers abroad, the exporting country's government, exporters abroad, the importing country's government, or importers. The distribution of these rents depends on the market structure for the good in question and the method of administration.

CONSUMER COST AND EFFICIENCY LOSSES

Quantitative restrictions hurt consumers by raising prices. The size of the loss to consumers can be measured using the concept of "consumers' surplus."[4] When the price was P_w, before the quota was imposed, consumers' surplus equaled the entire area below the demand curve, but above the P_wI line. When the quota is imposed and the price increases to P_d, consumers' surplus decreases by the area bounded by the points P_dBIP_w, the entire area outlined in bold on figure 2.1. This area represents the money payment that would have to be made to consumers to make them just as well off after the quota was imposed as they were before.

Part of the loss to consumers, the area P_dAEP_w representing increased profits of domestic firms, is a transfer from domestic consumers to domestic producers. Another portion of the loss to consumers, the area ABHF, is a transfer from consumers to the recipients of the quota rents. The remainder, the sum of the shaded triangular areas AFE and BIH, is a pure loss or "deadweight loss" due to economic distortions caused by the restriction. Area AFE represents the increased cost of producing Q_0Q_1 of the product in the importing country rather than importing it at a cost of P_w. Area BIH represents the efficiency loss when consumers are not able to purchase the amount C_1C_0 at the lower world price P_w. The sum of these two triangles measures the efficiency losses, or "cost of protection" to the domestic economy.

This efficiency loss is the minimum cost to the country of the restriction. If the quota rents or the increased profits from internal production do not go

---

4. Consumers' surplus is the difference between the maximum amount consumers would be willing to pay to get a given amount of a product and what they actually have to pay. The height of the demand curve shows the amount that consumers are willing to pay to get each unit.

to domestic residents, the portion transferred abroad can also be considered part of the country's loss from the restriction.

ADMINISTRATION OF QUOTAS

Assuming competitive markets and given supply and demand conditions, a particular quota level will result in the same protective effect, quota rent, consumer cost, and efficiency loss, regardless of how it is administered. The method of administration, however, may affect the composition of imports under quota (for example, by encouraging upgrading), their source, and the distribution of quota rents. An imperfectly competitive market structure in either exporting or importing may raise prices and consumer costs and increase the size and distribution of potential quota rents. In this section, we examine the distribution of quota rents, the denomination of quota levels (in value or volume terms), and the geographic distribution of the restraints (global or country-specific).

Distribution of Quota Rents

To determine the likely distribution of the quota rents, it is useful to think of a series of exchanges: the producer abroad sells to "exporters" (firms who buy domestically and sell abroad); these exporters sell to "importers" (firms who buy abroad and sell domestically). The distribution of quota rents will be determined by the prices that prevail in the exchanges between these groups. Who obtains the rents will depend upon four interrelated factors: (1) the market structure (that is, the degree of monopoly power) in the export and import industries and the industry producing the good abroad; (2) the type of restriction (import or export quota); (3) the method in which the quota is administered; and (4) the imposition of any other trade restrictions on the product by the governments of the importing or exporting countries.[5]

The distribution of the quota rents depends in large part upon the ability of producers, exporters, and importers to influence market price. In compet-

5. The distribution of the quota rents under various assumptions about market structure and type of QR is analyzed in detail in appendix A. This section summarizes the conclusions of that analysis.

itive markets, as analyzed in figure 2.1, the rents go to the firm that is able to import the good, which in turn will depend upon how the quota is administered.

As explained in chapter 1, the fundamental administrative issues arising from the imposition of a quantitative restraint are who administers the quota, the importing or exporting country, and how it is allocated. Once an import or export quota has been imposed, there are several alternatives for distributing the quota rights:

• The quota may be distributed randomly. The most frequently used method is first-come-first-served, which is common with unlicensed quota imports (for example, the quota on US imports of peanuts). Alternatively, licenses could be sold for a fixed fee until all were taken up.

• The quota may be allocated administratively; this option means dividing the quota according to some arbitrary formula. Import quotas are often distributed on the basis of historical shares, as with most US dairy quotas, while export quotas are often tied to performance criteria, including high-value exports or exports to nonrestrained markets. Again, a fixed fee could be charged for the license.[6]

• The quota may be auctioned.[7]

The first-come-first-served method of allocation requires little additional bureaucratic administration since there are usually no licenses and, thus, no need to distribute them. However, there are efficiency losses as a result of the need to devote extra resources to the nonproductive end of getting the goods in before the quota is filled (or having to wait in line if licenses are issued). This method was used initially when France imposed import quotas in the 1930s, but it was quickly abandoned when a stampede to the border overwhelmed customs officers. They could not keep track of imports at the various ports of entry quickly enough to immediately close the border when the quota ceiling was reached (Heuser 1939, pp. 82–84, 95).

---

6. Charging a fixed fee for an import license, however, would violate Article VIII of the General Agreement on Tariffs and Trade, see ch. 8. See Hamilton (1986d), Bark and DeMelo (1987), and Allen, Dodge, and Schmitz (1983) on the allocation of export licenses.

7. Kindleberger and Lindert (1978, pp. 152–54) identified similar options, which they listed in order of preference as competitive auctions, fixed favoritism, and resource-using application procedures.

The second range of options, requiring specific allocations according to historical share formulas, freezes the existing distribution system in place and maintains existing customer relationships. Although such methods provide the greatest degree of certainty to importers and exporters, they are the most rigid and inefficient. Administrative allocation also often requires the promulgation of lengthy and complex eligibility regulations, which may entail submission of extensive documentary evidence demonstrating eligibility.[8] This imposes a substantial administrative burden and additional costs both for the government and for firms seeking licenses.[9]

If the government simply allows imports on a first-come-first-served basis until the quota is filled, then whoever is able to bring the goods through customs first obtains the rents. If the government of the importing country administers the quota by simply issuing import licenses to importing firms, those importers are likely to obtain the quota rents. Exporters will still be competing among themselves to sell to the importers, which would keep the import price low and allow the importers to resell the product domestically at the higher price, thereby capturing the quota rents. If export quotas or VERs limit trade and are administered in the exporting country by giving licenses to exporters, then the quota rents would be expected to go to the exporters receiving the permits. Competition among importers to obtain the product and resell it at the higher price in the protected market will drive up the price importers pay. Thus, with competitive markets, those who receive the export or import licenses stand to gain.[10]

If the producing, exporting, or importing industries are not made up of a large number of competitive firms, the recipients of the quota licenses may

---

8. In the 1930s, for example, Greek import quota licenses were distributed on the basis of a number of factors: capital values of the firms; amount of taxes paid; rent payable on the firms' premises; size of staff; and number of proprietors, as well as the firms' imports in previous years (Heuser 1939, p. 104).

9. There may also be resources spent on lobbying by affected firms to influence the distribution of the licenses. Elimination of such lobbying activity would be an additional efficiency gain from auctioning quotas. See Krueger (1974), Bhagwati (1982), and Bhagwati and Srinivasan (1980) on "rent seeking."

10. Similar conclusions apply if the market structure is oligopolistic. Harris (1985) and Krishna (1985) have shown that if two producers of differentiated products (one foreign, one domestic) compete in the market within an importing country, a self-enforced export quota (VER) forces the foreign firm to raise its price enough to avoid exceeding the agreed export limit. In this type of model, the quota rents show up as greater profits of the foreign firm at the expense of domestic consumers.

not be able to obtain the rents. If importers, exporters, or producers abroad have market power (that is, the ability to set prices in international markets), the firms with market power will probably be able to appropriate the rents even if they do not receive the quota licenses.

To illustrate the importance of market structure, suppose that an import quota is imposed on a good produced abroad by a monopolist or exported by a single firm, and import licenses are given to importing firms. The quota increases the price at which the product sells in the protected market. The single producing or exporting firm can increase the price charged importers just enough to leave them some incentive to import, but no excess profits or windfall gains. The quota rents would then go to the monopoly producer or exporter.

At the other, less likely extreme, suppose an exporting country agrees to a VER and administers the quota by issuing export licenses, which it gives to producers or exporters. With competitive markets, these exporters would be expected to receive the quota rents. Suppose, however, that they are selling to a single importing firm. The importing firm could keep the price at which it offers to buy low, even though the price of the good within the protected import market is driven up by the quota. The quota rents would accrue to the monopoly importer.

The method of administering the quota system can determine the distribution of the rents in competitive markets by giving quota licenses to specific firms or individuals. It can also influence the distribution of the rents indirectly by influencing the market structure in importing or exporting.

An example of the latter is VERs that are not administered by the government of the exporting country through a formal licensing system, but through collaboration with industry or trade associations. The government may allow, actively encourage, or even require that the producers or exporters organize themselves to limit exports. This is widely believed to have occurred in Japan in the early textile export restraints of the 1950s and in Japan and the European Community with steel mill product restraints from 1969 to 1974.[11] Forcing an industry, in essence, to collude to limit export volumes virtually ensures that it will also collude to keep export prices as high as

---

11. For the Japanese experience, see Hunsberger (1964); in the most recent steel case, the US Trade Representative requested that the Department of Justice write letters explicitly approving the steel VERs and exempting the industry cooperation required to enforce them from US antitrust laws.

possible to fill the quota and thus garner the quota rents. In other words, a government's method of administering the quota can create a monopoly exporter where the market structure was previously more competitive.[12]

The preceding discussion on the likely distribution of quota rents leads to the conclusion that the greater the degree of control and administration of the quotas in the exporting country, the more likely it is that the rents will go to firms abroad. Likewise, the greater the degree of industry concentration or market power in production or exporting abroad, across countries as well as within individual countries, the more likely it is that the quota rents will go to firms in the exporting country.

Volume Versus Value Quotas

Quantitative restrictions can be denominated in value or in volume terms. If denominated by value, a certain maximum dollar, franc, or yen value of imports is allowed. If denominated by volume, a maximum number of units, pairs, tons, barrels, or square yards equivalent may be imported. In practice, all of the important quantitative restrictions on trade to the United States have been denominated in terms of volume. There are two reasons why the economic impact of value and volume quotas may differ.

The first has to do with the effect of changes in prices of imported goods, either due to changes in export prices or changes in exchange rates. If the quota is denominated in value terms in the importing country's currency units, an increase in the export price (or a depreciation of the importing country's currency relative to the exporting country's) will decrease the volume allowed under the quota. A fall in export prices (or an appreciation) will increase the quantity allowed.

The decision to denominate the restriction in value or volume terms will hinge upon the objective of the restriction. If quotas are imposed for balance of payments purposes, the authorities should be concerned primarily with limiting the value of imports, so a value-denominated quota would be

---

12. Murray, Schmidt, and Walter (1983) show that when an export monopoly is created by a quota arrangement, it may then have an incentive to exploit its monopoly power by "short-shipping," or shipping less than the quota limit. In this case the method of administering the quota would determine its economic impact because creating a monopoly exporter who shortships results in imports below the quota ceiling. The method of administering an import quota could affect the market structure in importing and provide an incentive for shortshipping.

appropriate. On the other hand, if the intention is to protect a domestic industry or maintain domestic prices in the face of falling world prices, a quota denominated in volume terms would be more appropriate.

The second difference between volume and value quotas is their impact on the composition of imports within the overall limit. If volume quotas are imposed on a product group consisting of different varieties, types, styles, or qualities of a product, the composition of imports may tend to shift toward higher valued items. This *upgrading* effect has been observed when US imports of textiles, footwear, steel mill products, and automobiles have been protected by QRs.[13]

One way of explaining the upgrading phenomenon is to note that importers will want to maximize their profits from the use of the licenses they hold. This implies that they will want to import items with the greatest difference between domestic selling price and import price. If the difference between these prices is higher on one variety than on another, they will shift license use to the variety with the greater price disparity. Importers can thus be expected to reallocate licenses among varieties, or subcategories of the overall quota, until the deviation of domestic price from import price, or the quota rent per unit imported, is equated across all varieties or types.[14]

This means the quota increases the price of all varieties of the product by exactly the same absolute amount. An import quota on all blouses, for example, would be expected to increase the domestic prices of all blouses above the world market price by, say, $5. Blouses that sell on the world market for $5 would sell domestically for $10, and blouses that sell on the world market for $10 would sell domestically for $15. The domestic selling price of the $5 blouse would increase by 100 percent, while the domestic price of the $10 blouse would increase by only 50 percent. Volume denominated import quotas thus tend to increase the prices of cheaper items *relative to* more expensive items, and shift consumer purchases toward higher valued items.[15]

---

13. On footwear, see Pearson (1983, pp. 36–46) and Aw and Roberts (1986); on autos, see Feenstra (1984); on textiles, see Keesing and Wolf (1980, pp. 32–33); on steel mill products, see Mintz (1973, p. 83).

14. To simplify the discussion, we do not mention other objectives of importers. The need to supply a full range of products, for example, would lead to a less than full shift of licenses to higher profit items and limit somewhat the upgrading phenomenon.

15. Falvey (1979) explains upgrading in this way. Rodriguez (1979) and Santoni and Van Cott (1980) explain upgrading from the cost side in a model where consumers demand the services

Newly imposed quotas in value terms will not shift the relative prices of lower and higher priced items. Importers who hold licenses to import a given dollar's worth of imports will allocate licenses among categories so that the quota rent per dollar's worth of imports is the same across all varieties imported. Prices of goods of different values will increase proportionately, so that no shift in the composition of imports from a relative price change would be expected.

The upgrading phenomenon is important because the shift in import composition can undermine the intent of the quota system. If a quota was imposed to prevent increases in imports from disrupting the domestic industry, the portion of the industry producing higher valued items might not be protected. This result is particularly perverse in an economy such as the United States, whose comparative advantage is typically in more sophisticated, higher value products. For example, under the voluntary export restraint on autos, the Japanese automobile industry upgraded very quickly from small, economical automobiles to larger, more luxurious models. Those models substantially augmented the Japanese automakers' profits and placed them in direct competition with the main source of profits for US companies much sooner than would otherwise have occurred. The shift in import composition could be prevented by denominating the quotas in value terms, but this method would still suffer from the disadvantage, discussed earlier, of changes in import value if export prices or exchange rates change. Imposing separate subquotas on narrowly defined product lines would also prevent upgrading, but this has the disadvantage of inflexibility should consumer tastes or production costs change over time.

Global or Discriminatory Quotas

The import quota considered in the preceding example was a *global* import quota. It simply fixed a maximum quantity that could be imported during a specified period of time, without any restrictions on the source of the imports.

---

from a product rather than the product itself, and more durable, higher valued items provide more services per unit. Upgrading increases the services per unit of imports. Krishna (1985) provides yet another interpretation. Different consumers demand different varieties, and a cutback on imports will necessarily remove some consumers from the market. If the consumers driven out of the market tend to consume the lower valued items, upgrading will be observed.

In practice, quantitative restrictions are very often discriminatory because they either subdivide the quota by country of origin or take the form of VERs that apply only to a limited number of suppliers.

Subdividing an overall import quota into separate subquotas for chosen exporting countries is one way to protect the domestic industry and pursue foreign policy objectives at the same time. Countries considered "friendly" or close allies can be given larger shares of the market. Changes in quota allocations can serve as carrots and sticks in the arsenal of foreign policy tools. Sugar quotas provide the most vivid examples. Cuba held the bulk of the US sugar import quota until relations between the two countries deteriorated. More recently, sugar quota was taken away from South Africa as part of the US sanctions against apartheid, and given to the Philippines to support the new Aquino government.

Even if some objective rule is used to distribute the quota among exporting countries, it is difficult to find a rule that is not discriminatory in some way. If the quota is divided on the basis of market share in some base period, early or long average base periods favor traditional suppliers over newly emerging ones; very recent base periods favor new suppliers over traditional ones.

Any arbitrary distribution of an overall import quota among exporting countries can result in losses to the importing country by guaranteeing market share for relatively inefficient suppliers or by fostering monopolistic behavior by favored exporters. Removing competition from suppliers in other countries may encourage exporters to engage in monopolistic behavior and make it more likely that the quota rents will go to them. If all exporting firms throughout the world had to compete with one another to supply under the quota, competition among suppliers would result in imports from the lowest cost exporters. Forcing importers to import from certain sources increases the cost of the imported product and contributes to an even more inefficient worldwide allocation of production. Emerging suppliers are often thrown into an "all others" category, which makes it harder for them to break into the market.

By their nature, VERs are also discriminatory because they restrict shipments only from those countries that agree to limit their exports, without limiting exports from third countries. It is normally the lowest cost sources of supply, whose exports are growing most rapidly, that face pressure to limit shipments. A VER drives up the price of the restrained good in the importing market, which in turn encourages increased imports from nonrestrained exporters. VERs do allow the emergence of new suppliers, but sometimes these entrants are competitive only because the quota system itself restricts competition. Increased exports from nonrestrained countries often lead to pressure to extend the controls to those countries. In fact, they have led to a steady increase in the number of countries covered under the Multi-Fiber Arrangement governing trade in textiles and apparel.

Comparing Quotas to Tariffs

Having discussed the economic effects of quantitative trade restrictions, it is useful to summarize the major differences between quotas and tariffs. The most important differences are the distribution of revenue and the implications of severing the connection between prices inside and outside the protected market.

A tariff is essentially a tax on imported goods. It increases the price of the imported good to domestic buyers by adding the tax to the import price. The tariff revenue is collected directly by the government of the importing country. A quota with the same impact on imports as an equivalent tariff will generate the same amount of revenue by causing a similar divergence between domestic prices and either import prices or production costs abroad.[16] If the government does not charge in any way for the right to import under the quota, this revenue is distributed among producers abroad, exporters, and importers. Thus, the first major difference between tariffs and quotas is that tariffs provide government revenue, but quotas, as usually administered, provide windfall gains to private individuals or firms.

The other major differences between tariffs and quotas arise because a binding quota implies that the price of the imported good will be determined by supply and demand conditions in the importing country alone. Changes in prices abroad will not be transmitted into the domestic market. This is the reason why quotas have been used to keep imports from undermining domestic agricultural price support programs and why industries seeking protection prefer quantitative restraints. It is also the reason why quotas can prove more distortionary than tariffs.

---

16. The area ABHF in figure 2.1, which represents the quota rents from an import quota limit of Q_1C_1, is equivalent to the revenue from a specific tariff of $P_d - P_w$ or a tariff rate of $(P_d - P_w)/P_w$.

As already noted, quotas allow no increases in imports even if domestic firms greatly increase prices once they are protected. A quota will allow a potentially monopolistic or oligopolistic industry to exploit its market power by eliminating any possibility that consumers could switch to imported goods in the face of price increases by domestic firms. Tariffs, on the other hand, give domestic firms a competitive edge, but they still allow consumers access to increased imports if domestic firms raise prices by much more than the competitive edge provided by the tariff. Quotas can turn potential monopolies into actual monopolies whereas tariffs cannot.

Under a quota system, imports cannot respond to changes in demand or cost conditions. In particular, if domestic demand for the imported good increases or domestic production costs increase, the quota limit does not allow increased imports to moderate price increases. The resulting domestic price increases will be larger with a quota system than if the industry had been protected with a tariff. Once a quota system is imposed, its distortionary impact can grow over time as domestic demand grows or as the domestic industry's competitiveness declines.

For these reasons, quotas are a less desirable method of protection than tariffs. If an industry must be protected, and if it can be protected with a tariff (that is, if it is not an agricultural program or other program in which the goal is a given price or level of production), tariffs are preferable to quotas.

In between these two is a hybrid alternative: tariff quotas. Tariff quotas combine the features of tariffs and import quotas. A maximum amount or quota is fixed for imports that can enter at a lower tariff rate; unlike a quota, however, imports can still enter the country over the quota ceiling, but only at a higher tariff rate. Whether the tariff quota acts like a tariff or a quota depends upon whether imports are below, just at, or over the quota level for the lower tariff rate.

If imports are below the level at which the quota would bind and the higher tariff rate would become applicable for additional imports, the tariff quota would have the same effect as a tariff at the lower rate. The imported good would be expected to sell at the import price including the tariff, and no quota rents would arise.

If the import level reached the ceiling for imports at the lower rate, but the higher tariff rate were sufficiently high to prevent further imports, the tariff quota would act like a quota. As with a quota, the equilibrium price of the good in the importing market would be the price at which the quantity supplied by domestic firms plus the quantity allowed in at the lower rate equaled the quantity demanded by domestic consumers. Quota rents would arise because this price can exceed the tariff-inclusive import price.

If imports exceed the ceiling for the lower tariff rate, the tariff quota again acts like a tariff. The domestic price of the product would equal the tariff-inclusive price at the *higher* tariff rate, and the link between domestic prices and world market prices would be restored. The difference, however, would be that quota rents remain for the importers who are able to import at the lower rate. They can sell in the domestic market at the price determined by the higher rate, but they have to pay only the lower rate.

Summary

As demonstrated, quotas create a gap between prices in the protected and world markets. This gap generates quota rents that can accrue to importers, exporters, producers abroad, or the governments of the importing and exporting countries if the quota licenses are auctioned or sold by governments. These quota rents are important to the discussion of auction quotas, because auctioning the quotas may transfer the rents to the government of the restraining country.

Who gets the quota rents depends upon the market structure in importing, exporting, and production abroad, and how the quota is administered. If all markets are competitive, the firms or individuals who receive the right to import under quota are likely to obtain the rents. Thus, import quotas that are administered by giving licenses to importers will leave the importers with the rents. Similarly, exporters that receive licenses under VERs or other export quotas would be expected to receive the rents under competitive market conditions.

If markets are not competitive, firms with market power (the ability to influence prices by their behavior) are likely to obtain the rents. If export industries abroad are concentrated, such as the steel or auto industries, the rents are likely to go to them. Self-administered export restraints are likely to increase cooperative behavior among exporting firms and thus are also likely to transfer the rents abroad.

When import relief is necessary, tariffs remain the least distortive and least costly instrument. In those situations in which quotas are imposed, we believe auction quotas would be less disruptive and less uncertain than a first-come-first-served system, more flexible and efficient than administrative allocation, and more equitable than either. Chapter 3 surveys the US experience with quantitative restraints. The other remaining chapters will examine the economic and administrative issues surrounding the auction option and the arguments for adopting this approach.

3 Quantitative Trade Restrictions in US Trade Policy

Quantitative restrictions (QRs) affect a large and growing proportion of US imports.[1] Of the eight major quotas currently in place, seven are allocated primarily by the exporters; only the quotas on certain dairy products are specifically allocated by the US government to US importers. Autos, carbon steel, machine tools, meat, and textiles and apparel are implemented via "voluntary" export restraints (VERs). Specialty steel industry protection is a mixture of increased tariffs, VERs, and import quotas. The sugar quotas are jointly administered by the US Secretary of Agriculture and officials in the exporting country. In addition to these major sectors, a very small quota on peanuts and a nonbinding quota on cotton are administered by the US Customs Service on a first-come-first-served basis, as is the tariff quota on tuna canned in water.

This chapter examines the eight major quota cases in some detail, drawing extensively on a recent Institute study on trade protection in the United States (Hufbauer, Berliner, and Elliott 1986). We first summarize the legal authority for imposing the QRs and then discuss how they are allocated and which groups probably capture the bulk of the rents in each case.

Domestic Legal Authority

Quantitative restraints affecting US imports have fallen into three main categories: import quotas to supplement agricultural price-support programs; QRs of various types imposed as escape clause relief; and voluntary export

---

1. Although import quotas were imposed on a few agricultural products in the 1930s, the United States did not use QRs widely until the 1950s (see appendix B). The list of trade restraints in appendix B and the discussion here do not include import controls imposed for foreign policy reasons (for example, the recent embargo on imports of crude oil and petroleum products from Libya).

31

restraints, usually negotiated on behalf of large, politically powerful industries threatened by imports.

The quotas on dairy products, peanuts, and cotton were imposed under the authority of section 22 of the Agricultural Adjustment Act of 1933 and on sugar under the headnote authority of subpart A of part 10 of schedule 1 of the Tariff Schedules of the United States (TSUS). These authorities allow the President to impose quotas or duties to prevent imports from subverting the objectives of price support and other farm programs.[2] Section 22 was used frequently, but in a more limited fashion, in the 1950s to limit imports of rye, barley, wheat, oats, tung nuts, and shelled filberts.

Section 204 of the Agricultural Act of 1956 gives the President authority to negotiate VERs on textile products and agricultural commodities and to impose import quotas on products from uncovered countries as long as a significant portion of world trade in the product area is already covered. This statute provides the domestic authority for the negotiation of VERs on textiles and apparel under the rubric of the Multi-Fiber Arrangement and has been used from time to time to avoid imposition of unilateral import quotas on meat (as required by the Meat Act of 1979, originally passed in 1964), when imports threaten to exceed a designated ceiling.

Import quotas, orderly marketing agreements, and tariff quotas, as well as tariffs, have been employed to protect industries under section 201 of the Trade Act of 1974. This "escape clause" authorizes the President to provide temporary and degressive protection to industries that have been found by the US International Trade Commission to have been injured by imports. Although intended to serve as the primary avenue of import relief, the specialty steel industry is the only one of the eight major sectors currently protected by QRs that received relief under the escape clause.[3]

---

2. Section 22 limits the size of the quota (or fees) to no less (more) than 50 percent of the volume (value) of imports in a base period, and it does not allow both quotas and fees to be imposed simultaneously. The headnote authority is much broader; it does not restrict the maximum level of the quota and allows fees to be imposed simultaneously.

3. In 1983, Harley-Davidson was granted five years of escape clause relief in the form of a tariff quota. This case is not included here or in appendix B, however, because the tariff quota was designed to preserve the market share of smaller European suppliers (by setting the quota level well above their expected sales), while protecting the domestic industry from Japanese imports (by setting its quota level well below expected shipments). Thus, the Japanese were the only suppliers having to pay the higher overquota tariff on most exports. In early 1987, Harley announced that it had regained a competitive position and opted to forgo the final year of protection. See Hufbauer and Rosen (1986), and Hufbauer, Berliner, and Elliott (1986).

The VERs on carbon steel, autos, and machine tools were negotiated pursuant to the President's executive authority to conduct foreign affairs. The steel restraints are backed up by the Steel Import Stabilization Act of 1984 (Title VIII of the Trade and Tariff Act of 1984), which authorizes the President to enforce steel QRs negotiated under bilateral restraint agreements. Such enforcement initially involves passive customs controls (for example, requiring valid export licenses as a condition of entry into the US market). However, if the quotas set under the bilateral restraint agreements are exceeded, the President can embargo further shipments until the next quota year.

The machine tool restraints rest on a finding under section 232 of the Trade Expansion Act of 1962, which authorizes the President to control imports judged to be a threat to the national security. Although this authority was not actually invoked in negotiating the export restraints with Japan and Taiwan, the finding remains valid and may be used to impose import quotas at any time against suppliers not in compliance with "suggested" guidelines. No US statutory authority underpins the auto restraints; furthermore, since 1985, that VER has not been sought by the United States and thus has been truly "voluntary" by Japan.

Quota Allocation

Prior to 1970, the standard US approach to quantitative restraints was to declare an import quota, usually dividing it among the major suppliers and occasionally by specific product category, but doing little else administratively. About a third of the quotas imposed in this period were allocated globally (i.e., one quota for all countries), while more than three-fifths were "global" in terms of category coverage (see table 3.1). Licenses were seldom required, and any additional allocation among individual suppliers was left to the exporting country. Formal licensing procedures with quota shares allocated to domestic entities have been used only twice by the United States, from 1959 to 1973 under the Mandatory Oil Import Program and since 1953 under the dairy program.

During the past 20 years, voluntary export restraints have become the most popular form of protection, with presidents seeking to preserve free trade images even as they respond to pressure from politically powerful industries,

TABLE 3.1   **Dividing quotas among countries and categories**

Country coverage	Category coverage	
	Global	Category-specific
Global	Long-staple cotton	Clothespins
	Peanuts	Stainless steel flatware
	Shelled filberts	Petroleum[a]
	Alsike clover seed	
	Canned tuna	
Country-specific[b]	Sugar	Machine tools*
	Automobiles*	Carbon steel*
	Color televisions*	Specialty steel
	Meat*	Nonrubber footwear*
	Lead and zinc	Textiles and apparel*
	Wheat	Dairy products
	Tung nuts and oil	
	Rye and rye flour	
	Oats	
	Short-staple cotton	

* Voluntary export restraints.

a. There were no specific country allocations, but there were exemptions for Canada and Mexico (overland suppliers) and other provisions that encouraged imports from other Western Hemisphere suppliers, relative to Middle Eastern suppliers, for national security reasons.

b. There are actually two different types of country-specific quantitative restraints: discriminatory QRs that cover only certain suppliers (marked with an asterisk); and QRs that cover all suppliers but are subdivided among them.

such as textiles and apparel, carbon steel, and autos. In addition to being country specific, these restraints are often category specific as well, and export licenses are usually required for entry into the United States. Table 3.2 elaborates on the matrix in chapter 1 and extends it back in time to summarize the administration of US quantitative restraints during the past 40 years.

"VOLUNTARY" EXPORT RESTRAINTS

In over a third of the cases listed in table 3.2, and 8 of 10 since 1964, the President negotiated VERs and allowed the exporting country to administer them.[4] These export restraints usually are backed up with US Customs Service monitoring, which, depending on the underlying legal authority, may result in unilateral embargoes if the negotiated ceiling is exceeded. VERs currently limit US imports of textiles and apparel, autos, carbon and some specialty steel products, and machine tools. While meat restraints are not currently in force, the ceiling set by the Meat Act of 1979 serves to inhibit imports since quotas can be imposed or negotiated any time imports threaten to exceed the trigger level.

The Multi-Fiber Arrangement (MFA) governing textile and apparel trade has been in force since 1974, although controls on cotton textiles extend back to a VER with Japan in 1957. As of the end of 1986, the United States maintained 39 bilateral export restraint agreements with developing-country suppliers and Japan—as well as consultation agreements with four other countries—under the umbrella of the MFA (US Congress, House Committee on Ways and Means 1987a, p. 78). Each agreement sets quotas for individual items; some bilaterals contain more than 100 different product categories, others only a few. Overall, the United States has more than 1,300 quotas by product and by country under MFA bilaterals. US imports from developed countries except Japan are not subject to quantitative restraints; however, imports of textiles and apparel from all countries are subject to tariffs, which average 10 percent on textiles and 22.5 percent on apparel. MFA quotas are administered in the exporting countries, generally by allocating quotas to exporting firms on the basis of historical market shares.[5] Presentation of official export visas is required at the US border. The use of "antisurge" and "call" provisions affords some additional control by the importing country.

The first of the 1980s wave of VERs was directed at Japanese automobiles. Despite a negative USITC finding for import relief under section 201 in November 1980, the United States negotiated a VER with Japan to limit shipments of automobiles to the United States. Japanese exports were cut back to 1.68 million units for the period April 1981 to March 1982. The agreement was renewed annually until 1985, when the Reagan administration decided not to request an extension of the auto restraints. In the face of trade threats from Congress and the industry, however, the Japanese government

---

4. These figures include the textile and apparel VERs, which began in 1957 but have been extended repeatedly both to new products and new suppliers. The figures exclude both specialty steel cases because they were a combination of import quotas and VERs.

5. See Hamilton (1986d) for descriptions of export quota allocations in the ASEAN countries (Malaysia, Indonesia, Singapore, Thailand, and the Philippines).

TABLE 3.2 **Allocating US quantitative trade restraints**

Administering country	Allocated by license[a]	First-come-first-served allocation[b]	
		By country	Globally
Exporting	Sugar (1948–74)[c]		
	Textiles and apparel (1957–)		
	Carbon steel (1969–74)		
	Specialty steel (1976–80)[d]		
	Footwear (1977–81)		
	Color televisions (1978–82)		
	Autos (1981–)		
	Sugar (1982–)		
	Carbon steel (1982–)		
	Specialty steel (1983–)[d]		
	Machine tools (1987–)		
	Meat (intermittent)		
Importing	Dairy products (1953–)	Short-staple cotton (1939–)	Long-staple cotton (1939–)
	Petroleum (1959–73)	Wheat (1941–74)	Shelled filberts (1952–53)
		Barley (1954–55)	Peanuts (1953–)
		Oats (1954–55)	Alsike clover seed (1954–59)
		Rye and rye flour, and meal (1954–61)	Canned tuna (1956–)
		Tung nuts and oil (1957–62)	Stainless steel flatware (1959–67)
		Lead and zinc (1958–65)	Clothespins (1979–84)

unilaterally extended the restraints, although expanding the level significantly. These restraints remain in place, but their restrictiveness has probably declined as a result of the expansion in volume and the large appreciation of the yen.

In 1982, the United States negotiated a VER with the European Community limiting exports of carbon steel products to the US market in order to avoid the imposition of antidumping and countervailing duties. This arrangement was supplemented by additional bilateral restraint agreements with 17 key suppliers in 1984–85 as part of the President's steel program, devised after he determined that import relief under section 201 would not be in the nation's economic interest (USITC 1987, p. vi). The bilaterals set separate quotas for individual steel products for a five-year period extending to 30 September 1989.

Administration of the steel agreements typically combines informal negotiations (among steel producers and between the industry and government to determine market shares) with formal export licensing arrangements. Congress gave the President authority to enforce the restraint agreements in the Trade and Tariff Act of 1984. The US Customs Service used this authority to embargo further shipments of carbon steel pipe and tube from the EC in November 1984 when imports reached the ''agreed'' level.

In the most recent case, machine tool imports were determined to be a threat to national security under section 232 of the Trade Expansion Act of 1962. As in the steel case, however, the President chose to negotiate VERs

a. Includes export licenses and ''administrative guidance'' by exporting-country governments to determine export shares, as well as US import licenses. Licensed quotas do not have to be country-specific; in practice, all but the petroleum controls have been. All of the restraints administered by the exporting countries, except the two sugar cases and some of the specialty steel quotas, were voluntary export restraints.

b. Exporting-country governments may have been involved in allocating quota among individual exporters under some of the country-specific ''first-come-first-served'' quotas, but we have no evidence to that effect.

c. Under the Sugar Act of 1948, quotas were allocated to the exporting country, which, in turn, allocated them among individual exporters with no documentation required at the US border. Certificates of eligibility are issued by the Secretary of Agriculture under the more recent quota program, but an official in the exporting country must execute them and make the final allocation.

d. The early specialty steel restraints included country-specific quotas on all suppliers but Japan, which negotiated an orderly marketing arrangement. The more recent specialty steel case is a mixed one, involving export licenses from the European Community on all products and from other countries on certain products, imports of which they agreed to limit in return for having the extra 201 case duties waived. Other suppliers are subject to country-specific import quotas.

with major suppliers rather than take statutory action. The United States concluded VERs with Japan and Taiwan in December 1986, to be administered via export licensing. In addition, the United States notified West Germany and Switzerland—major suppliers that would not agree to VERs—that increased shipments over the levels recorded in recent years would result in the imposition of US import quotas on national security grounds. Similar demands were made of seven smaller suppliers of machine tools to the US market.

Finally, the Meat Import Act of 1979 requires the President to impose quotas when the Secretary of Agriculture calculates that the statutory import ceiling may be exceeded. In such cases, country-specific quotas are set based on historical shares. To avoid the "automatic" imposition of US quotas, the President has negotiated VERs with principal suppliers under the authority of section 204 of the Agricultural Act of 1956. The most recent instance was in 1982–83, when VERs were concluded with Australia, New Zealand, and Canada to ensure that imports remained below the trigger level.

UNILATERAL IMPORT QUOTAS

Nearly half of the quantitative restraints in appendix B were unilaterally imposed import quotas subdivided by country, but not administered through a formal licensing procedure; a smaller fraction were not allocated even among countries. No licenses were issued or required, and imports were usually on a first-come-first-served basis unless the exporting country elected to allocate the quota among individual suppliers. The dairy quota program is the only current case of quotas allocated among individual importers via formal licensing procedures.

Country-specific import quotas with no US licensing procedures were imposed in the 1950s on lead and zinc under the escape clause, and on wheat and several other agricultural products under section 22. Imports of some types of specialty steel from all sources other than the EC have been handled in this manner since the industry won escape clause relief in July 1983. The relief is mixed: increased tariffs for stainless steel sheets and strip, and stainless steel plate; and quotas on stainless steel bar and wire rod, and alloy tool steel. The higher duties on sheet, strip, and plate were waived for countries agreeing to restrain exports of those products as part of their voluntary export restraints on carbon steel. In addition, import quotas were lifted on shipments from the EC countries in return for their agreement to voluntarily limit those exports. Import quotas on shipments from other sources remain in place and are subdivided by country. No import licenses are required, although export licenses are issued by countries limiting shipments under voluntary restraint agreements.

The sugar quotas imposed in May 1982 are subdivided among supplying countries by the Department of Agriculture according to average shipments in a base period, and they were originally administered on a first-come-first-served basis.[6] The informal method of administration created problems almost immediately, including "uncertainty among exporters, operators, and US importers as to whether a given cargo [would] be able to enter the United States against the quota, or [would] have to be entered into warehouse," surges early in the quota year, and the possibility of transshipment.[7]

To address problems arising from the first-come-first-served allocation, the Secretary of Agriculture was authorized in August 1982 to issue certificates of eligibility to import. The Secretary determines the timing and the quantity allowed under each certificate, above a minimum, and issues them to a designated official in the exporting country. That official executes the certificate and issues it to exporters, who must present it to Customs officials at the US border.

The US Customs Service currently administers global quotas on peanuts and some cotton and dairy imports on a first-come-first-served unlicensed basis. Tariff quotas also are usually administered in this manner (for example, the two-tiered tariff on canned tuna). Although computers have helped to ameliorate tracking problems associated with determining when quotas administered on a first-come-first-served basis have been filled, this method still requires extensive customs monitoring and can result in disruptive import surges.[8]

---

6. Longstanding quotas had lapsed when the Sugar Act of 1948 was allowed to expire at the end of 1974. Sugar imports averaged 5 million short tons annually from 1977 to 1981 before the quotas were imposed. The 1987 quota reduced imports to 1 million short tons. Without changes in the sugar price-support program, the quota could eventually be reduced to zero.

7. *Federal Register*, 11 August 1982, p. 34777.

8. Escape clause relief provided to the specialty steel industry from 1976 to 1980 included country-specific quotas administered on a first-come-first-served basis and an orderly marketing agreement with Japan. Import quotas were imposed on all other suppliers, with specific allocations for major suppliers—the European Community, Canada, and Sweden—and baskets for most-favored-nation (MFN) suppliers and all others. Implementing regulations allowed no more than 60 percent of the quota to be entered in the first six months of each quota year with any

Unlike the other US quotas now in place, dairy quota rights are given to US importers, not to foreign suppliers. Import licenses generally are allocated to US importers based on their import performance in the past. A small portion of the quota pool is available to nonhistorical importers. Quota rights entitle the holder to import a particular product from a particular country. Currently, there are 17 product categories which, for the most part, are supplied from the European Community and 13 other countries.[9]

Historical eligibility to import is based on the average annual quantity of the article entered by the licensee from the specified country of origin during a representative base period. Historical licenses are not transferable and may be revoked if there is a failure to import for up to three years, not necessarily consecutive, within a five-year period, unless the shortfall can be satisfactorily explained to the licensing authorities. These allocations may also be reduced or temporarily suspended if imports fall to less than 85 percent of the quota share in any one year.

Eligibility for nonhistorical licenses requires the submission of notarized certification, with supporting documents, attesting to involvement in either manufacturing or marketing of the item for which the license is requested. The applicant must maintain a bona fide business in the United States and must be represented by a person, principal, or agent "upon whom service of judicial process may be made." The licensee cannot be related to any other license holder, either personally or through business relationships.

Even nonhistorical licenses are allocated first to eligible applicants who have a "history" of importing in the prior year.[10] Any remaining quota is allocated among applicants with no import history on the basis of the date of the postmark on their applications. Eligibility for nonhistorical licenses must by renewed each year and will not be approved if imports have fallen below the 85 percent threshold.[11]

"excess" placed in customs warehouses. Nevertheless, exporters from the EC and from countries in the basket categories, rushing to get their products in first, filled some quota categories within days. The surges created significant problems for domestic users of imported specialty steel who faced uncertain supply and increased storage and financing costs (USITC 1979).

9. See Import Regulation I, Revision 7, for details (*Code of Federal Regulations*, Title 7, Part 6).

10. Preference is given to those who held licenses for the same article from the same country of origin in the prior year and then to importers who held licenses for the same article but from a different country of origin.

11. Historical license holders and importers who can establish eligibility under the nonhistorical license provisions are also eligible for supplementary licenses, which are available for selected categories and destinations.

Who Collects the Rents?

As noted earlier, assuming competitive markets, the greater the degree of control exercised by the administering country, the greater the chances that it will capture the quota rents. Most of the industries affected by US quantitative restraints have been relatively competitive on both the import and export sides. Therefore, the distribution of the quota rents has been determined largely by the method of administration, which in all but one existing case has been controlled primarily by the exporters. US practice contrasts starkly with that in other countries where import quotas allocated among importers are far more common (Nogues, Olechowski, and Winters 1986).

Often, the United States requires submission of export licenses (sometimes called visas) for products under voluntary restraint agreements (for example, the restraints on footwear and color televisions in the late 1970s and all the current VERs). The licenses are usually distributed by the exporting country to exporters on the basis of export performance in a representative period; transferability of the license is limited. Issuing licenses reduces competition and strengthens the market position of exporters receiving them, thus making it even more likely that they capture the rents. Occasionally, the exporting country will choose to administer the restraints informally by encouraging cooperation among suppliers. This may create an informal export cartel as is believed to have happened with the early steel and textile restraints. Again, the exporters receiving specific allocations probably collect the rents.

There are at least three documented cases in which transferable quota licenses have commanded a price when traded, thereby indicating that the license recipients have received at least part of the rents. The emergence of quota brokers in Australia and New Zealand to facilitate the exchange of import licenses under those countries' auction quota systems is one example. Another is the markets in Hong Kong and Taiwan for licenses to export textiles and apparel under the MFA.[12]

Finally, there is the mandatory import quota program for petroleum. As noted earlier, it was in effect in the United States from 1959 until 1973. Licenses to import crude petroleum, or "quota tickets," were allocated to US refineries on the basis of their crude oil inputs. Inland refineries that did

---

12. For a discussion of quota ticket prices in Hong Kong, see Hamilton (1986b) and Morkre (1984). Although less widely known, an active quota ticket market in Taiwan has also emerged (Hamilton 1986e).

TABLE 3.3   **Estimated rents from US quantitative restraints**
(million dollars)

Industry	Year of estimate	Estimated quota rents[a]	Likely recipient
Ongoing cases			
Textiles and apparel*	1986	4,000	Exporters
Automobiles*	1984	2,200	Exporters
Carbon Steel*	1984	2,000	Exporters
Sugar	1984	410	Exporters
Dairy products	1983	250	Importers
Meat*	1983	135	Exporters
Specialty steel	1984	50	Exporters
Machine tools*	1987	n.a.	Exporters
Total		9,045	
Recently expired cases			
Petroleum	1971	2,000	Importers
Carbon steel*	1974	330	Exporters
Nonrubber footwear*	1981	250	Exporters
Color televisions*	1982	150	Exporters

* Voluntary export restraint; n.a.   not available.
Source: Hufbauer, Berliner, and Elliott (1986); Cline (1987).
a. Because of the methodology used, which based the estimates on imports from all sources, the "quota rents" in the VER cases include any windfall profits gained by uncovered suppliers as a result of the higher US price. Such profits are not quota rents, since no quota exists on those imports, but are closer to the surplus gained by domestic producers as a result of the QR. See chapter 2.

not use imported crude could not legally sell their quota tickets, but they could import the crude oil and barter with a coastal refinery, exchanging imported for domestic crude. Based on the ratio of domestic crude received to imported crude, the value of the quota tickets in 1969 has been estimated at $1.17 per barrel. At the time, the world market price of crude oil was about $2.10 per barrel, so this rent, which went to the refineries receiving quota tickets, represented revenue equivalent to that from a 56 percent tariff (Bohi and Russell 1978, p. 290).

In cases where there are no licenses or even less formal allocations via administrative guidance or industry consultation, the distribution of the rents is less clear. As we have noted, if there were a monopoly situation in importing, exporting, or production abroad, the monopolist would probably be able to capture the rents, with or without licensing. Evidence collected by various sources indicates, however, that importing in the relevant products is competitive.[13] Collusion under a global quota would also be difficult since it would require cooperation among countries as well as among individual exporters. It would be easier for exporters to capture the rents under a country-specific quota, especially if the industry were very concentrated or the government encouraged cooperation as under some VERs (Hamilton 1986d, p. 218).

In summary, we would expect that individuals receiving specific allocations, either by license or informal agreement, would capture the rents in those situations. Under less structured quotas and assuming competitive markets, the distribution is likely to be more mixed, with exporters perhaps having an advantage if the quota is country specific. Table 3.3 estimates the size of the quota rents for important past and current quantitative restrictions on US trade, as well as the likely recipients based on the way in which the quotas were administered and the structure of the industries involved. The estimates in the cases involving voluntary export restraints are larger than the amounts the government could expect to capture from an auction because they are based on imports from all sources. Since we do not recommend extending an auction quota system to suppliers who are currently uncovered, the capturable revenues would be less than the total gains to foreigners listed here. Chapter 4 includes our estimates of the revenue that could be captured by an auction.

---

13. There are approximately 500 licensed importers of cheese, 160 firms importing significant quantities of steel, 400 importers of footwear, and nearly 40 importers of raw sugar (Christie 1986; USITC 1982, 1984, and 1985). Approximately 45,000 persons or firms imported textiles and apparel in 1986 (unpublished customs data).

4 The Economics of Auction Quotas

Chapter 2 examined the economic effects of quantitative trade restrictions (QRs) in general, with special emphasis on the creation of quota rents. The distribution of the rents was shown to depend upon who received quota licenses, and the market structure in importing, exporting, and the industry producing the product abroad. Redistribution of the rents is the major economic difference between allocated and auctioned quotas.

Questions have been raised, however, concerning the government's ability to capture the rents through an auction or, if it did, whether they would be significant. Regardless of the potential revenue, some observers argue that an auction quota would be worse than an allocated quota because it would impose an additional cost on consumers, disrupt import markets, and be more likely to result in monopolization. This chapter examines each of these issues in turn. It concludes with a brief comparison of auction quotas and tariffs and shows how auction quotas could facilitate the conversion of existing quantitative restraints to tariffs.

Transfer of Quota Rents to the Government

Would the government of the importing country be able to capture the quota rents by auctioning import licenses? A competitive auction probably would transfer the rents to the government. If a large number of firms are engaged in the importing and internal distribution of a restricted good, the auction will have numerous independent bidders or potential bidders. Competing firms would bid up the price of a quota ticket toward the expected value to them of holding the permit, which would be equal to the expected difference between the domestic selling price of the imported good and the full cost of purchasing and importing it, including any tariff.

If the price paid for the quota ticket were less than the expected windfall profits from buying in the world market and selling internally, some windfall

45

profits would remain. Other potential bidders who are aware of these expected profits would have an incentive to participate in the auction to obtain the import permits and thus the profits or rents. Competition among bidders to obtain the permits would drive the bids up to a level at which no excess profits remain, thus transferring all of the rents to the government.

If an allocated quota system has restricted trade in a particular product for some time, potential bidders will be able to observe the prices at which goods are selling internally with the restriction in place. They would then have an idea of the price at which they could expect to sell the product domestically to compare with prices offered by exporters. If these existing quotas were converted to auctioned quotas, traders would have a fairly good idea what they could afford to bid for the licenses and still retain an acceptable profit from importing.

Some uncertainty about the effects of a given quota, especially on postrestraint prices, would cloud bidding in the first few auctions of newly established quotas. Traders would have to rely on their knowledge of the market to estimate the amount by which the quota would increase domestic prices. If the quota does bind, domestic prices will be expected to increase, but the precise amount will depend upon demand and supply conditions inside the protected market. In the initial auctions, traders may bid on average too high or too low, finding themselves with losses in the former case and the government with revenue below the actual quota rents in the latter case. As the effect of the quota on the price at which importers can sell reveals itself over time, and as firms gain experience with the auction system and the operation of secondary markets in quota tickets, this uncertainty will diminish. Continued competition would be expected to drive the bids toward the size of the quota rents as bidders obtain better information over time.[1]

The government may not be able to capture the rents even with a large number of competitive importers, if there are only a few exporters or producers of the restricted good abroad. Knowing that importers will be able

---

1. If there are a few firms involved in trading a product, and new firms cannot easily join them because of the high costs of setting up trading facilities or exclusive franchise arrangements, the government may not be able to obtain the quota rents by simply auctioning off the quotas to the highest bidder or bidders. Taking the extreme case of just one importing firm (an import monopoly), the firm would have no incentive to bid more than a minimal, token bid for the quota. If the single firm can obtain the quota with a minimal (or even a zero) bid, the quota rents would go to that firm. Collusion among a few importers would have the same effect. Appendix A treats the case of an import monopoly in detail.

to sell at higher prices because of the restrictions, exporters could simply increase the prices at which they offer the product to importers, if collusion among them is feasible. Competitive participants in the auction will bid only as much as the extra windfall profits they expect. If those expected profits are kept low because export prices are kept high, the importers have no incentive to bid any more than a small amount for the quotas. The quota rents would go to the exporters or producers abroad.

The government may also find itself unable to capture all of the quota rents through a simple auction if the exporting country or countries react to the quota auction by imposing measures to capture some of the rents for themselves. Bidders will offer bids only up to the difference between the domestic selling price and the cost of the goods to them. An export tax imposed by an exporting country would drive up the cost of the goods and would lower bids. Some of the quota rents would be transferred to the coffers of the exporting country.

If there were competition *among* exporting firms and *among* exporting countries to fill the import quota, it would be more difficult for any single firm or government to capture the rents. This is another reason for "globalizing" quotas rather than dividing them by country of origin.[2]

In theory, the government could counter monopoly power in foreign production, exporting, or importing—and ensure itself of at least some of the quota rents—by insisting upon a minimum bid. The announcement of the quota auction could simply state that only bids over a certain dollar amount will be considered. Alternatively, a more radical method would be to offer the quota permits to the single importer, exporter, or foreign producer at a stated price in an "all or nothing" offer. As shown in appendix A, however, minimum bids run the risk of reducing imports below the quota ceiling if set too high, and "all-or-nothing" offers set too high could eliminate trade completely.[3]

---

2. See ch. 2 for other negative effects of country-specific quotas. Note that discriminatory quotas—i.e., those not applied on a most-favored-nation basis—are prohibited by the General Agreement on Tariffs and Trade (GATT), which is one reason for the prevalence of VERs. Nevertheless, we would prefer to maintain *existing* discriminatory quotas rather than to extend protection to currently unrestrained countries. See chs. 9 and 10 for a fuller discussion of these issues and our recommendations for "globalizing" existing quotas only within the universe of covered suppliers.

3. As a practical matter, deciding upon the level at which to set the minimum bid or "all-or-nothing" offer would require substantial information about the market for the product involved

The important point is that the government could expect to obtain the quota rents by simply auctioning quota licenses to the highest bidders, unless importing, exporting, or production abroad is controlled by so few firms that collusion and price fixing among them is a real possibility, or unless the exporting country could successfully react to the auction with restrictions of its own. Then the government might not be able to appropriate the quota rents by auctioning quota licenses; in this case, the revenue considerations also argue for the use of a tariff rather than a quota.

How much revenue could the United States expect to collect from an auction quota system? In table 4.1, we estimate that the total potential revenues from converting existing quantitative restraints to auction quotas would have been about $5.1 billion in early 1987. Note, however, that this is a point estimate. Exchange rate changes and other market factors affect the restrictiveness of quantitative restraints and therefore the size of the quota rents. Thus, any estimates of potential auction revenues, including our own, are subject to change as market conditions fluctuate.

Because our auction revenue estimates assume perfectly competitive markets, they probably overestimate somewhat the revenues that could actually be captured. For two major reasons they differ from our estimate in chapter 3 that about $9 billion annually in rents went to foreigners in 1984–85.[4] First, the auto and meat restraints, which had estimated rents of more than $2 billion in 1984-85, are not included in the current estimate of capturable revenue.[5]

Second, the higher estimate treated the loss to the United States from

---

and the cost conditions of the importer (or exporter or producer abroad if the monopoly power lay there). If the minimum bid is set too high and no one bids for the quota licenses, the opportunity to import during that time period would be missed. If the government starts lowering minimum bids in response to no bids, the single or few importers would have an incentive to refrain from bidding in the hope that the required bid would be lowered further.

4. This figure is also slightly different from our earlier published estimate of gains to foreigners of $10 billion. That figure included nearly $3 billion in potential auction revenue from reform of the maritime program that we have excluded here. The resulting $7 billion was then revised upward by $2 billion due to an update of the textiles and apparel number. See Hufbauer and Rosen (1986); Hufbauer, Berliner, and Elliott (1986); and Cline (1987).

5. As noted in ch. 2, the United States has no authority to impose an import quota on automobiles; furthermore, it would not be practical to convert a VER applied to only one country because that country could readily capture the rents from exporters and preclude the transfer of rents to the importing country. Conversion of the meat VERs would also be inappropriate because of the on-and-off nature of the restraints.

TABLE 4.1   **Potential auction revenues**
(million dollars)

Sector (year)	Revenue estimate
Textiles and apparel (1986)	3,000
Carbon steel (1986)	1,270
Machine tools (1987)[a]	320
Sugar (1987)	300
Dairy products (1987)	200
Specialty steel (1986)	60
Total	5,150

Source: Cline (1987); Hufbauer, Berliner, and Elliott (1986); US Department of Commerce (1987b); USITC (1987); IMF (1987).
a. Unpublished USITC data, reported in *National Journal,* 14 February 1987, p. 371.

higher quota-induced prices on imports from uncovered suppliers in the cases of "voluntary" export restraints (VERs) as quota rents.[6] The gains to uncovered suppliers, however, are different from the quota rents that go to restraining suppliers, and could not be captured by an auction. The estimated capturable revenue from the restraining suppliers alone in the textile and apparel and steel cases would be about $1.7 billion less than the total transfer to foreign suppliers in these cases.

Our total revenue estimate largely conforms to recent estimates by the Congressional Budget Office (1987), which calculated the potential auction revenues to be $3.7 billion, $3.9 billion, and $4.7 billion in 1987, 1988, and 1989, respectively. The major difference in the two estimates is on the steel and textile and apparel quotas. The CBO assumes that the declining dollar has resulted in substantially higher import prices, thereby reducing the restrictiveness of the steel VERs and lowering their tariff equivalent to only 8.6 percent. CBO concludes that potential auction revenues in this case would be only $700 million in 1987, compared with our estimate of $1.3 billion. While capturable rents have declined recently due to diversion to

6. As shown in ch. 2, a quota that effectively restricts supply creates a gap between domestic and world prices. Even nonrestraining suppliers will be able to raise the price they charge in the protected market and thus will earn windfall profits similar to the producer's surplus described in that chapter. See also Hamilton (1986d, pp. 214–29).

uncovered suppliers, the effects of the dollar depreciation have not to date fully passed through to import prices. As a result, our estimate of the quota rents in the steel case is higher for 1987 than is the CBO estimate. On textiles and apparel, the difference is due to differing estimates of the tariff equivalent of quota protection.

Auction Quotas Versus Allocated Quotas

Three major economic arguments have been raised against auctioning import quotas: they would impose additional burdens on consumers by increasing prices; they would create uncertainty and disrupt normal trading relationships with foreign suppliers abroad; and they would foster monopoly or increased market concentration in the importing and distribution of the restricted good. To evaluate these objections it is essential to distinguish between the adverse impact of the quota system per se and the potential adverse impact of *auctioning* the quotas rather than allocating licenses by administrative means or allowing imports on a first-come-first-served basis.

ADDITIONAL BURDEN ON CONSUMERS?

As shown in chapter 2, any quantitative restraint will increase prices to consumers by reducing the supply of imports to the domestic market. The relevant question is whether auctioning the quotas would drive up the price even further.

Traders are only willing to bid for import licenses because the quotas increase domestic prices relative to world prices. The size of the expected divergence between domestic and import prices determines the size of the bids, not vice versa. If importers found that they had bid too high for the quota and tried to incorporate the extra cost into the selling price, the resulting price would be above the equilibrium price. They would have to cut prices to sell all of the goods imported. Auctioning the quotas would not increase the price of the imported good to consumers. It would simply transfer the quota rents to the government. As such, auctions do not add to consumer costs; indeed, auctions can lower the costs to the domestic economy to the extent that the rents are transferred from foreign exporters back to the United States. The transfer of rents to the government further lowers the cost to the economy to the extent that the revenues offset the costs of administering the quota.

DISRUPTION OF IMPORT MARKETS?

Another alleged drawback to a system of auction quotas is disruption of trade caused by increased uncertainty. Importing firms are engaged in buying, shipping, storing, and selling imported goods. They are not experienced in dealing with auctions, predicting the price effects of quantitative restrictions, or operating in markets for the exchange of quota tickets. Introducing an auction quota system would involve them in all of these new activities in which they have little or no expertise.

Market disruption and uncertainty are inherent in the use of quantitative restrictions, and they are inevitable no matter whether the quotas are auctioned, allocated, or administered in some other way. If trade is restricted by quotas, importers initially will not know for certain how much quota they will be allocated (or how much their suppliers would be allocated under an export quota) or whether they will beat other suppliers to the border (if quotas are on a first-come-first-served basis).[7]

Quota auctions could entail additional uncertainties, particularly at the beginning of the process until participants become familiar with the newly instituted procedures.[8] Any new procedures that change traditional ways of doing business cause anxiety and some problems at the outset. For example, importers would not know how much they would be able to import—or, indeed, whether they would be able to import at all—until the results of the auction are announced. Given the long time lags that may be involved in determining specifications for goods, negotiating contracts, and producing and shipping goods, this increased uncertainty could disrupt the normal trading relationships between importers and their suppliers and even lead to "panic bidding" to avoid being completely closed out of the market.

---

7. By contrast, if trade is restricted by a tariff, the tariff rate is certain and known to importers beforehand. Apart from possible disputes over tariff classification, importers know exactly what extra charge they will have to pay, and they can take this into account when deciding what products to import and when negotiating contracts with suppliers. They do not have to worry about whether, or when, they will be able to bring the goods into the country.

8. Similar concerns were raised when floating exchange rates were introduced, but exporters and importers soon learned how to hedge their risks.

Importers unfamiliar with the impact of quantitative restrictions may bid too high (and incur some losses) or too low (and find themselves without quota). But this is part of the normal commercial risk raised by quotas, and increased experience with the operation of the auctions and the opportunity to observe the actual impact of the quotas on domestic prices should reduce these errors. Quota brokers could be expected to facilitate the exchange of quota tickets among firms that found themselves with too much or too little quota. Quota ticket brokers have emerged in Hong Kong, which permits the transfer of export quota tickets used to administer the MFA, and in response to the Australia and New Zealand auction quota systems.[9] The existence of a secondary market in quota tickets would allow importers to correct their mistakes, albeit possibly at a cost.

The notion of disruption of normal import markets and panic bidding can also be interpreted another way. Think of the importer as a firm. If the importer is not successful in a quota auction and cannot obtain quota permits on the secondary market, it cannot import during that time period. This will force its output down to zero, but not necessarily its costs. If the importer has fixed costs in the short run, it will suffer a loss in the short run equal to the fixed costs if it cannot import at all. Under these circumstances, an importer would be willing to bid up to the expected quota rents *plus* its fixed costs to get import licenses. In the short run, bids might overestimate the true size of the quota rents if fixed costs are important for the importer. This problem underscores the importance of a secondary market to enable firms to secure quota tickets after the initial auction.

The disruption of trading relationships during the initial phases of auction quotas could be minimized by transitional measures. For example, some proportion of the quota could be reserved on a first-refusal basis for importers of record in some base period or firms that previously were allocated quota. The price of the quota tickets would be determined by an auction for the remaining portion. Such a procedure would mitigate panic bidding by ensuring existing importers of at least some of the quota. Such transitional measures would entail efficiency losses, however, by making it difficult for new, potentially more efficient, entrants to get quota (also thereby reducing potential competition). It would be preferable, although not necessary, to scale such measures down over time as the quota is liberalized.

---

9. See Morkre (1984); Hamilton (1986b); and ch. 7.

MONOPOLIZATION OF IMPORTING?

A third major objection to auction quotas is that the auction process would encourage increased concentration (perhaps even monopolization) of importing and distribution of the restricted good. As shown in appendix A, a firm that realizes that increased profits could be made by monopolizing importing would have an incentive to outbid firms that correctly forecast the size of the quota rents under competitive conditions. The single firm that then controls the market can reap monopoly profits by "shortshipping," that is, actually bringing in and selling domestically an amount less than its quota ticket holding. This further restriction of trade puts even higher burdens upon consumers than does the original quota.

Monopolization of importing through the auction process would be a serious concern if it were likely to occur in practice. We think it is improbable in the US context because of the size and competitive nature of the markets involved. The threat of such monopolization could also be mitigated by actively applying existing antitrust provisions and by including specific regulations and limitations in the quota auction designed to prevent a single firm from cornering the import market.[10]

For example, the government could impose "use-it-or-lose-it" requirements on quota rights, whereby firms would be penalized if they did not use or transfer the quota they acquire in the original auction or in the secondary market. Firms could be penalized with a monetary fine, by excluding them from future auctions, or by other means (for example, by not allowing them to write off as legitimate business expenses quota they purchase but do not actually use or transfer). Such an approach has two disadvantages, however. The possibility of penalties would tend to depress the bids. More importantly, if market conditions change so that the quota no longer binds, penalties for *not* using or selling the quota obtained in the auction give firms an incentive to import at a loss, as long as the loss is less than the penalty they would incur by not importing. Under these circumstances, penalties for shortshipping

---

10. If one firm did gain control of imports through the auction, it could not exploit its monopoly power unless it further increased prices by restricting sales of the imported good to an amount below the quota ceiling. If the firm does not fill the quota, this should be evident from customs data. If the firm tries to disguise the shortshipping by importing but not selling the full amount, it will have to store the unsold portion indefinitely or dispose of it in some other way. The firm could conceivably reexport the excess, but reexportation could be prohibited in the quota regulations.

would act like an import subsidy.[11] It is inconsistent at best to impose a quota to reduce imports, and then issue regulations to administer the quota that can have the same effect as an import subsidy.

Transitional measures allocating established importers some proportion of the quota on a first-refusal basis would also contribute toward prevention of monopolization of the quotas. Such historical setasides would help buffer firms against uncertainty by limiting the size of the quota pool subject to auction.

If concentrated markets for the quota goods pose a threat to competition, other antimonopoly provisions could be instituted to limit the proportion or amount of quota that could be bought by any one firm. Restrictions for antimonopoly purposes could be stated in terms of maximum amounts that any firm could actually import under quota during a specific time period. Any such maximum, however, should be large enough to preserve flexibility to adjust to changing market conditions. Customs data would be readily available to check on the activities of importing firms, so no additional data collection would be required to verify compliance with the regulations.

Any restrictions on the amount that a firm could bid for or import are, of course, difficult to enforce because of the possibility of setting up dummy corporations and the time and effort involved in verifying interrelationships among companies. Nonetheless, the threat of antitrust action or other penalties (such as exclusion from future auctions) if the subterfuges are discovered should deter most firms from trying to circumvent the limitations.

Auction Quotas Versus Tariffs

As chapter 2 pointed out, one of the differences between quantitative restrictions and tariffs is that a tariff transfers revenue to the government of the importing country, while a quota leads to windfall gains to importers, exporters, or producers of the product abroad. Because auction quotas transfer the "tariff-equivalent revenue" to the government, it might be tempting to think that auction quotas and tariffs would have the same economic impact. If the industries producing the traded good (and its substitutes at home and abroad) and the firms trading the product in international markets are all competitive, and if there are no changes in demand or supply conditions at

---

11. See Anderson (1986) for a discussion of "use-it-or-lose-it" requirements in this context.

home or abroad, an auction quota and a tariff that result in the same level of imports will have exactly the same impact. But these two would differ except under these very limited circumstances.[12]

Auction quotas are like tariffs in that they transfer revenue to the government, but they retain the other detrimental effects of quotas: they allow domestic firms to exploit their market power without fear of increased imports, and they are more inflationary than tariffs in times of increased domestic demand for tradable goods. Thus, tariffs are preferable to quotas when imports must be restricted, particularly for cyclical industries and industries that consist of only a few firms.

Auction quotas could serve as a useful intermediate step in converting an established quota system into a system of tariffs. If the quota were suddenly replaced by a tariff set at some arbitrary level, it might be either more or less restrictive than the original quota. To ease the transition from quotas to tariffs, an auction could help determine the level of tariffs that would be required to result in the same quantity of imports. If all of the relevant markets are competitive, the bids for the quota would thus provide information for setting tariff rates in the conversion from quotas to tariffs.[13]

Whether quotas can be usefully converted to tariffs depends very much upon the underlying rationale for the quota. If quotas are used simply to provide domestic producers with a competitive edge over firms abroad, a tariff can achieve that objective. If, however, quotas are used to keep imports from undermining domestic price support programs, as with the dairy and sugar quotas, this objective may be difficult to achieve with an ad valorem tariff. As noted in chapter 2, any decline in the price of a product in the world market will tend to be transmitted into the imported country if a tariff alone protects the domestic market. A quota insulates the domestic market

---

12. In terms of figure 2.1, which assumes that all markets are competitive, an auction quota of Q_1C_1 and a tariff per unit of P_wP_d will have exactly the same impact. Area ABHF would be either tariff or auction revenue if all markets are competitive and firms correctly foresee the impact of the quota. Price, output, and consumption effects will be the same under both the auction quota and the tariff.

13. Remember, however, that the bids may underestimate the tariff equivalents if importing, exporting, or production abroad is highly concentrated, for the reasons cited earlier in the discussion of whether the government would be able to capture the quota rents through a straightforward auction. Likewise, the bids may overestimate the size of the tariff equivalents if importing firms operate in the short run with high fixed costs, for the reasons discussed in the discussion of panic bidding.

from price fluctuations abroad. This consideration may make it impossible to convert certain agricultural quotas to tariffs and still achieve the original objective of the quota. There is no reason, however, why such quotas should not be auctioned. This achieves the objective of domestic price support while transferring the quota rents to the government.

Summary

Auctions could capture a significant share of the rents that are generated by quantitative trade restrictions. We estimate that about $5.1 billion could be raised by the US Treasury if existing QRs were converted into import quotas administered and auctioned by the United States.

The positive revenue effect of auction quotas results from a redistribution of the quota rents between exporters, importers, foreign producers, and the government, and not from an increase in the level of protection and cost to consumers in the importing market. The price consumers are willing to pay is set by the supply-demand conditions created by the quota. The auctioning of quotas does not effect that price unless the quota is underutilized (thereby further restricting supply). The auction premium merely transfers some of the excess profits from the importer, exporter, or foreign producer to the importing government.

Auctions could create some additional uncertainty in the marketplace at the outset until participants become accustomed to the bidding process. However, bidders can quickly adapt to new procedures, as will be shown in chapters 5 and 7 with regard to US auctions in nontrade areas and Australian and New Zealand quota auctions. In addition, safeguards can be built into the auction procedures to reduce uncertainty and ease the transition from allocated to auctioned quotas. Specific proposals in this regard are detailed in chapter 8.

In a similar fashion, auction procedures can be designed to guard against monopolization. While such market power would be difficult to accumulate in the US market given its size and the diversity of suppliers, auction guidelines could be instituted that, when coupled with antitrust regulations, would mitigate remaining concerns in this area.

5 Auctions in Nontrade Areas

Auctions are commonly used by local, state, and federal governments in the United States to allocate government-held property rights to private parties (or to select private suppliers for government contracts). Currently, the federal government auctions surplus government property, natural resources on public lands, and financial securities. In addition, the Reagan administration has proposed using auctions to distribute Federal Communications Commission (FCC) licenses, Federal Aviation Administration (FAA) slots at airports, and parts of the federal loan portfolio. Increased use of auctions (and user fees) has been proposed by the administration, primarily for revenue reasons, but also on equity and efficiency grounds.

This chapter describes the auction systems that the US government uses in policy areas other than trade. The number and variety of these other auctions demonstrates that the government is no stranger to auction procedures; indeed, in most cases, market approaches are the preferred means of allocating publicly held assets. The free allocation of import quota rights is a rare exception to this rule. These cases also illustrate specific auction procedures that could be usefully incorporated in proposals for designing an auction quota system (see chapter 8).

US Government Auctions

The government regularly disposes of a wide variety of surplus property and confers rights to exploit public resources for private gains. It has two primary objectives in these transactions: to find the most equitable means of choosing among eligible applicants and to ensure that the government receives fair market value for the asset. Auctions have been frequently chosen as the best means of achieving these goals. Auctions are currently used for the sale of leases on offshore and onshore public lands to exploit minerals, primarily oil, gas, and coal. The right to cut timber in national forests is also sold via

57

auction, as are surplus government property (including excess supplies from the national defense stockpiles) and US Treasury securities.[1] Recurring concerns in these auctions have been that the bidding will be dominated by one or a few large firms or that firms will collude to lower bid prices. As detailed below, specific auction procedures have been designed to address these concerns.

MINERAL LEASES ON FEDERAL LANDS

The authority and procedures for auctioning onshore leases of mineral rights on federal lands are found in the Mineral Lands Leasing Act of 1920, as amended, and its implementing regulations. Offshore oil and gas leases were first granted via auction by Gulf Coast states, beginning with Louisiana in 1936 and followed closely by Texas. In 1953, Congress, buttressed by a Supreme Court ruling, passed the Submerged Lands Act, which limited state jurisdiction to areas within three miles of the coast (except in Texas and Florida) and extended federal jurisdiction to 200 miles offshore. The Outer Continental Shelf Lands Act of 1953 addressed the problem of existing state-awarded leases within the new federal jurisdiction and established guidelines for federal leasing of such lands for mineral production (Mead et al. 1985, pp. 8–9).

Of the more than 100 million acres of federally owned land currently under lease to private interests for mineral production, the vast bulk is in onshore oil and gas leases. Prior to the oil price plunge in 1986, federal onshore oil and gas leases produced about 5 percent of total annual US production, while offshore continental shelf (OCS) leases accounted for approximately 9 percent of US oil and 20 percent of US natural gas production annually. Coal production from just 1 million acres of leased federal lands accounts for 10 percent of the annual total.[2]

---

1. Congressionally chartered and government-owned financing corporations, such as the Government National Mortgage Association and Federal National Mortgage Association, also use auctions to select mortgages to be pooled and dealers to sell securities based on those mortgages in the secondary market. However, because those associations are run as corporations rather than government agencies, we have not included them here.

2. The Bureau of Land Management and US Geological Survey estimate that 25 percent of US oil and gas, 50 percent of coal, 80 percent of oil shale, and 50 percent of geothermal energy reserves are on federal lands (leases of geothermal steam lands are authorized by the Geothermal

Both the Mineral Lands Leasing Act and the OCS Lands Act limit the size of the lease any individual or single entity may control, but they allow the consolidation of leases if that will facilitate the extraction of the minerals "in an efficient, economical, and orderly manner as a unit." They also set the length of the leases (five years for producing tracts, unless minerals are still being profitably produced, and ten for nonproducing tracts) and the minimum royalty rate (12.5 percent of recovered production for oil and gas and for coal leases). They authorize the Secretary of the Interior to regulate both rental fees and royalties. The Mineral Lands Leasing Act allows onshore oil and gas royalties to be paid in kind, with any commodities so collected to be subsequently disposed of through sealed bids or public auction.

The implementing regulations outline the specific leasing procedures. All coal and OCS leases, and leases on a "known geological structure of a producing oil or gas field," are subject to competitive bidding procedures (McDonald 1979, p. 11). Notice of tracts for lease must be published in the *Federal Register* and in at least one general circulation newspaper in the affected area at least 30 days prior to the day of the sale. The notice must include the time and place of the sale, how it is to be conducted (sealed bid or oral auction), description of the tract, conditions of sale, and an indication of where more detailed information may be found.

The leases are awarded to the "highest responsible qualified bidder," on the basis of the cash bonus offered plus a fixed annual royalty rate of not less than 12.5 percent of the value of production saved, removed, or sold. The bonus is an up-front payment that the bidder pays in order to get the lease; until a discovery is made, the lessee must also pay rental fees on the tract. Once minerals are found, the rental payments are suspended and royalty payments must begin. On OCS leases, the bidder may be allowed to offer the royalty rate he or she is willing to pay, plus a fixed cash bonus. The choice of bidding variable is at the discretion of the Secretary of the Interior.[3]

The Secretary may refuse to accept any bid if, in the Secretary's judgment, even the highest is below the "fair market value" of the tract. The Secretary may also cancel any lease obtained by fraud or misrepresentation, or any

---

Steam Act of 1970). 80 percent of the onshore leases remain unexplored, and the 29.8 million acres leased offshore represent less than 5 percent of the total offshore acreage under federal jurisdiction (Hagenstein 1984).

3. The earlier Louisiana system determined successful bids on the basis of two bid variables, a cash bonus and royalties. If the high bids on the two variables were split, the winner was chosen at the discretion of the State Mineral Board.

nonproducing lease the owner of which has not complied with the provisions of the OCS Lands Act. Producing leases can be canceled only following appropriate court proceedings for noncompliance (McDonald 1979, pp. 16–18; Mead et al. 1985, p. 14).

The Bureau of Land Management uses sealed bids exclusively (although some states use oral auctions to assign oil and gas leases on state land). The bids must be accompanied by a certified check, money order, or cash equal to one-fifth of the bonus bid; evidence of citizenship; and evidence of authority of the person bidding. "All bidders are warned against violation of the provisions of Title 18 USC Section 1860 prohibiting unlawful combination or intimidation of bidders" (*Code of Federal Regulations,* Title 43, section 3302.4). All bids are publicly announced and recorded at the time they are opened, but successful bids are not announced until after the bids have been evaluated to ensure they represent at least fair market value.[4] Within 15 days of receiving notice or 30 days after the sale, whichever is later, successful bidders must pay the balance of the bonus bid and the first year's rental; failure to do so results in the loss of deposits. Deposits are returned to unsuccessful bidders.

The OCS regulations also allow joint bidding except by the eight largest companies. This provision has been criticized as anticompetitive. There is some evidence, however, that it increases competition by allowing small bidders, who otherwise might be unable to participate because of limited capital or other resources, to join with larger companies and thereby share the risk (McDonald 1979, pp. 14–19; Mead et al. 1985, pp. 68–69).

Nearly all OCS leases awarded from 1954 to 1977 were based on the highest bonus offered with a fixed royalty rate of 16.67 percent and rental payments on nonproducing tracts. In 1978, Congress amended the OCS Lands Act in response to charges that the leasing system did not, in fact, produce competitive results, that the government had not received fair market value, and that the major oil companies had an advantage under the current bidding system. The amendments specified eight alternative bidding systems, including royalty and bonus bidding, and required that 20 percent to 60 percent of the tracts offered each year during the subsequent five-year period be offered on a basis other than the traditional bonus with fixed royalty rate.

As of September 1983, the leasing system automatically reverted to

---

4. Even in an oral auction, the winner would not be announced until the bid had been evaluated to determine whether it represented fair market value (McDonald 1979, p. 77).

provisions under the 1953 legislation because, given the lack of evidence to support the earlier charges of collusion, Congress chose not to extend the new requirements. Comparative empirical analysis of leases granted in the two periods suggested that the traditional bonus bidding system had been effective in promoting competition among bidders and in capturing the economic rents for the government. Internal rate of return analysis revealed a before-tax rate of return on OCS leases slightly below the average for all manufacturing, while the after-tax rate of return was about the same. Further analysis revealed no advantage of big firms over small firms in bidding, and there has never been a case of alleged bid rigging in the history of OCS leasing (Mead et al. 1985, pp. 54, 68, 83).

The 1978 amendments also established two compensation funds intended to force leaseholders to internalize all costs associated with their drilling operations. The Offshore Oil Pollution Compensation Fund is financed out of a fee of not more than three cents per barrel on oil produced from leases, not to exceed $200 million. The Fund is to be used to pay for or compensate others for oil-spill removal costs, the processing and settlement of claims arising from a spill, and all administrative and personnel costs of the government due to spills. The second, the Fisherman's Contingency Fund, is not to exceed $1 million, and it compensates fishermen for damage to fishing gear or other economic losses due to drilling activities (Mead et al. 1985, p. 21).

Only a very small portion of onshore oil and gas leases are sold competitively since it is difficult to identify geological structures likely to contain oil or gas. Noncompetitive leases are awarded either on a first-come-first-served basis or randomly via lottery. Noncompetitive bids for leases must be accompanied by a $75 nonrefundable filing fee and the first year's dollar per acre rental fee, which is refunded to losers. Winners are selected at random by computer and must pay the remaining rental fees on the lease within 15 days of notice that such payment is due. If oil or gas is discovered, rental fees increase, and a minimum royalty payment of 12.5 percent is added (McDonald 1979, pp. 13–14).

The lottery system allows parties unrelated to the oil and gas industry to apply for licenses because they do not need to have the detailed knowledge necessary to submit a competitive bid. This has led to the creation of a thriving secondary market in leases. In fact, the Bureau of Land Management, which runs the sales, has estimated that less than 5 percent of lease winners actually engage in oil and gas development activity. In addition to speculators, some of these individuals are agents for firms in the industry, filing the lease applications and financing the advance rental deposits. An analyst of the system, however, interviewed "oil operators [many of whom] complained bitterly about the nuisance and expense associated with securing lease assignments from lessees who know nothing about the real prospects on their land but who are naturally intent on making the largest possible profit" (McDonald 1979, p. 76).

Groups as diverse as the General Accounting Office and the Sierra Club have urged Congress to require that all leases be sold competitively to ensure that the government receives fair market value (Comptroller General 1970, p. 76). Senator Dale Bumpers (D-Ark.) has introduced such legislation each year since 1979 to no avail. The executive branch has typically resisted such suggestions out of fear that an auction requiring an up-front payment for all leases would inhibit exploration on tracts where the probability of finding mineral deposits is unknown. In 1987, the administration decided to work with Senator Bumpers and others in Congress on a compromise proposal (S 66) whereby all onshore oil and gas leases would be subject to competitive bidding procedures. However, a backup lottery would be authorized for leases not attracting bids.

From 1953 to 1982, the federal government received $41.3 billion in bonus payments from the auctions and $17.3 billion in royalty payments and $302 million in rental payments from OCS leases. The value of rents, royalties, and bonuses in the OCS account in fiscal 1986 was nearly $5 billion, while that for onshore leases was just under $1 billion. Revenue from the OCS leases is greater "because resource values on the OCS are high. But, it has also been due to the fact that all OCS leasing is competitive, while most federal leasing of oil and gas onshore is not."[5]

STUMPAGE RIGHTS ON FEDERAL LANDS

Like the right to exploit mineral resources on public lands, the right to harvest federal timber is sold competitively, usually by oral auctions but occasionally by sealed bids. More than one-fourth of each year's softwood timber harvest

---

5. Hagenstein (1984, p. 79). See also Mead et al. (1985, p. 47) and Office of Management and Budget (1987b, pp. 6c-29, 6c-30).

comes from federal lands. National forests have about half the national total of softwood timber and 20 percent of the high-quality timberland.

Unlike the mineral leasing procedures, under which the leasing authorities retain the right to reject any bid considered too low, an auction of federal timber begins with an appraisal of the fair market value of the stumpage to be sold. Under the oral auction procedures, bidders must qualify by submitting a sealed bid at or above the appraised price and posting a minimum deposit or bond "as evidence of ability to meet stated sale requirements." On the sale date, which has been advertised 30 days in advance, the selected timber stand is sold to the highest bidder in an oral auction. Payment is not usually made until the timber is harvested (Mead et al. 1981; Muraoka and Watson 1985, pp. 202–4).

The auction winner must remove the timber before a designated date, generally within three to five years. Failure to complete a contract may result in a reappraisal of remaining timber on which the firm has to pay the reappraised value plus the original bid premium, or the original bid price, whichever is higher. Firms that fail to complete contracts may also be barred from future sales. In the past, nonfulfillment of contracts was rare, and punitive action was limited to repeat offenders; a recent increase in the frequency of defaults has led to the introduction of additional penalties (Muraoka and Watson 1985, pp. 204–5).

Concern about the status of small firms has led to the creation of provisions for small business setaside sales. Setaside sales are not triggered unless firms defined as "small"—those independently owned and operated, not dominant in the field of operation, and having fewer than 500 employees—have been unable to purchase a predetermined share, based on purchases in a designated five-year period, of federal timber offered for sale during a given 12-month period. Setaside sales are sales in which only small bidders, as defined above, are allowed to participate. There have been allegations, tentatively supported by empirical evidence, that the setaside sales involve relatively more valuable tracts, yet tend to elicit lower average winning bids than do regular sales (Mead, Schniepp, and Watson 1981, pp. 217–47; Schniepp 1985, p. 227).

There has been only one conviction for bid rigging in the federal timber sales. There have been repeated allegations of collusion to lower bids in the public auctions, however. Experimentation with sealed bids did result in higher average winning bids but public auctions continue to be used because of a strong preference on the part of the industry (Mead, Schniepp, and Watson 1981, pp. 217–32; Mead 1967, pp. 219–23).

SURPLUS GOVERNMENT PROPERTY

Surplus government property includes personal property (for example, typewriters and automobiles), real property (land and buildings), and excess supplies from the national defense stockpiles. Surplus property, once identified as such, may be sold to the public, and it is almost always sold on a competitive basis. The General Services Administration (GSA) administers all such sales.[6]

GSA will offer surplus real property first to other federal agencies, then to state and local governments at the appraised price for public use. If no other government entity is interested, the property is offered to the general public using the appraised value as the minimum bid. The sales are usually by sealed bid, although public auctions are used occasionally. Similar procedures are used to dispose of surplus personal property.

Sales procedures for national defense stockpile surpluses depend on the market for the commodity in question. Sealed bids are the preferred method if the market is sufficiently competitive. Bid results are announced publicly so that participants will know who bid what. For commodities offered regularly to knowledgeable bidders, the bids tend to cluster around a minimum level. For commodities for which demand is sporadic, the price highly volatile, or for which there are few buyers, alternative methods are used. For example, an "off-the-shelf" price is used for sales of tin, a commodity for which the price fluctuates daily on the London metal exchange. Manganese ore, on the other hand, is used mainly by steel companies who contract for their needs a year at a time. Negotiated offers are accepted for this and other commodities with very few buyers. The revenues go into a special fund that is used to replenish stocks as necessary. The fund has a statutorily set limit; when that ceiling is reached, commodities cannot be sold for money. This provision recently led the GSA to negotiate with ferroalloy users to trade raw materials for finished products.

TREASURY SECURITIES

Each week the Department of the Treasury auctions billions of dollars in short-term financial securities.[7] In the second quarter of 1986, for example,

---

6. Other agencies, such as the US Customs Service, auction seized and unclaimed property or hire professionals to do it. Unclaimed effects of dead seamen may also be auctioned.

7. Longer term notes and bonds are auctioned quarterly. The Bank of England recently conducted

an average of $25 billion in bids was tendered in the weekly auctions for 13-week T-bills. An average of $7.1 billion in bids was accepted, 85 percent on a competitive basis (US Department of the Treasury, *Treasury Bulletin*).

In the Treasury auctions, interested parties submit sealed bids based on the yield they would be willing to accept. Acceptance of bids begins at the low yield (highest price) and continues to the high yield (low price) that "clears" the market, the point at which all available securities have been allocated among eligible bidders. No single bidder in the competitive auction can be awarded more than 35 percent of the public offering (the remainder after Federal Reserve Banks' needs have been satisfied). If there is more than one tender at the high yield rate, the remaining securities are uniformly prorated among the bidders who submitted offers at that price. Noncompetitive bidders automatically receive what they ask for as long as it is less than $1 million and they are willing to accept the price that emerges from the auction, based on the average of the competitive bids.

There are two sets of books in which these transactions are recorded: the Treasury Direct Book-entry Securities System, held at the US Department of the Treasury; and the commercial book-entry system, held at Federal Reserve Banks. Securities under the Treasury Direct system are purchased by investors planning to hold them until maturity. These securities cannot be sold or traded unless they are transferred to the commercial book-entry system, which supports the secondary market. Participants in the Treasury Direct system are usually small investors making noncompetitive tenders who must make full payment at the time they submit their tender. Competitive bids in this system are extremely rare.

Bidders in the commercial system are usually banks and large investment houses who plan to resell the securities in the secondary market. Successful bidders in this system must make full payment at the time of settlement. The banks often have accounts with a Federal Reserve Bank that will be debited at the time of settlement if they bid successfully. Securities dealers, who do not have Federal Reserve accounts, often contract with the banks to use their accounts for this purpose. If there is no account to be drawn on, payment must be made by cashier's check or certified check for bills, which require

---

its first experimental auction of UK government bonds, which the *Financial Times* (14 May 1987, p. 1) reported had "passed off relatively smoothly, if undramatically." The spread among bids accepted by the Bank indicated a lack of expertise, as might be expected in the first auction. Nevertheless, the average competitive bid accepted was quite close to the lowest accepted price.

three to five days to settle, and either of those means or a personal check for notes or bonds, which take one to two weeks to settle.

Four people with calculators in Treasury's Bureau of the Public Debt oversee both auction systems and determine the final allocation of winning bids in all the auctions. A larger staff at the New York Federal Reserve Bank, however, actually collects the vast majority of commercial system bids, organizes them, and estimates what the high yield will be before sending them to Treasury.

PROPOSED AUCTION OF FCC LICENSES

The Federal Communications Commission is charged with assigning licenses for use of the airwaves. Currently, this is done through a combination of hearings and lottery. Recently, however, the administration proposed that Congress give the FCC authority to use auctions to assign non-mass media portions of the unassigned spectrum.

For many years, a hearings process was the dominant method used by the FCC for allocating construction permits and operating licenses to radio and television stations and other users of the airwaves, for example, cellular phone companies. This process is extremely lengthy and costly, to both the FCC and seekers of licenses. In 1982, Congress authorized the use of lotteries as a means of reducing the administrative burden; the FCC began implementing this option in late 1984. The *New York Times* (3 December 1984) greeted this move with enthusiasm, but noted that auctions would be an even better option:

The flaw in the [lottery] plan is that it doesn't let the public gain the profit. If space on the spectrum is really comparable to, say, oil under public lands, why not sell it instead of giving it away? Instead of a lottery, why not an auction? Revenues would go into the Treasury or, conceivably, be dedicated to public television and radio subsidies.

In fact, the lottery proved nearly as difficult and costly to administer as the hearings process, because the relatively low entry requirements and free transferability of licenses elicited a surge of applications.[8]

---

8. Mark S. Fowler, former FCC Chairman, noted that prior to introduction of the lottery, there were only 1,200 applications for the top 90 markets. "Following the decision, more than 5,000 applications were filed for markets 91 through 120. For markets 121 to 305, we received approximately 90,000 applications. And we expect over 100,000 applications for remaining markets" (Fowler 1986, p. 4).

As a result, the administration asked Congress in May 1985 to permit the FCC to use auctions in allocating licenses and permits. Congress took no action in 1985 or 1986 and the proposal was reintroduced in the President's budget for fiscal 1988. FCC Chairman Mark S. Fowler testified in favor of the idea in October 1986, noting that "not only would auctions generate revenues for the Treasury, they would also significantly reduce private and government administrative expenditures and delays that deprive the public of communications service and waste valuable resources" (Fowler 1986, p. 1). Director of the Office of Management and Budget James C. Miller endorsed the proposal on similar grounds, noting that:

Auctions . . . would ensure that a license is assigned to the applicant who places the highest monetary value on it and who, for that reason, has the greatest incentive to put it to good use. . . . At a time when we are all looking for new and innovative ways both to make the Federal Government more effective and efficient and to bring the Government's books into balance, the Commission's proposal, in my view, merits your serious and favorable consideration. (Miller 1986)

The FCC staff prepared a study on the concerns raised by opponents of auctions, in particular "that auctions might lead to greater concentration of ownership of FCC licenses or that they might favor those with deep pockets." The report noted:

If [large] firms were willing and able to monopolize spectrum under auctions, they could also do so under the current selection schemes by purchasing licenses from parties that won the initial assignment. . . . Apparently no firm has sufficient wealth to buy up all the spectrum. (Kwerel and Felker 1985, p. 11)

The report analyzed the potential design of an auction. It favored an oral auction with minimum bids if there were few bidders, but noted that problems in estimating the value of the license might outweigh the benefits of setting a reservation price if competition were intense. Similarly, it favored an oral auction over sealed bidding because bidders could react in an oral auction to other bids, therefore the license would be more likely to go to the one who values it the most. The report did not recommend a setaside for small bidders since monopolization was not considered a serious threat for the reasons mentioned earlier (Kwerel and Felker 1985, pp. 22–26).

Fowler concluded in his testimony that auctions "were an idea whose time has come." He said that the proposal offered "an opportunity for bipartisan action by Congress that can provide benefits to consumers and taxpayers." The administration's FY 1988 budget estimated that an auction of selected

FCC licenses could raise $600 million (Fowler 1986, pp. 5-7; Office of Management and Budget 1987b, p. 2-41).

Trade as an Anomaly

In the preceding cases, the government regularly sells public assets or the rights to exploit them.[9] In addition, the government charges fixed user fees and excise taxes for other economic goods and services that it provides in more than 40 programs administered by 36 different federal agencies (see appendix C).[10] Overall, the federal government will collect an estimated $35 billion in proprietary receipts from the public in FY 1987 from auctions and other sales of government property and assets, and "fees and other charges for services and special benefits" (Office of Management and Budget 1987b, pp. 6c-30).

When the government intervenes in the market to achieve a public goal, as in the cases we have described, it either creates or appropriates something of economic value, which it then must find a way of allocating. In a similar fashion, the government creates an asset with an economic value—a quota right—when it imposes trade restrictions. As shown in chapters 2 and 3, however, these assets are distributed *without charge,* enabling importers, or more frequently exporters or producers abroad, to reap windfall profits or quota rents. Quota rights are a rare example of economic assets that the government gives away rather than charges for or sells. In this regard, the treatment of property rights created by restrictions on trade is an anomaly.

Why should particular individuals reap these benefits free of charge, while others are excluded and the public foots the bill? Consumers pay the rents no matter who is collecting them or how they are distributed. Equity considerations argue that those rents be collected by the government rather

---

9. Although the administration has not yet received congressional approval to auction FCC licenses, it does charge a fee for them.

10. A recent survey defined a user fee program as one "that provides goods and services to identifiable private beneficiaries who can be effectively excluded from such benefits if they do not pay the fee." In addition to cases involving tangible property, examples include certain recreation facilities in national parks, Coast Guard services, and maintenance of coastal and inland waterways and harbors, which are available to all but which only a few use. Other examples are licensing and inspection "services," which are required to ensure the health and safety of US citizens, but without which the affected businesses would not be able to operate (Administrative Council of the United States 1986).

than by a few individuals and that they be used for a broader public purpose (for example, reducing the budget deficit or retraining workers who have lost their jobs due to changing economic trends).

Why does the government give away quota allocations while regularly selling the right to cut timber or exploit minerals on federal lands? Chairman Fowler (1986, p. 4), testifying in favor of auctioning FCC licenses which he estimated to be worth billions of dollars to those currently holding them, asked committee members to "imagine for a moment the furor, if the oil and gas companies had been given [mineral] leases for nothing." Prompted by environmental and other groups, Congress has, in fact, frequently criticized various resource disposal procedures for allegedly allowing private interests to exploit public resources without returning fair market value to the public.

The obvious difference is that oil, gas, and timber are tangible commodities with a clear economic value, while the costs of quantitative restraints to the economy and the windfall to a few individuals are often not understood. Trade policy officials focus more on the administrative and political problems created by the restraint than on the efficiency and equity questions arising from its imposition. The quota rents are either ignored or are used to compensate adversely affected exporters in other countries.

Implications for Auction Quotas

There are several useful lessons to be learned from government practices in allocating government benefits. First, quota allocations are a rare deviation from the presumption that the government should receive fair market value for the exclusive economic assets it distributes to individuals for private benefit. Second, auctions work. They have been conducted in these sectors for many years, and they are an established and accepted part of the landscape. Finally, as in the auction quota debate, collusion and market concentration have been recurring concerns, but safeguards built into the auction procedures have ameliorated those concerns.

There are a number of common elements in the different auctions intended to prevent potential monopolization, guard against collusive bidding, and ensure that the government receives fair market value. Procedures aimed at encouraging competition include:

● where applicable, limits on the size of bids (for example, limits on the size of mineral leases, timber stands, and the proportion of an offering of Treasury securities available to any single bidder)

- specific setasides or other special provisions for small and/or noncompetitive bidders, as in the timber and Treasury auctions, and joint bidding in OCS auctions

- use-it-or-lose-it requirements, which are implicit in the fixed time limits of the mineral leases and the timber auction contracts

- the use of sealed bids in the majority of cases because they are less vulnerable to collusion than public auctions (see chapter 8) and, in many ways, easier to administer.

The common features aimed at getting fair market value from the auctions are:

- sealed bids, which empirical evidence suggests result in higher bids and thus more revenue for the seller

- minimum bids, which are implicit in the mineral lease auctions (where the government reserves the right to refuse any bid) and explicit in the timber and GSA auctions (where opening bids must be above the appraisal value)

- use of security deposits and prompt payment requirements with penalties for nonfulfillment of contracts, where applicable.

Features of government auctions that contribute to smoother functioning of markets are the ready availability of information and the presence of secondary markets, where appropriate. Sales must be published in the *Federal Register,* usually well in advance, and in other publications as appropriate. After the auction, the results, including losing bids, are publicly announced. Information about the item being sold and about bidder behavior in prior auctions is critical to the ability of bidders to formulate their bids. Secondary markets are equally important in giving bidders an opportunity to correct mistakes made in the initial auction. Such markets exist for Treasury securities and for noncompetitively sold oil and gas leases.

Many of these features could be usefully incorporated in an auction quota system. Others, such as the minimum bids and use-it-or-lose-it requirements, would not be appropriate for reasons discussed in chapter 4. Our proposals for specific auction quota procedures are presented in chapter 8.

6 Auction Quota Debates from the Past

The illogic of giving away billions of dollars annually in quota rents has not gone completely unnoticed by policymakers. Although never implemented in the United States, auction quotas have been discussed on several occasions. Indeed, the President was granted authority to auction import licenses, with some exceptions, in section 1102 of the Trade Agreements Act of 1979, but he has never chosen to exercise it. Even earlier, auction quotas were considered repeatedly as a means of allocating oil import quotas and once as a remedy in an escape clause case. Since enactment of section 1102, auction quotas have been recommended in two other escape clause cases.

When proposed, auction quotas were never the center of the debate, and failure to adopt them seems to have reflected other priorities, not the relative merits of auctioning. This chapter summarizes the various situations in which auction quotas have been considered and the rationales and procedures proposed for their implementation on those occasions.

Proposals to Auction Oil Import Quotas

Perhaps because the potential quota rents are so large, and more recently out of a conviction that quota rents should not go to foreigners already extracting sizable monopoly rents, the possibility of auctioning import licenses has recurred most frequently with oil. Three administrations in office in the 1960s considered auctions in connection with the Mandatory Oil Import Program (MOIP), which used quotas to control oil imports from 1959 to 1973. In the mid-to-late 1970s, proposals to control the supply and distribution of oil imports through competitive bidding procedures were offered repeatedly in Congress as a means of countering the monopoly power of the Organization of Petroleum Exporting Countries (OPEC). Finally, auction quotas resurfaced as one of three options proposed by the Carter administration for allocating

71

oil import quotas in 1979 when the issue was briefly revived in a period of rapidly increasing oil prices following the Iranian revolution.

THE MANDATORY OIL IMPORT PROGRAM

In 1957, President Dwight D. Eisenhower, motivated by national security concerns following disruption of foreign supplies after the 1956 Suez crisis, asked US companies to "voluntarily" restrain oil imports (a rare example of a voluntary *import* restraint). He imposed mandatory quotas in 1959 when the voluntary program failed.[1] The program had two major goals: to maintain the domestic price at a level sufficient to keep high-cost wells in operation and encourage exploration and development of reserves; and to encourage imports of Western Hemisphere oil relative to Middle East oil, which was viewed as more vulnerable to interdiction.

The import ceiling, originally set at 9 percent of domestic production, was later changed to 12.2 percent of estimated domestic consumption in the current period. Quota rights were allocated to refiners in the United States based both on inputs of crude and unfinished oils in the previous year and on import shares under the voluntary program, so that no refiner would suffer a drastic cut in imports.[2] There was no official secondary market, but inland refiners with no way to use imported oil were allowed to trade their imported crude to coastal refiners for domestic oil supplies. A sliding scale was used to give small refiners a larger than *pro rata* allocation; over time, other special allocations were made for overland imports, petrochemicals, and for shipments from Puerto Rico and the Virgin Islands for development purposes. The growing list of exceptions and special allocations often resulted in imports over the ceiling, thereby creating considerable discontent with the program, especially among independent producers and refiners.

As early as 1963, an interagency task force, made up of representatives from the departments of State, Treasury, Defense, Justice, Interior, Commerce, and Labor, noted that the free distribution of oil import quota

---

1. Authority to limit imports for reasons of national security was included in the Trade Agreements Extension Acts of 1954 and 1955 and later incorporated in section 232 of the Trade Expansion Act of 1962.

2. For similar reasons, we recommend a historical setaside for importers of record at least during the transition to an auction system.

allocations under MOIP "place[d] the federal government in the role of distributing a considerable economic advantage, perhaps $1 million per day."[3] While noting that tariffs are preferable to quotas, the task force suggested that "fees and auctions are among the methods which might be used" as alternatives to the present system.[4]

In 1968, the Department of Interior solicited public comments on the auction idea. In hearings on the operation of MOIP before the House Subcommittee on Mines and Mining, J. Cordell Moore, Assistant Secretary of Interior for Mineral Resources, conceded that the comments received in the first two months were running 99 to 1 against the proposal. Subcommittee Chairman Ed Edmondson (D-Okla.) opened the hearings by noting skeptically:

the Secretary of the Interior has been talking—and surveying industry opinion—about a radically new idea for raising Federal revenues by auctioning of import quotas. The auction proposal, while possibly attractive to some interests and undoubtedly a possible source of revenue for Government, would almost certainly be ruinous for many companies and would assuredly result in price increases for the consumer. (US Congress, House, Committee on Interior and Insular Affairs 1968, p. 1)

The one organization in favor of an auction system was the Texas Independent Producers and Royalty Owners Association (TIPRO). Its dissatisfaction with the existing system stemmed from concerns that the quota level was insufficiently restrictive to raise foreign prices to the domestic level and that the allocation method unintentionally promoted monopolization of the market by the majors, sometimes leading to "product price wars and other measures which place domestic independents in grave jeopardy" (US Congress, House, Committee on Interior and Insular Affairs 1968, p. 236). TIPRO claimed that the concentration of the benefits of cheaper imported oil in the hands of the large international companies "fails to neutralize the economic advantage of foreign oil."

As independent producers of domestic oil, TIPRO wanted a system that supported domestic prices and raised the price of imports with greater certainty than under the current system. It presented an auction proposal that included

---

3. Hufbauer, Berliner, and Elliott (1986) estimate quota rents to have been $2 billion in 1971, about $5.5 million a day.

4. The Kennedy task force report is cited in documents accompanying testimony by the Texas Independent Producers and Royalty Owners Association (US Congress, House, Committee on Interior and Insular Affairs 1968, pp. 237–38).

incentives to use domestic crude and preferences for small inland refiners to guard against monopolization by the large integrated companies. In addition, it required minimum bids under certain circumstances. There were three categories of refiners with different bidding requirements for each. Eligible firms in the most favorable category were those not refining foreign crude in the United States and those "which do not contribute to domestic oversupply of products by refining in excess of logically devised standards" (US Congress, House, Committee on Interior and Insular Affairs 1968, p. 239). This group, mainly small independent refiners, would not have to bid or pay for their allocation and would be allowed to enter into exchange agreements with other eligible importers.

The other two main categories would consist primarily of the major integrated companies, based on the proportion of imported crude in their refinery runs. Those using less than 15 percent of imported crude would be in the more favorable category and would be required to meet a lower minimum bid. Companies using larger proportions of imported oil would be subject to minimum bids of up to 600 percent of the 1967 tariff level. TIPRO also recommended that the quota tickets be divided among specific source continents to avoid undermining the national security objective of discouraging excessive reliance on cheaper Middle Eastern sources.

Fred Hartley, President of the Union Oil Company of California, added a new wrinkle in a presentation before the National Petroleum Refiners Association in April 1968. He recommended auctioning 10 percent of the allocations and using the weighted average price of the tickets to set the price for the remainder, which would be sold to refiners and chemical companies based on refinery capacity without a sliding scale or any special allocations. The administratively set "formula" price would actually be somewhat below the average bid price, and small companies would be allowed to purchase tickets at 50 percent of the formula price.

The strongest opposition to the auction proposal came from refiners, including independents, who were collecting quota premiums or who feared increased input costs and a lower profit margin. Unlike the producers, who were interested in the highest possible domestic crude oil price, the refiners were interested in the margin between crude and product prices. Free allocation of the quota to refiners was, in effect, a subsidy. Several inland refiners testified that they used the rents to offset the cost of the more expensive domestic oil. If forced to rely entirely on domestic sources, they claimed they would lower the price they were willing to pay for crude rather than raise the price of their products to consumers, thereby undermining the price objective of the quota program. It is unclear, however, why the refiners would not already have cut the price they were willing to pay for crude or raised product prices, while still collecting the rents, if that were feasible.

The independents also feared that they would not be able to compete in an auction with larger, integrated companies and would find themselves at a competitive disadvantage from having to rely solely on the more expensive domestic oil. As noted earlier, this implies that they did not believe the quota ticket price would be bid up to the full difference between domestic and imported crude prices and, therefore, that the winning bidders would still be capturing some of the rent. This fear would be justified only if the market position of the international companies were sufficiently strong.

As for the majors, those submitting statements to the committee objected primarily to the rent transfer to the government. Several claimed that the rents were intentionally granted to the industry to provide it with the additional funds needed for exploration and development of reserves.[5] Companies also feared supply disruption and market distortions, and adverse reactions from previously favored Western Hemisphere suppliers.

Although vigorous opposition from the petroleum industry deterred the Johnson administration from pursuing the auction idea, dissatisfaction with the existing quota system continued to grow. In 1969, President Richard Nixon appointed a special cabinet task force, headed by then Secretary of Labor George Shultz, to study "The Oil Import Question" (Cabinet Task Force 1970). The task force considered several options for controlling oil imports, including the auction alternative.

Although favoring a conversion to tariffs, the task force pointed out several advantages of an auction over administrative allocation under competitive market conditions:

- elimination of the current inefficient, ineffective system of allocation

- quota distribution via a market mechanism

- greater competition within the industry.

---

5. Section 232 import relief is imposed for very different reasons than escape clause relief, which is supposed to give an industry a breathing space to adjust, usually by downsizing. Nevertheless, this example illustrates an alternative method for providing adjustment assistance to an injured industry. See chapter 10 for a fuller discussion of ways of using quota rents to fund adjustment assistance.

Nevertheless, the task force did not recommend an auction as an alternative for allocating the aggregate quota, even if the first-best tariff option were rejected. If the President opted to retain the quota, the task force recommended replacing the anticompetitive historical share and sliding scale allocations with "the uniform distribution of a fully convertible ticket" subject to government monitoring.[6]

In rejecting the comprehensive auction alternative, the task force cited the possibilities that it would raise consumer prices and favor low cost, potentially less secure Middle Eastern suppliers. The task force accepted industry arguments that the refiners were passing along some of their cost savings from the free allocation system to consumers, though it offered no evidence to support that conclusion. It also noted that the "danger" of excessive reliance on Middle Eastern sources could be addressed in the structure of the auction.

The task force did offer several suggestions as to how an auction might be used in more limited fashion, either in conjunction with the tariff option or to rationalize the existing quota. First of all, the task force implicitly conceded that excessive reliance on the Middle East could be a problem under the task force's proposed "retariffication" option as much as under an auction. It suggested using an auction as a "security adjustment mechanism" as part of the tariff plan. Whenever projected imports from the Middle East exceeded 10 percent of total domestic demand, the task force recommended auctioning import licenses for that maximum, with importers paying the license price as determined in the auction on top of the higher proposed tariff (Cabinet Task Force 1970, pp. 80, 82, 87, 138).

The task force also suggested other limited uses of an auction system in administering the quota within the existing structure. One alternative was to substitute a "partial auction" for the sliding scale. Under this system, similar to the earlier TIPRO plan, quotas would be allocated directly to small refiners with only the remainder auctioned, in whole or part, to the integrated companies. An even more limited possibility was that of auctioning the allocations to northern tier refiners whose imports of Canadian oil were exempt from restrictions and whose allocations were based on historical shares of a decade earlier. The task force's report also stated that an auction

---

6. The task force did not specify to whom or how the initial distribution would be made (Cabinet Task Force 1970, pp. 86–87).

might be a more equitable (i.e., unsubsidized) means of distributing petroleum product quotas. A separate auction of product licenses would also solve the potential problem of diversion of imports from crude to higher value products.

President Nixon rejected all the recommendations and no changes were made in the oil import system until April 1973 when he replaced the quota with a license-fee system. These fees quickly lost significance in the face of rapidly rising world oil prices and the Arab oil embargo.

COUNTERING OPEC

Although OPEC contributed to the demise of oil quotas in 1973, it helped revive the issue very quickly thereafter. In 1975, concerns about "national vulnerability to economic disruption [exacerbated by] dependence on foreign oil" led to efforts by the President and Congress to forge a comprehensive energy policy (US Congress, House, Committee on Ways and Means 1975, p. 6). Similar concerns were revived in 1979–80 when the second oil shock occurred. The central goal of many of the proposals was to shift market power from OPEC to the United States.

The House Ways and Means Committee submitted a proposal (HR 6860) in 1975 that included an oil import quota to be administered via a double auction quota system: the first auction would allocate among foreign exporters the right to ship oil to the United States; the second would allocate the right to import it. The committee recommended creation of a Federal Petroleum Purchasing Agency with "the exclusive right to import crude oil and oil products into the United States." It suggested that the agency "could promote competition for the US market among producing countries through allocation of import purchase orders by auctioning them under sealed competitive bids. Such a system would reward the lowest bidder, tend to lower the costs of imports, and expose the OPEC cartel's problem of excess capacity." The agency would then allocate freely transferable import tickets among potential importers by auction (US Congress, House, Committee on Ways and Means 1975, pp. 6–8). The House of Representatives approved HR 6860, but the bill failed to pass the Senate.

In 1979, the disruption caused by the Iranian revolution and rapidly increasing oil prices led to an agreement at the Tokyo Economic Summit in June to limit oil imports. President Jimmy Carter pledged at the summit to hold imports to 8.5 million barrels per day (mmbd) through 1985. In July

1979, President Carter proposed a comprehensive energy plan, including an import ceiling of 8.2 mmbd for that year and 8.5 mmbd annually through 1985.[7] Congress was leery of the effects of a quota, and several variations on the federal purchasing agency idea were proposed in the Ways and Means Committee as alternatives.

Nevertheless, the departments of Energy and Treasury developed three options for controlling imports: an auction quota; a license-fee system; or free distribution of quota tickets to refiners, as in the 1960s. The preliminary auction plan called for quota tickets to be allocated first to the highest bidder with bids filled down to the clearing level. Bidders would be allowed to make multiple bids (different prices for various quantities), and the tickets would be freely transferable.

In October 1979, Acting Assistant Secretary of Energy C. William Fischer discussed the import restraint options in hearings before the House Committee on Ways and Means, Subcommittee on Trade (1979). Representative Sam Gibbons (D-Fla.), although concerned about the effects of a quota no matter how administered, expressed a preference for seeing the auction option tried. He was worried, however, that an auction could result in excess refinery capacity if those refineries needing them did not succeed in getting tickets. Representative Henson Moore (R-La.) stated his fear of monopolization of the market by the larger corporations, while Representative Thomas J. Downey (D-N.Y.) worried that an auction would create additional upward pressure on prices and queried whether such a system would favor larger corporations with "deep pockets." Fischer responded that the secondary market should take care of any misallocation in the initial auction, while potential monopolization could be addressed with a setaside provision for small bidders. He also pointed out that oil prices in the US market would rise only at the point at which the quota became binding and that that would occur regardless of how it was administered.

Subcommittee Chairman Charles A. Vanik (D-Oh.) raised the issue of uncertainty of supply of imports under an auction system and the potential impact of that uncertainty on refinery investment decisions. Fischer responded:

A market type system, which is the system that we are talking about here, does have its uncertainties because it is controlled basically by price and supply and

---

7. The United States had imported an average 8.5 mmbd in 1977 before the addition of Alaskan oil supplies. Demand had rebounded to the 8.5 mmbd level in January 1979 but subsequently dropped back to between 7.9 mmbd and 8.1 mmbd (*Congressional Quarterly Weekly*, 7 July 1979, p. 1337).

demand relationships in the market. . . . Any time you have an administratively imposed allocation system, you are always working against a historical base, a historical set of numbers of what the supply-demand relationships have been. And that is always by definition in error. It never accurately reflects the current situation. (US Congress, House, Committee on Ways and Means, Subcommittee on Trade 1979, pp. 45–46)

In this period, however, many members of Congress, and users of petroleum and petroleum products, were opposed to quotas, regardless of their allocation. A Congressional Research Service report had predicted that an 8.5 mmbd quota would begin to bite in 1982 with increasing shortfalls through 1985. It also predicted that the most likely outcome was a 1985 shortfall of between 500,000 and 800,000 barrels per day resulting in a differential of $10 per barrel between domestic and world oil prices and a total cost to consumers of $72.5 billion.[8] The estimated macroeconomic effects included GNP growth 2 percent lower than otherwise, 500,000 fewer jobs, and a 2 percent increase in the consumer price index.

In the end, congressional opposition and changing economic conditions combined to forestall the imposition of quotas. High oil prices, improved conservation measures, and a deep recession dampened demand for imports to below 7 mmbd in 1980 and to just over 5 mmbd on average in 1982–85, well below the proposed quota levels. An oil import fee was proposed in 1980 (and again in 1987) to further encourage conservation, but quotas have not been revived as an option.[9]

Auction Quotas and the Escape Clause

On three occasions in the past decade, auction quotas have been recommended as an option for providing import relief under the escape clause of section 201 of the Trade Act of 1974. In 1977, a minority of commissioners on the US International Trade Commission (USITC) recommended auctioning sugar

---

8. The Congressional Research Service (1979) roughly estimated that $32 billion of this would go to the US Treasury and $40.5 billion to the domestic industry under an auction system.

9. The oil import figures are derived from various issues of the *Survey on Current Business*. The national security finding used to establish MOIP was updated by Treasury Secretary W. Michael Blumenthal in April 1979 when the administration wanted to impose import fees on oil. The finding continues to provide the authority for the President to impose quotas or fees on oil imports if he so chooses; he would not, however, have the authority to auction import licenses under that finding. See the discussion on section 1102 at the end of this chapter.

quotas; in 1985, a majority recommended auction quotas for nonrubber footwear. Both times, however, the President rejected any form of relief. In 1984, the Federal Trade Commission (FTC) recommended auction quotas to the USITC as a third-best remedy, after adjustment assistance and tariffs, in the carbon steel case; it repeated the recommendation before the administration's interagency trade policy review committee after the USITC had recommended a combination of quotas and tariffs. The President rejected statutory relief in that case as well and instead negotiated "voluntary" export restraints (VERs).

In each case, advocates of global auction quotas argued that this approach would result in a more efficient allocation of quota and lower welfare costs; by contrast, country-specific allocations would freeze the pattern of supply, while first-come-first-served allocations could lead to disruptive import surges. In addition, auctions would lower the costs to the economy, although not to consumers, to the extent that the quota rents could be repatriated to the United States.

In the 1977 sugar case, in addition to the advantages already cited, US International Trade Commissioners Will Leonard and Italo Ablondi favored an auction for reasons specific to the sugar industry. Cane sugar refiners are the primary importers of raw sugar and, therefore, would be likely to capture the bulk of the rents generated by a global quota administered on a first-come-first-served basis. Leonard and Ablondi feared that these refiners might lower their prices below the quota-induced level, thereby passing along some of the the quota premium to consumers, in order to meet competition from the high fructose corn syrup industry. The commissioners concluded that "this use of the premium will prevent the full upward adjustment of domestic sugar prices, and the protective quota will fall short of achieving the objective—the target price."[10]

Instead of either a first-come-first-served or country-specific quota, Leonard and Ablondi recommended establishment of a global quota "to be allocated on the basis of nontransferable import licenses to be auctioned by the Secretary of Agriculture from time to time as appropriate under such regulations as the Secretary of Agriculture shall prescribe, such regulations to provide for the equitable distribution of the imports among importers."[11] They noted "that

---

10. See "Views of Commissioners Leonard and Ablondi with Respect to Import Relief" in USITC (1977, p. 44).

11. The dual requirement for both an auction and an "equitable" distribution among importers may reflect a concern about potential monopolization (USITC 1977, p. 44).

the administrative costs of a remedy providing for an auction of import licenses would be much less than for administering a country-by-country quota'' and that the revenues from the quota rents, which they estimated at $250 million, would go to the US Treasury and could be used to pay for administering the relief, thus "to some extent offset[ting] the total cost to society. . . ." (USITC 1977, p. 56).

A majority of commissioners recommended country-specific quotas without addressing the licensing issue or to whom the specific right to import should be granted (USITC 1977, pp. 5–6). In the end, President Carter rejected the USITC recommendation, but he did raise tariffs under authority of headnote 2 of the Tariff Schedules of the United States.

In 1984, the Federal Trade Commission recommended auction quotas to the USITC in remedy hearings in the carbon steel escape clause case. In addition to allowing the government to capture estimated rents of $134 million[12] and permitting a more efficient allocation, the FTC favored an auctioned global quota over an allocated quota because it would have "the advantage of not creating a possibly new group [of quota right holders] who would devote resources toward the maintenance of steel quotas."[13] The administration rejected both sets of proposed remedies and negotiated VERs with major suppliers.

In 1985, four of five USITC commissioners recommended auction quotas as the appropriate remedy for the shoe industry.[14] The majority concluded that import licenses distributed by auction would "create greater certainty, regulate the flow of imports, and preclude the build up of excess inventories (beyond that allowed under the quota) in Customs warehouses because importers will bring only that quantity of merchandise permitted under the license." Furthermore, as noted in other cases, the auction would reduce the costs to the US economy, although not to consumers, by transferring quota

---

12. The Congressional Budget Office (1984, p. 46) also noted that import licenses could be auctioned in order to capture the quota premium for the government. Hufbauer, Berliner, and Elliott (1986) estimated that the quota rents from restraints in effect since 1982 against the European Community and Japan, the major suppliers, were $2 billion annually. The FTC estimates reflect just the additional cost of extending restraints to other suppliers, not the cost of the existing restraints against the EC and Japan.

13. The Federal Trade Commission (1984, pp. 29, 31) did not foresee the government becoming so "hooked" on the revenue as to support retention of the quotas.

14. Commissioner Susan Liebeler recommended that relief be in the form of tariffs but concurred in the opinion that an auction should be used if quotas were imposed.

rents from foreigners to the US Treasury, revenues that could be used to "defray the costs of administering the program. . . ."[15]

USITC Chairwoman Paula Stern amplified the case for global auctioned quotas, noting that they

● "substitute the price mechanism for fiat in allocating scarce import rights," in this way resembling the effects of a tariff

● are more transparent

● are more "effective" (i.e., more restrictive) than country-specific restraints or orderly marketing arrangements (OMAs) that allow for diversion to unrestrained countries and encourage upgrading by restrained suppliers.[16]

Stern also pointed out that auction revenues could be dedicated to an adjustment program for the injured industry and its workers (USITC 1985, p. 132). Again, however the administration rejected the recommendation, and in this case elected not to provide any relief at all.

In December 1986, the General Accounting Office (GAO) echoed several of these arguments in analyzing the potential effects of auction quotas as a remedy in section 201 cases (Comptroller General 1986, pp. 2–3, 18–21). The GAO noted that auctioning would allow the government, rather than foreign producers, to capture the rents, thereby reducing the costs to the US economy, and that it "would distort trade less than administratively allocated quotas" by allowing new, potentially more efficient suppliers to enter the market. The report expressed skepticism that an auction system would be more burdensome to monitor and enforce than an administratively allocated quota; moreover, auction revenue could be used to offset the cost of administering the quotas. It concluded that the "potential advantages of auctioned quotas, relative to the known disadvantages of . . . allocated quotas, could be significant." It recommended that the Department of Treasury "experiment with auctions of import licenses in selected cases and evaluate their effectiveness, administrative feasibility, and potential for wider application." The study further recommended that the US Trade Represent-

---

15. See "Views of Chairwoman Paula Stern and Commissioners Alfred E. Eckes, Seeley G. Lodwick, and David B. Rohr on Remedy" in USITC (1985, p. 119).

16. The third point pertains to global quotas whether they are auctioned or not. Also, upgrading could still occur if the quotas were volume based and the bids were on a dollar per volume basis. See ch. 4 on the upgrading issue and "Additional Views of Chairwoman Paula Stern on Remedy" in USITC (1985, pp. 131–32).

ative explore with other nations whether auction quotas could facilitate the negotiation of a General Agreement on Tariffs and Trade (GATT) safeguards code (see chapter 9).

Congress and Auction Quotas

Congressional attitudes toward auction quotas over the past decade have fluctuated between skepticism and hesitant acceptance. The House recommended and the Senate rejected the idea in the drafting of sugar legislation in 1978; both considered auctions as options in energy debates throughout the 1970s; and the full Congress finally incorporated auction authority in the Trade Agreements Act of 1979.

After the President rejected the 1977 USITC recommendation to protect the sugar industry, Congress attempted to do so legislatively. The House Agriculture Committee passed the Sugar Stabilization Act of 1978, HR 13750, which mandated the use of quotas and fees to achieve the target price and granted the President explicit authority to allocate the quotas via auction (*New York Times*, 2 August 1978). Treasury Department officials endorsed quota auctions as a second-best solution, if Congress would not give the President authority to use a variable fee to control sugar imports.[17] An alternative Ways and Means bill, HR 13848, "A Bill to Carry Out the Obligations of the United States under the International Sugar Agreement," reflected the administration's position in favor of variable fees and a lower support price, but it also included auctions as a means of allocating backup quotas as necessary.

In the end, the House approved the Agriculture Committee's bill with Ways and Means Committee amendments on the price support level and with auctioned quotas as a backup to fees. The Senate further amended the legislation inter alia by raising the support price and requiring that any quotas imposed be global and administered on a first-come-first-served basis. The amended legislation was submitted to a conference committee, which retained the Senate provisions on quotas and made other modifications that were ultimately unacceptable to the House (US Congress 1978). The House rejected the conference report, and no sugar legislation was passed.

---

17. A simple tariff was not recommended in this case because it could not have reliably achieved the price objective for domestic sugar.

The auction quota proposal was seldom mentioned in either the committee hearings or the floor debate on the various bills, so it is difficult to surmise the reasons why it was offered. Representative Vanik, however, repeatedly referred to the positive revenue effects of relying on fees to control sugar imports; one could thus conclude that auctions were also proposed primarily for revenue reasons. In addition, given a presumption in both houses that any sugar quota imposed should be global, an auction may also have been viewed in the House as a means of allocation superior to the first-come-first-served method recommended by the Senate.

In 1979, Congress finally included explicit, although limited, auction quota authority in section 1102 of the Trade Agreements Act, which explicitly permits the President to "sell import licenses at public auction under such terms and conditions as he deems appropriate." To address concerns about potential monopolization, Congress specified that the implementing regulations "shall, to the extent practicable and consistent with efficient and fair administration, insure against inequitable sharing of imports by a relatively small number of the larger importers."

The authority is not comprehensive, primarily due to lingering concerns over potential petroleum quotas under section 232 and heavy lobbying by the food processing industry. Thus, section 22 of the Agricultural Adjustment Act of 1933, meat imports under section 204 of the Agricultural Act of 1956, or any act implementing international agreements relating to cheese or dairy products are explicitly exempted from the auction authority. The Meat Act of 1979 and section 232 of the Trade Expansion Act of 1962 are also not included.[18] The exemptions and exclusions mean that the legislation would have to be amended for the President to auction import licenses for existing restrictions on machine tools, dairy products, or meat.

Import licenses can be auctioned under sections 201 (the escape clause), 301 (retaliation against unfair trade practices), and 406 (disruption due to imports from nonmarket economies) of the Trade Act of 1974; headnote authority of the tariff schedules; the International Emergency Economic Powers Act; the Trading with the Enemy Act; quantitative restraints on other than meat products under section 204 of the Agricultural Act of 1956; and "any Act enacted explicitly for the purpose of implementing an international

---

18. The House Ways and Means Committee report also explicitly states that the authority does not apply to petroleum or petroleum products (US Congress, House, Committee on Ways and Means 1979, p. 186).

agreement,'' except those relating to dairy products. As such, this authority could apply to the sugar quotas, which are under headnote authority rather than section 22, the specialty steel quotas under the escape clause, and the carbon steel and textile and apparel VERs if those restraints were converted to US-administered import quotas. The auto VER could not be auctioned, since no domestic authority exists to impose import quotas.[19]

Under existing authority, however, the conversion of the VERs on carbon steel and textiles and apparel to auction quotas would require the acquiescence of the United States' trading partners. Abrogation of the steel agreements would cancel the authority to auction steel import quotas since that authority applies in this case ''explicitly for the purpose of implementing an international agreement.'' Section 204, which provides the legal basis for the textile and apparel agreements, authorizes the President to impose import quotas if a majority of trade in the product is already covered by negotiated restraint agreements. If unilateral conversion to auction quotas led to the abrogation of those agreements, the President would no longer have authority to impose import quotas. These legal requirements underscore our recommendation in chapter 10 that any conversion of existing quantitative restraints to auction quotas be negotiated rather than implemented unilaterally.

Reports by both the House Ways and Means and Senate Finance committees on section 1102 pointed out that an auction might be ''a more desirable method to achieve the purposes of particular quantitative restrictions. . . .'' In particular, the House report stressed the advantages of moving to a more market-oriented system, while the Senate report noted the desirability of capturing the quota rents (US Congress, House, Committee on Ways and Means 1979; US Congress, Senate, Committee on Finance 1979). However, the President has not established implementing regulations to guide the imposition of auction quotas, much less advocated their use in the distribution of quota rights. For this reason, and for the revenue considerations noted in chapters 1 and 10, Congress revived the debate on auction quotas in 1986 and 1987. The contemporary debate has centered on whether to make the

---

19. Auctioning licenses to import automobiles under the current VER would not be desirable in any event since only one country is involved, thereby making it easier for that country to take steps to retain the quota rents. Moreover, many observers believe that, with liberalization of the restraint level and the substantial appreciation of the yen, the VER on automobiles no longer has any major restraining effect.

use of auction quotas mandatory and, if so, whether the mandate should apply only to future cases or to existing cases of quantitative restraints as well.

Summary

On several occasions over the past 25 years, auction quotas have been proposed as a market-oriented approach to administering quantitative trade controls. That the proposals have never been implemented reflects less the merits of the idea than the fact that auctions were never central to the decision whether to impose or modify a quota system.

The only cases in which auctions were an important part of the debate were the two oil quota programs. The auction proposal was defeated in the 1960s because of the vigorous opposition of the refiners who were capturing the rents. In 1979, auctions were again proposed, but the issue became moot when oil imports plunged and quotas became unnecessary. In every other case, import quotas were rejected as not being in the national economic interest, regardless of how they might be administered.

Proponents of auction quotas repeatedly stressed the efficiency and equity of an auction system. First, it would not require arbitrary administrative decisions about the allocation of benefits that would unavoidably discriminate against someone. Second, it would encourage the use of global quotas, which do not discriminate among countries and which allow importers to buy from the most efficient suppliers. Finally, it would allow the government to capture the quota rents, thereby reducing the cost to the American economy (although not to consumers, as noted in chapter 2).

7 Auction Quotas in Australia and New Zealand

In the 1980s, Australia and New Zealand instituted systems for auctioning import quotas. Both programs are designed to provide a more transparent system of protection, to convert existing quantitative controls into their tariff-rate equivalents ("retariffication"), and to liberalize import controls on a selective basis.

Australia and New Zealand are the only countries that have used auctions to distribute import licenses, in addition to allocations based on historical market shares and other allocation methods. Sufficient data now exist to analyze the results of these "experiments" with import auctions. This chapter will compare the import auction systems in Australia and New Zealand, examine the results of the auctions, and explore whether there are lessons that can be derived to instruct US trade policy.

Comparison of the Australian and New Zealand Auction Systems

Given the similarities and proximity of their economies, it is not surprising that both Australia and New Zealand have adopted a similar approach to their import problems by introducing a system of import quota auctions. There are important differences, however, between the type of auction, the administrative provisions, and the product coverage in both systems (see table 7.1). Some of the differences reflect the history of import protection in each country; others have resulted from the trial-and-error modifications instituted in light of the ongoing experience with auctions. In both countries, the import auctions are only a part of broader industry plans set by the government.

Product coverage. The Australian system aims to unravel the web of quotas on selected manufactured imports that was instituted in the 1970s. Auctions of import licenses are held for 24 categories of textiles, clothing,

TABLE 7.1   **Comparison of Australian and New Zealand import auctions**

Issue	Australian policy	New Zealand policy
Type of auction	Sealed bids. Lowest premium that clears pool is the premium rate for all bidders.	Sealed bids. Each bidder pays what he bids.
Value vs. volume quota	Of 24 categories, 21 are volume based.	Almost all are value based.
Global vs. country	Global licenses with limited exceptions for ANZCERTA quotas.	Global licenses with limited exceptions for ANZCERTA quotas.
Dollar vs. ad valorem bids	Ad valorem bids.	Dollar bids.
Minimum bids/size of licenses	No minimum bids.	Bids for small units of licenses (NZ $2000).
		No minimum bids, but bids below 7.5 percent make item eligible for license on demand in future.
Duration of licenses	One year generally; four-year quota entitlements also offered for motor vehicles.	One year; "continuity" licenses also available for 50 percent of the value of the license for an additional year.
Transferability of licenses	Base quota freely transferable; transfer of more than 20 percent of auction quota can trigger review.	Auctioned licenses freely transferable upon notification to the government.
Antispeculation provisions	Security deposit required equal to 10 percent of estimated average unit value of imports; forfeited if goods not imported.	Security deposit of 20 percent of bid within 14 days of notification of successful bids; balance due within three months.
	No penalty for underutilization of base quota.	Companies that use less than 75 percent of auction quota can be barred from future tenders.
		Each bidder limited to 20 percent of auction pool.
Product coverage	Textiles, clothing, footwear, and passenger motor vehicles (not all imports).	All imports subject to QRs (less than 10 percent of total imports).

and footwear (TCF), and for passenger motor vehicles. The auctions cover licenses for a small, but growing share of the total imports of these goods; most licenses, however, are still allocated administratively according to historical market shares.

Coverage under the New Zealand system is more diverse, reflecting the comprehensive nature of the import licensing policy that has been in place since 1938. Auctioned licenses are offered across the entire range of items subject to quantitative import controls. Licensing requirements currently apply to about 16.5 percent of total imports. Approximately one-quarter of all licenses issued are auctioned; of these, motor vehicles and apparel account for the largest share.

Type of auction. Both countries use sealed bidding rather than oral auctions. In Australia, tariff quotas are used to protect industry. Licenses are auctioned for imports under quota; other imports may still enter, although at a higher overquota tariff. The Australian auctions solicit bids from eligible importers, distributors, and manufacturers in the form of the ad valorem premium over the base tariff rates that they are willing to pay to receive a license for a certain volume of imports of a particular category of goods. The lowest bid that clears the tender pool becomes the "premium rate" for all licenses for that category. The TCF licenses are valid for one year; 21 of the 24 categories are denominated in volume terms and the rest in value terms. For imports of motor vehicles, auctions are held for both one-year and four-year licenses denominated in volume terms.

The New Zealand system differs in several significant ways from the Australian program. With one exception, the quotas are value based; some volume-based quotas had applied until recently but are now being phased out. Sealed bids are submitted, and the bidder pays what he bids.[1] Bids take the form of cash payments for quota tickets that entitle an importer to enter NZ$2,000 worth of a specific category of goods. The total available quota is divided into an equal number of these NZ$2,000 value units. Auctioned licenses are valid for one year; "continuity" licenses, which give the holder the right in the following year to 50 percent of the value of the license of the current year at the same rate, are available but their "take up" or use

---

1. The situation differs slightly for licenses tendered subject to the Australia–New Zealand Closer Economic Relations Trade Agreement (ANZCERTA). If the amount put up for tender is undersubscribed, no premium is payable. If the amount is oversubscribed, the amount bid is payable as with global tenders.

varies by product from very little to 100 percent (as occurred in motor vehicles for the 1987 quota).

In both systems, almost all tendered licenses are global, i.e., they permit imports from any country. Global quotas encourage imports from the most efficient suppliers, thus providing stronger price competition for domestic industries. In addition, global quotas make it more difficult for the exporting countries to siphon off a share of the quota rents.[2] Proceeds from the auctions are not earmarked for specific programs and go into the general Treasury revenue pool. Both countries, however, fund industry adjustment programs out of general revenues as part of their overall industry assistance plans.

The quota categories themselves provide in many instances flexibility to import a broad range of products or similar products made of different materials. Compared with US quotas on textiles and apparel, which are divided into more than 100 product categories, the systems in Australia and New Zealand provide "broadbanded" quotas. Such broadbanding is a key element of their policy of industrial rationalization. It enables importers to concentrate their imports on particular items (presumably the more profitable ones), thus focusing import competition on the weakest lines of domestic production.

Transfer of licenses. Another important element in both systems is transfer provisions for import entitlements. Such provisions seek to promote greater utilization of licenses by providing flexibility to meet changing market conditions. At the same time, however, they restrict the size of transfers and holdings of tender quota by individual firms in an effort to forestall, for example, speculation and preemptive bidding by large companies.

Auctioned licenses in New Zealand are fully transferable. This tends to limit "panic bidding" because if one fails to get all the licenses needed, there is still an opportunity to buy more from other license holders. By contrast, in Australia transfers of auctioned quota above 20 percent of holdings are subject to review by the Australian Customs Service. In practice, however, such reviews do not control the unlimited transfer of import entitlements because of the difficulty in regulating the activities of "shelf companies" and of "quota brokers."

---

2. Although Australian and New Zealand firms may be considered "price takers" in the world market, their ability in most cases to source from any foreign supplier of a restricted good enables the importer to seize the quota rents. Moreover, both governments effectively capture a substantial share of the potential rents by maintaining high base tariffs on most imports subject to quantitative restraints.

Antispeculation provisions. Both governments attempt to control speculation and underutilization of quotas by requiring security deposits and by setting usage requirements. In Australia, winning bidders must put down a security deposit equal to 10 percent of the average unit value of the volume of goods for which they hold the import entitlement. Failure to import results in the forfeiture of the deposit. Similarly, New Zealand requires a security deposit of 20 percent of the license fee (recently increased from 10 percent) within 14 days of notification of a successful bid. The balance is due within three months.

Given the low level of security deposit required, it could be profitable for domestic producers with sufficient market power to preempt competition by bidding high for import licenses and then to not import. The cost of the forfeited deposits would be made up out of the profits earned by increasing prices on the import-competing domestic goods. However, there would be incentives to shortship, if a firm has sufficient market power to affect prices, regardless of whether quota rights are auctioned or allocated administratively (see chapter 2 and appendix A).

To forestall such manipulation, New Zealand tried at first to place limits on how much of the total pool each bidder could acquire (usually 20 percent)—much like the US Treasury does for its securities auctions (with a 35 percent limit). This was meant to protect the small bidder, but analysts of the New Zealand system concluded in 1984 that restrictions on bidding were not needed because efficient small firms should be able to obtain funds in capital markets to finance their bids (Syntec Economic Services 1984, p. 66). In addition, the New Zealand government required importers to fill at least 75 percent of their license or be barred from future auctions for two years. Neither discipline has proven very workable, and the "use-it-or-lose-it" rule has never been invoked. Both requirements are easily evaded through bids by subsidiary or dummy companies, or by simply changing the name of the bidder. Other problems with use-it-or-lose-it requirements are examined in chapter 4.

The Australian Experience

The following sections will examine the results since 1982 of auctions of import quotas for textiles, clothing, and footwear products, and for passenger motor vehicles.

TEXTILES, CLOTHING, AND FOOTWEAR QUOTAS

Australia was an original signatory to the Multi-Fiber Arrangement (MFA) in 1974, but it soon dropped out because it was unable to control a surge of imports through selective bilateral agreements. Since the mid-1970s, the Australian textile, clothing, and footwear industries have been protected by global tariff quotas with extremely high penalty duties that preclude most overquota imports.[3] Most TCF tariffs are high (40 or 50 percent) and not bound in the General Agreement on Tariffs and Trade (GATT).

In 1980, Australia adopted a seven-year plan for the period 1982–88 to rationalize production and phase down quantitative controls on 29 TCF categories. Legislation was enacted enabling some import licenses for 24 of the TCF categories (all except handicrafts items) to be distributed by public tender. The first auction took place in 1981 for licenses for calendar year 1982 imports; a global quota was set based on import performance during the period June 1978 to June 1980. Most of the quota (85 percent) was allocated according to historical shares; the remaining 15 percent was auctioned (Industries Assistance Commission 1981, p. 113).

In subsequent years, the global quota has been generally increased by a combination of two factors: a small, annual quota expansion factor designed to promote gradual import liberalization, and a market growth factor based on estimates by the TCF Advisory Committee (the Elix Committee) of prospective growth in domestic demand. All market growth is allocated to imports; however, conservative forecasts of growth in the domestic market can offset the impact of the small quota expansion factor and result in small increases or even declines in quota levels.

Have the auctions of TCF quotas succeeded in meeting either of their goals of retariffication and liberalization? Including the auction for 1987 import licenses, quota levels for all TCF categories have increased by 30.6 percent since the start of the seven-year plan, or by an annual average of about 6 percent. Growth in apparel and footwear has far outpaced that in textiles. But there have been marked differences by category. Some have had almost no growth in quotas (for example, woven manmade fiber fabrics, cotton bedsheeting); others have had enormous growth (the quota for leather

---

3. Most penalty rates are in the form of specific duties, whose ad valorem equivalent in 1984 was estimated by the TCF Advisory Committee to range from 110 percent to 440 percent. Those estimates, however, were based on average unit-value imports. For some high unit-value imports, the specific duty confers a very low penalty (Industries Assistance Commission 1986, p. 14).

T A B L E 7.2   **Growth in total quota levels: Australia**
(percentage change from previous year)

Category	1983	1984	1985	1986	1987	Total 1982–87
Textiles	5.0	1.2	3.2	7.9	3.1	18.4
Apparel	6.7	0.3	15.3	9.0	5.6	42.0
Footwear	4.9	1.6	11.9	11.6	9.0	45.0
Total	5.9	0.7	12.4	9.5	6.1	30.6

Note: Weighted by 1981 average unit values.
Source: Australian Department of Industry, Technology, and Commerce (1986a).

coats has increased by almost 300 percent). In addition, the year-to-year growth in quota levels has been uneven, ranging from a low of 0.7 percent in 1984 to 12.4 percent in 1985 (see table 7.2). For individual categories, the variance often has been much greater (for example, pantyhose dropped 6.7 percent in 1984 and rose 52 percent in 1985).[4]

Along with the growth in quota levels, there has been a shift in the share of quotas from historical allocations (base quota) to auction quota. Almost 38 percent of all quotas are auctioned, up sharply from the 17 percent level (weighted by 1981 average unit values) achieved in the first year of the plan (see table 7.3). The shift to auction quota has been most marked in footwear and apparel. Again, however, the situation differs significantly by quota category. In three categories, auction quota is more than 70 percent of the total (pantyhose, leather coats, shorts and male swimwear).[5] By contrast, in three categories of textiles, auctions account for less than 17 percent of the total quota (towelling, woven, manmade fiber fabrics; cotton bedsheeting). In 11 of the 24 categories, more than 40 percent of the quota is auctioned.

The results of the auctions are summarized in table 7.4. Overall, premia were slightly higher in the 1987 auction than in 1982. However, 9 of the 24 categories had premium rates of 6 percent or less in 1987; three categories had premia over 80 percent. Overall, bids for textile licenses have been fairly

4. In 1984, the quota for 9 of the 29 categories actually decreased by 0.7 percent to 6.7 percent. Since then, however, declines have occurred in only two quota categories: towelling in 1985 by 0.5 percent and woven coats in 1986 by 5.5 percent (Australian Department of Industry, Technology, and Commerce 1986a).
5. During this period, the tender quota to total quota ratio for leather coats jumped from 19.0 percent to 78.8 percent; the ratio for pantyhose rose from 42.8 percent to 84.6 percent.

TABLE 7.3   **Auction quotas as a share of total quotas: Australia**
(percentage)

Category	1982	1983	1984	1985	1986	1987
Textiles	15.1	18.2	18.6	21.9	24.7	26.9
Apparel	17.6	22.1	22.1	31.3	35.7	38.7
Footwear	17.0	20.8	21.6	29.6	36.2	41.4
Total	17.1	21.1	21.4	29.4	34.1	37.6

Note: Weighted by 1981 average unit values.
Source: Australian Department of Industry, Technology, and Commerce (1986a).

constant and lower than apparel and footwear, except for the items with slow quota growth.

What effect has this had on consumer prices? While prices have gone up, the increases have been due to the underlying protection of the quota; they have not varied with the annual changes in the auction premia. For example, the variation in the tender premia for shoes (which jumped from 50 percent in 1982, to 126 percent in 1985, to zero in 1986, and to 30 percent in 1987) has not led to wild swings in the price of shoes in Australia. Rather it has been only one of many variable costs for importers affecting how much of the quota rents they are able to retain.[6]

In the aggregate, auction premia for the 24 categories of imports increased each year from 1982 to 1985, despite the modest growth in quota levels. The sharp decline in the Australian dollar in early 1985 led to a sharp reversal in this trend in the 1986 auction; the 1987 premia show only a small increase. Clearly, the depreciation of the exchange rate has tremendously affected importers, sharply curtailing their quota rents in many product categories.

However, while the Australian dollar has dropped dramatically against the yen (and Japan is Australia's largest trading partner), it has fallen less so vis-à-vis other East Asian countries, especially those that supply TCF products. This helps explain why several apparel categories still had extremely high premia in the 1987 tender (for example, pajamas, 100 percent; shirts and blouses, 97 percent; foundation garments, 81 percent).

Some of the high premia represent the genuine scarcity value of imports;

---

6. US retailers have incorrectly argued that such variation in auction premia create volatile prices and destabilize the retail market. In fact, the volatility is in the level of windfall profits garnered by importers and retailers (Mangione 1987).

TABLE 7.4   **Auction premia: Australia**
(percentage)

Category	1982	1983	1984	1985	1986	1987
Textiles	19.6	18.4	16.7	26.0	17.5	18.3
Apparel	28.0	49.0	50.3	68.8	26.4	33.3
Footwear	41.0	66.1	86.9	100.0	1.4	31.0
Total	29.9	48.6	54.2	71.3	19.0	31.1

Note: Weighted by 1981 average unit values.
Source: Australian Department of Industry, Technology, and Commerce (1986a).

in some cases, however, high bids may reflect attempts by companies to lock out competitors. There is anecdotal evidence of cases where companies garnered a large share of auctioned quotas. But overall there have been few instances of market suppression because allocations of base quota have provided a buffer to forestall monopolization and to protect historical trading relationships. In addition, overquota imports can be entered by any supplier if the penalty tariff is not prohibitive.

Concerns about quota abuse arise in large part because Australian industry is so highly concentrated. However, in 1987, there were about 1,900 tenderers for all 24 quota categories. (This compares with over 45,000 importers of textiles, apparel, and footwear in the United States.) Of those, 1,256 were successful, including 589 "new entrants."[7] Ten firms account for over 50 percent of the winning bids in 21 of the 24 categories (and for over 75 percent in 14 of 24). Ten of the categories had fewer than 25 successful bidders. Domestic manufacturers accounted for 26 percent of the winning bids, retailers for 19 percent, and other importers for 55 percent in 1987.

The Australian system of base plus auction quota encourages upgrading of imports that enter under base quota and lower unit-value imports for goods that enter under auctioned quota. In general, higher priced imports come in under base quota, which is subject only to the regular tariff. The ad valorem bids for auction quota tend to skew the composition of imports toward low-priced goods because importers will use auction quota (which is subject to

---

7. "New entrants" are new registrants, even if their corporate holdings link them to other bidders. Australian Customs officials acknowledge that there is no effective way to police limits on bids by individual tenderers because of the ease of registering "dummy" corporations or surrogates to bid for another company.

the auction premium on top of the base tariff) to ship low-priced goods. As a greater share of the quota is auctioned, upgrading should become less pronounced. In a survey of 12 of the quota categories, a government report found the average unit import value for base quota in 1985 to be substantially higher—on average more than double—than auction quota in all categories except towelling (Australian Department of Industry, Technology, and Commerce 1986b, p. 181).

The Australian auction system creates incentives for excessively high bids. Domestic producers who are also traditionally large importers have an incentive to bid aggressively for auction quota because they can spread the cost of the auction premium over their domestic production and their base quota and lower their average unit cost for imports. In addition, excessively high bids may result from the desire by new entrants to ensure quota access and by current importers to maintain market share. (Such pressures increase as the ratio of auction quota to base quota also increases.) These excesses could be mitigated if auctions were held more frequently (to increase opportunities for new entrants), if all licenses were freely transferable, and if there were an efficient secondary market.[8]

Finally, the burden of adjustment for domestic industry under the Australian auction system falls in the out-years of their industry plans. For example, TCF quotas are being slowly phased out as the overquota penalty tariff begins to decline to the in quota rate from 1989 to 1996. As the difference between the two rates narrows, the quotas become less restrictive. Given past experience, however, companies do not know if the political support for liberalization will continue over time. In Australia, for example, delays in the liberalization schedule could be instituted by invocation of a new safeguards clause in the TCF plan. The risk that imports will remain controlled while planned liberalization is postponed is a real one. Industries that ''buy'' relief in return for a future liberalization schedule have an incentive to overturn the bargain through the political process. This is the ''Chinese menu'' problem, cited in chapter 1, which we will address again in chapter 10.

---

8. In a concentrated market like Australia's with loosely enforced antispeculation laws, recourse to a secondary market to secure additional import entitlements may be limited. As one critic of auctioning noted, ''the secondary market doesn't work if your competitors don't want to sell to you.''

MOTOR VEHICLE QUOTAS

Given its relatively small domestic market of 450,000 to 500,000 units, Australia has a diverse domestic industry composed of five assemblers producing 13 models of cars. In 1984, Australia initiated a new policy to restructure the motor vehicle industry and to promote import liberalization. The auctioning of import quotas is only one part of the government's complex industry plan. The objectives are to set an environment for the rationalization of domestic production down to three assemblers with six models by 1992; to encourage local sourcing by maintaining local content requirements and by allocating subsidies for Australian research and design; and to stimulate exports. To promote these objectives, the government is both phasing out quantitative restrictions on imports and rewarding domestic producers with duty-free import allocations based on local content and export performance. Such subsidies, however, create market distortions that run counter to the trade liberalization objectives.

Quantitative controls have been applied to motor vehicle imports since January 1975 to restrict imports to 20 percent of the domestic market. The level of the quota is determined each year by the Automotive Industry Authority based on the projected change in domestic demand. Imports under quota are levied a 57.5 percent tariff; through 1985, overquota imports were subject to a penalty rate of 100 percent. Including some four-wheel drive and other vehicles, the total import share actually averaged about 22 percent during the period 1982–84.[9]

The plan establishes a schedule for the phased reduction of the penalty rate for overquota imports from 100 percent in 1985 down to the regular tariff of 57.5 percent in 1992.[10] During that period, Australia will effectively "grow out" of quotas. Although the quota level will be held constant at about 23 percent of the domestic market, overquota imports are likely to increase as the penalty rate decreases. Once the penalty rate merges with the existing 57.5 percent tariff in 1992, the quota will be eliminated.

Import licenses, which had been allocated on the basis of historical performance, will be increasingly subject to auction.[11] In 1985, importers

---

9. The annual shares were 21.4 percent in 1982, 23.0 percent in 1983, 22.1 percent in 1984, and 22.7 percent in 1985 (Automotive Industry Authority 1986, p. 59).

10. The penalty rate would decrease to 95 percent in 1986, 90 percent in 1987, 85 percent in 1988, 80 percent in 1989, 72.5 percent in 1990, 65 percent in 1991, and 57.5 percent in 1992.

11. The government experimented with an auction of import licenses for calendar year 1980.

received six-sevenths of their 1984 licenses as base quota—each domestic assembler also received an allocation of 6,000—and the rest was auctioned for one year.[12] Over the period 1986–88, base quota will be phased out, and the entire quota will be auctioned starting in 1989.[13]

In light of the experience with the TCF tenders, the motor vehicle plan provides for both one-year and four-year entitlements. Most of the base quota that is subsequently tendered during the 1986–88 period will be in the form of four-year entitlements. A limited amount of one-year entitlements will continue to be auctioned to provide a "shock absorber" for companies to adjust imports to changing market conditions.

The initial motor vehicle tenders elicited very high bids. One-year licenses sold at 94.5 percent in 1985 (just 5.5 percent under the penalty rate)[14] and 81 percent in 1986. The first four-year licenses for the period 1986–89 sold at 68 percent. Since that auction, however, imports have been battered by the sharp drop in the Australian dollar against the yen (from 209 yen in December 1984 to 100 yen in July 1986), which is noteworthy since Japan accounted for 83 percent of imports of completely built-up motor vehicles in 1985 (Automotive Industry Authority 1986, p. 62). Indeed, in the 1987 auction, most of the one-year licenses were not bid for, and those that were sold brought a zero premium. Interestingly, Hyundai dealers picked up the licenses because of the price advantage Korean imports gained against their Japanese competitors as a result of the exchange rate changes.

Other integral parts of the motor vehicle plan are the local content requirements and the export facilitation credits. Domestic assemblers are required to source 85 percent of the value of their components domestically. If this goal is met, producers are allowed to import components or cars duty-free up to a value equal to 15 percent of their domestic production.[15] The

---

11 percent of the total quota was auctioned; those licenses provided a continuing (i.e., multiyear) import entitlement. The following year, however, Australia reverted to historical allocations (Industries Assistance Commission 1981, p. 116).

12. Importers include domestic assemblers that import cars under local content and export performance incentive schemes, and representatives (distributors) of foreign companies—Mazda, Honda, BMW, Mercedes, Suzuki, Jaguar, and Hyundai.

13. In 1986, 25 percent of base quota was auctioned; the share rose to 50 percent in the 1987 auction and will rise to 75 percent and 100 percent in 1988 and 1989, respectively.

14. In 1985, 3,083 units or 3 percent of imports came in over quota and paid the 100 percent penalty tariff.

15. In 1985, duty-free imports totaled 16,758 units or 15 percent of total completely built-up imports.

local content requirement can be reduced through credits earned by increasing the local content *of exports* over the 1979 base-year level. Those credits (up to a maximum credit of 15 percent starting in 1987) are then applied to a formula to reduce the required imported content value of production.[16] Given the high tariffs, this scheme provides a substantial subsidy to domestic producers and increases pressure for importers to work together with assemblers to rationalize production and distribution.

The New Zealand Experience

New Zealand's domestic production has long been protected by a system of import licensing and tariffs. A comprehensive system of import licensing was instituted in the midst of a currency crisis in 1938 to conserve foreign exchange for essential imports and to service the foreign debt; tariffs have been levied since the 1840s. Tariffs have been generally low for intermediate and capital goods and high for consumer and final goods.

Since its inception in 1938, the licensing system has been liberalized gradually and spasmodically. In 1963, licenses were required for 75 percent of total imports; that total declined to 30 percent in the early 1970s and dropped to only 16.5 percent by February 1987 (Caygill 1987). The coverage of the licensing requirement differs by category of import. In 1982, only 28 percent of imports of all manufactured goods were subject to licenses, while 51 percent of imports of machinery and transport equipment required licenses (Syntec Economic Services 1984, pp. 25–26).

The New Zealand auction system has sought three main objectives: to provide information on the level of protection afforded by the import licensing system; to move away from allocations of import licenses based on historical market share; and to replace licenses with tariffs. The last objective also implies a substantial commitment to import liberalization in light of the current government's program to reduce tariffs on items not subject to industry development plans (IDPs) toward a maximum level of 25 percent.[17]

---

16. If the required domestic content level is not achieved in any quarter, the assembler is subject to a penalty in an amount equal to 25 percent of the value of the excess imported content.

17. In September 1985, the government announced unilateral tariff cuts from existing rates of 5 percentage points and 10 percentage points effective 1 July 1986 and 1 July 1987, respectively, for all tariffs above 25 percent except items subject to IDPs. As of 1 July 1987, 91 percent of imports will have tariffs of 40 percent or less; tariffs will be 10 percent or less for more than half of imports (and 32 percent will be duty free).

Three types of auctioned licenses exist: licenses for goods not subject to IDPs;[18] licenses under IDPs; and licenses for goods subject to the Australia–New Zealand Closer Economic Relations Trade Agreement (ANZCERTA). Auctions were first introduced on a trial basis in 1981. Six rounds of auctions took place between April 1981 and February 1983, covering NZ$71 million in licenses. More than half of the licenses auctioned were for apparel items (Syntec Economic Services 1984, pp. 55–56).

In 1984, the government introduced "global" auctions (i.e., for all products subject to import license except those covered by industry development plans) and increased import quotas to at least 10 percent by value of the domestic market. This minimum level then was to increase by 2.5 percentage points to 5 percentage points per year (later amended to 5 percentage points) with all additional quota offered at auction.

Through the first 33 rounds of auctions, a total of NZ$2,221 million in import licenses has been tendered (see table 7.5). Over half has been for global tenders; the rest has been divided almost equally between industry plan and ANZCERTA quotas (NZ$484 million and NZ$487 million, respectively). Significant liberalization has occurred in the first and last categories; the record under IDPs has been mixed.[19]

Under global auctions, the value of licenses offered has grown from NZ$438 million in the first global round of auctions in November 1984 to about NZ$720 million in the second global round in October 1985.[20] However, only about half of the licenses actually were taken up (NZ$221 million or 50 percent in 1984 and NZ$325 million or 45 percent in 1985). While the value of the licenses offered rose by 64 percent, the aggregate premia bid fell from NZ$15 million to NZ$12.7 million.[21] As a percentage of the licenses

18. Currently, 18 industries are covered by IDPs: textiles, clothing, tobacco, packing, wine, plastics, shipbuilding, writing instruments, starch, footwear, tires, canned fruit, electric motors, glassware, general rubber goods, ceramics, electronics, and motor vehicles.

19. The government plans to reduce or eliminate quotas for industries covered by IDPs. Electric motors were liberalized in 1986; electronics products will become exempt from licensing in 1987; plastic goods in 1988; tires, glassware, and starch in 1989; and rubber goods and canned fruit in 1990. Fixed dates have not been set, however, for the abolition of licenses for textiles, clothing, footwear, and motor vehicles. Liberalization in these sectors has been slowed because of the need to coordinate actions with Australia under ANZCERTA (Caygill 1987).

20. The third general round closed at the beginning of 1987 and results are currently being analyzed by the New Zealand government.

21. Data for premia bid for and actually paid are not yet available for the second global round. Only NZ$10.4 million out of NZ$15 million was paid for in the first global round; the rest was retendered.

TABLE 7.5   **New Zealand auction results: 1981–86**

Year (March–March)	A Total license tendered (million NZ dollars)	B Premia invoiced	B/A (percentage)
1981–83 Rounds 1–5A	71.47	13.36	18.7
1983–84 Rounds 6–12	206.37	12.75	6.2
1984–85 Rounds 13–21	705.65	75.79	10.7
1985–86 Rounds 22–33	1,237.54	n.a.	n.a.
Subtotal Rounds 1–25	1,162.16	122.97	10.6
Total Rounds 1–33	2,221.03	n.a.	n.a.

n.a.   not available.
Source: Department of Trade and Industry, New Zealand, unpublished data.

taken up in the global rounds, the premia invoiced represented on average an ad valorem rate of 6.8 percent and 3.9 percent, respectively.

However, there is a discrepancy between premia invoiced and premia paid. Over the first 20 rounds of auctions (March 1981 to February 1985), a total of NZ$77.4 million of premia was bid, but only NZ$64.2 million or 83 percent actually was paid. Bids did not bind companies to actually take up the licenses. Because firms were required to post only small security deposits, bidders tendered for more license than they needed (some at high premia to ensure that they were not closed out of the market), and then they either did not pick up the licenses right after the auction or sacrificed the 10 percent security deposit three months later. Licenses that were not taken up (i.e., where successful bids were made but security deposits were not provided) were retendered—a procedure that dampened the average premium paid for import licenses, although it did not significantly affect quota utilization.

New Zealand recently amended its auction rules to require a 20 percent security deposit within 14 days of notification of a successful bid, with the balance of the premium due within three months. Import licenses are not issued until the full amount is paid. If the deposit is not paid or the balance not received within three months, the license is made available in most instances as residual license at the average successful premium. Bidders are no longer barred from future tenders for nonpayment of premiums. Data are not yet available to examine whether the increased security deposit has affected the take-up of licenses.

When the average successful premium for an item over both global rounds averaged 7.5 percent or less, or when items only tendered in the second round attracted premiums of 1 percent or less, the items became available on demand and will become exempt from all licensing requirements within one year. Pursuant to this requirement, 400 out of about 660 categories subject to auctions moved to license on demand on 1 July 1986. In his budget speech on 31 July 1986, Finance Minister Roger Douglas announced plans to phase out import licenses by mid-1988 for all items except those subject to IDPs as part of a general reform of import policy.

Perceived Problems with Australian and New Zealand Auctions

The most prominent concern of government and business in Australia and New Zealand does not involve the auction process per se, but focuses instead on the impact of exchange rate changes on the level of protection. This is a general trade policy problem that arises under a floating exchange rate regime.

The recent depreciation of the Australian and New Zealand dollars has increased the cost of imports dramatically. In New Zealand, the fall in the dollar led to an across-the-board increase in the restrictiveness of the value-based quotas because of the rise in import prices in terms of national currency. Unlike August 1984, when value-based quotas were increased to compensate for the devaluation of the New Zealand dollar, the New Zealand government did not increase the amount of licenses available to importers following the recent depreciation. In Australia, motor vehicle quotas became almost redundant (for a while, at least) as importers were forced to cut back shipments because of the sharp price increases resulting from a depreciation of more than 50 percent against the yen.

The recent exchange rate changes have provoked calls to accelerate the pace of import liberalization. In New Zealand, the depreciation of the dollar has strengthened the government's case for proceeding with unilateral tariff cuts, although it has had less of an effect on protection under IDPs. Similar questions have been raised about the slow pace of liberalization under the TCF quotas in Australia. Industries have opposed accelerated liberalization because of their concern that, if the currencies appreciated, the level of protection would be sharply eroded. However, in December 1986, the Australian government announced a new program to phase out quotas and to cut tariffs on TCF imports by 1996 (although tariffs above 50 percent will remain for many items even after the seven year phase-in). The reforms are scheduled to begin in March 1989, but they could be revised if the import liberalization leads to a contraction of more than 15 percent in local production (Sherwell 1986).

Extensive interviews with government and business representatives, as well as academic observers, did point to four major problem areas that arise or are perceived to arise as a result of the auctioning of import licenses in Australia and New Zealand. Some relate to the specific procedures of the auctions; others are endemic to any system of quantitative import control. The nonexhaustive list of problem areas includes uncertainty as to access to quota; the underutilization of quotas and the impact of speculation; market disruption in individual products within broadbanded categories; and unfair pricing practices.

UNCERTAINTY

The problem most often cited was uncertainty about whether a company would be able to obtain the quota it needs through an auction system. Bidding involves risk and cost; a company obviously would prefer to receive an import entitlement for free. Furthermore, bidding complicates planning. One-year licenses may not provide the certainty desired to invest heavily in multiyear marketing and distribution strategies. "Continuity" licenses provide only limited relief, particularly in industries where demand changes as frequently as textiles and apparel.

To ease this problem, the Australian government has provided multiyear licenses in limited cases as part of a broader industry assistance program. Such a solution tends to promote the rationalization of industry (what the Australian government wanted when it introduced a four-year license as part of its 1984 motor vehicle plan), but it discourages new entrants. In this sense, security of access for traditional suppliers means greater uncertainty of access for new, and potentially more competitive, suppliers. Small suppliers and new entrants could be accommodated, however, if the government set aside a portion of the tender for noncompetitive bids by small traders (as is done in US Treasury securities auctions).

An additional problem in Australia, which could arise under any quota system, has been the method of calculating "growth expansion factors" for quotas. The use of annual forecasts of the domestic market to determine the growth, if any, in imports is wide open to political pressure and creates uncertainty as to whether the level of imports will increase or decrease. As noted earlier, the Australian experience with TCF quotas demonstrates the large variance in annual growth rates *by tender category*. Aggregated data mean little to the company manager planning for next year's business in a particular line of goods.

If a government is committed to a program of retariffication and import liberalization, it is preferable to impose automatic annual adjustments in quota levels unrelated to domestic demand levels. Domestic industry can plan ahead with greater certainty, and importers can enter multiyear contracts without the risk of not being able to enter goods in the out-years of the contract. To be sure, domestic industries may lose market share if demand turns down and competitive imports continue to grow. However, two factors should guard against an overly rapid decline in the industry: first, the natural brake imposed by the maximum annual growth in quota levels; and second, the availability of escape clause relief if imports are causing serious injury to the domestic industry. In the cases of Australia and New Zealand, policymakers might find industry more willing to proceed with, or accelerate, planned import liberalization *if* there was a more effective safeguards clause to backstop them. Indeed, such a provision has been a prerequisite for acceptance of liberalization commitments by virtually all GATT members throughout the postwar period, and has been incorporated in the recent decision to phase out TCF quotas in Australia by 1996 to help gain support for the liberalization program.

UNDERUTILIZATION AND SPECULATION

Underutilization of licenses can cause problems if it reduces competition for domestic industries, limits consumer choice, and increases prices. It can result from attempts to abuse market power by shortshipping (i.e., securing quota and not importing), or it can simply be the result of quota redundancy caused by a depreciation of the exchange rate or slow growth in domestic demand, or a host of other factors. To increase the costs of shortshipping, New Zealand increased required security deposits from 10 percent to 20 percent; Australia is considering similar measures. While there has been evidence of market suppression in a few categories of auction quotas, underutilization of licenses on the whole has not been a serious problem.

While widespread, speculation also has not been a problem. Brokering quota tickets has become a growth industry, as it has on the export side in Hong Kong. But there is nothing wrong with speculators taking a position in quota tickets in an auction or in a secondary market. In fact, they may make the market work better (as long as there are safeguards against the underutilization of quota). Government efforts to regulate activity through individual limits on auction quota holdings and through requirements on transfers in the secondary market have been ineffectual. Indeed, such requirements may be counterproductive since they force companies to engage in inefficient transactions to secure import entitlements.

An import license is a property right and should be treated accordingly, i.e., it should be freely transferable. For this reason, governments should encourage the growth of a private secondary market in quota tickets. Such a market would promote quota utilization by providing access to additional supply or the means to sell excess tickets obtained through the initial auction. Moreover, the existence of a secondary market may reduce the need to bid aggressively for quota tickets because additional tickets can be acquired if needed.

In highly concentrated markets like Australia's and New Zealand's, one or a few companies could gain control of the bulk of the quota tickets to preclude competition. Two measures could then be taken: high penalties could be imposed for the nonuse of quota; and allocations of a portion of the quota pool could be made to traditional importers (i.e., base quota) with the rest auctioned off (though holders of base quota should pay for their tickets at the average auction price). These procedures could help mitigate the risk of preemptive bidding.

MARKET DISRUPTION

Domestic producers also expressed concern about the potential for market disruption in specific products if import pressures rise too quickly or if importers concentrate shipments on a few items within the broadbanded tender categories. In Australia, this problem can be exacerbated for low-priced goods because of the incentive to import down-market goods under auction quota (which is subject to higher ad valorem duties than base quota).

The logical answer to such concerns is the availability of a credible and effective safeguard or escape clause. Indeed, the New Zealand business community sees the development of a new safeguards system as an essential complement to plans for further import liberalization. To be sure, it increases the political risk that the liberalization schedule will be postponed in the future. But a safeguard or escape clause probably needs to be instituted to garner domestic political support for liberalization and to encourage an orderly transfer of resources to more competitive lines of production.

UNFAIR PRICING PRACTICES

Auctions of import licenses in both Australia and New Zealand create incentives to underinvoice imports. In Australia, with ad valorem volume-based licenses, lower import prices mean lower duties; with New Zealand's value-based licenses, lower import prices mean more goods can be shipped under the license. In both countries, charges of manipulative pricing practices are prevalent.

American-style complaints against alleged predatory pricing practices by Japanese firms are commonplace. In some cases, dumping probably occurs; in others, importers negotiate prices with suppliers so that goods under quota cost less and freely traded goods cost more. This price averaging does not appear to conflict with existing trade laws as long as the reduced prices of quota goods are above the home-market price in the exporting country (i.e., not dumped). However, such determinations often are hard to make when dealing with exports from China and from large trading companies in other Asian countries.

Implications for US Trade Policy

The main purpose of the Australian and New Zealand auction quota programs has been to undo the harm caused by the imposition of extensive quantitative import controls. It was generally recognized that industry had become inefficient and uncompetitive under the quotas[22] and that industry specialization had to be pursued on a broad scale. A key element of that process was increased import competition, phased in gradually through the expansion and auctioning of import quotas.

The competitiveness of US industries that have been protected from import competition for decades has also eroded. Could the use of auction quotas provide a means to gradually restore competition to important sectors of the US economy? While the US market is quite different and much larger than those of Australia and New Zealand, those countries' experience with auctions has relevance for US trade policy in several important respects.

AUCTION QUOTAS CAN PROMOTE IMPORT LIBERALIZATION

The Australian and New Zealand systems demonstrate that it is possible to gradually grow out of longstanding quantitative restraints in various sectors including textiles and apparel. In Australia, quota levels on TCF products already have expanded significantly and are scheduled to be phased out by 1996 (although there will undoubtedly be political pressures to delay the planned liberalization). The pace of quota liberalization in New Zealand has been much quicker. Neither program is perfect, and the situation of the industry and the trade pressures are quite different from those facing US industry.[23] But the use of auctions has contributed to import liberalization and is worth examining if the United States decides to embark on a gradual program of import liberalization for existing QRs.

GLOBAL QUOTAS AND BROADBANDING ARE DESIRABLE

Both Australia and New Zealand auction global licenses with broadbanded quota categories. Global licenses allow importers to source from the most

22. Reflecting that concern, current proposals in Australia to provide protection for other industries (for example, iron and steel) have focused instead on the provisions of subsidies and tariffs.

23. Given the high level of tariffs in the TCF and motor vehicle industries, there was less concern that retariffication in Australia and New Zealand would denude these sectors of significant protection. Most US textile and apparel products also benefit from high tariff protection, although the tariff levels generally are much lower than in either Australia or New Zealand.

competitive foreign supplier. Broadbanded quota categories serve two important functions: they allow flexibility to alter the mix of imports to meet changes in fashion or market trends; and they "encourage greater concentration of domestic activity in the more efficient areas of local production" (Australian Department of Industry, Technology, and Commerce 1986b, p. 193).

The complexity of import quota auctions increases substantially, and the welfare gains decline, when quotas are set for narrow product ranges and by country. Almost all QRs in the United States are country specific; such a system reduces competition among foreign suppliers, raises costs to US importers, and makes it easier for exporting countries to siphon off some or all of the quota rents.

ADMINISTRATION OF AUCTIONS IS MANAGEABLE

Any quota will require administrative resources. There was surprisingly little indication that the auction approach presented a major bureaucratic burden for the government (beyond those already existing because of the basic policy of import control). In fact, New Zealand employs only six people and one large computer to administer its auction system. These people notify 10,000 firms on a master list of every round of auctions, process the bids, award the licenses and receive deposits, and publish the auction results. The administrative costs of the auction programs have been much more than offset by the revenues generated by the auctions.

AUCTIONS DO NOT DISRUPT IMPORT MARKETS

After an initial bumpy transition period, the auction systems in Australia and New Zealand have worked fairly well. Tariff quotas in Australia have been significantly liberalized, and licensing substantially eliminated in New Zealand, without major problems. Most complaints about auctioning stem more from the imposition of the underlying QR than on its method of allocation.

As with any QR, importers have had to learn the new system, but after a few auctions their bidding has become more precise. Of course, bids have fluctuated widely in response to changing market conditions, but this has not had much effect on final consumer prices. In addition, the auction systems have been adjusted in light of the initial Australian experience. Potential problems have been mitigated, for example, by removing many impediments to a secondary market, by raising security deposits to discourage shortshipping, and by reducing distortions due to upgrading.

The introduction of auction quotas in the United States could draw on this experience as it pertains to conditions in the US market. In most instances, potential problems with auctions that arose in Australia and New Zealand are less relevant because of the large size and diversity of the US market. The possible design of a US auction quota system is presented in the next chapter.

8 Designing an Auction Quota System

In designing an auction quota system, specific provisions must address the type of auction, how to determine the auction price, the type of bid, eligibility to bid, the frequency of the auctions and duration of licenses, the transferability of licenses, and appropriate measures for smoothing the transition to the new system. Our proposal assumes that a relatively unfettered secondary market would be an essential feature of any auction quota system. The specific recommendations in this chapter draw on the discussion of auctions in chapters 4 and 6, the experience of the United States with auctions in nontrade areas, and relevant lessons taken from the Australian and New Zealand experiences. Where feasible, auctions of global quotas are preferable to country-specific quotas, as are broadbanded quotas to specific product quotas, for the reasons cited in the previous chapters; either could be accommodated under the auction design proposals set out below.

Given the minimalist approach in most cases to administering US quantitative restrictions (i.e., let the foreigners do it), this proposal may seem complicated. Allowing the very exporters with whom American industry is trying to compete to administer US quotas and thereby capture the rents hardly seems a practical solution, however. If the United States did decide to administer more QRs domestically, many of the issues addressed here in the context of auction quotas would also have to be resolved under a system of allocated quotas: volume or value basis, eligibility to hold quota, duration of licenses, and transferability. Indeed, depending on the degree of country and category disaggregation, an auction system could be considerably less complex than the current allocated quotas for steel and textiles and apparel, which comprise precise limits for numerous specific categories and numerous countries, in the latter case leading to the application of over 1,300 separate quotas in early 1987.

111

Type of Auction

Auctions can be conducted orally or by sealed bid. In an oral auction, the seller or seller's agent and interested bidders gather at a specific place and time, and bids are made to determine who will purchase the item. Given the size and complexity of most potential quota auctions, however, an oral auction simply would not be feasible. Moreover, empirical analysis indicates that a sealed bidding procedure is less vulnerable to collusion. For these reasons, we recommend sealed bidding. This is the type of auction used by Australia and New Zealand in their auction quota systems and by the US government in most of the auctions it administers.

In a sealed bid auction, the interested parties submit written offers by a specified deadline. Bidders do not have to be physically present at the auction to participate. After the deadline, the bids are opened, and the item is awarded to the highest bidder.

The argument that sealed bidding is less open to collusion is based on the rationale that collusive agreements must be policed by the participants to be sustainable. If a group of bidders has agreed to keep bids artificially low, this must mean that the submitted bids are lower than what each bidder would actually be willing to pay. Each individual would have an incentive to cheat on the agreement by bidding slightly higher than the agreed price, if it were possible to do so without being detected. In an oral auction, departures from agreed bids would be immediately obvious, and the other parties to the collusive agreement could then bid up the price to the point at which there is no gain to the rebel bidder. This threat, plus the threat of punitive bidding to ensure that the rebel bidder does not succeed in future oral auctions, helps to keep everyone in line. By their nature, sealed bid auctions are not as conducive to such policing and punishment by collusive groups since no one will know who bid what until after the auction is over.

On the other hand, the lack of information about one's competition means that bidders cannot react to their competitors bids and adjust their own bids accordingly. This may result in miscalculations that allow a less efficient bidder to win over a more efficient one. Sealed bidding can also present a problem when many items are being sold simultaneously. For example, a bidder may want to import shirts and, if unsuccessful in the auction for cotton shirts, may want to bid for quota to import synthetic shirts. If forced to bid simultaneously, the bidder could end up with quota in excess of his needs, with a greater financial commitment than anticipated. This assumes, however, that the auction is a one-shot deal. Both problems would be mitigated if the bidder had recourse to a secondary market, which would allow for the correction of such miscalculations in the initial bidding. Indeed, we regard a secondary market as an essential component of any auction system.[1]

Determining the Auction Price

Given a sealed bid auction, how should the government determine the auction price for successful bidders? In a single-item auction, bidders usually pay what they bid. In a multiple auction, with many bidders and many items being sold simultaneously, more than one winner is probable. Under these circumstances, either a uniform or discriminatory (pay what you bid) pricing system may be used. Further, a uniform price may be set at the level of either the lowest accepted or highest rejected bid.

To clarify the incentives facing bidders under the various pricing schemes in a sealed bid auction, it is useful to analyze the expected behavior of bidders in oral auctions. There are two types of oral auctions: the ascending bid or "English" auction and the descending price or "Dutch" auction. In an English-style oral auction the price each bidder is willing to pay for the item is stated, and higher bids are offered until no one is willing to raise the bid further. The last remaining bidder then pays the amount he bid. In the English auction, bidders necessarily gain information during the auction process as to how much other bidders are willing to bid. Each bidder drops out of the auction process when the price goes above the maximum amount he is willing to pay. A bidder can raise his bid to be sure that he will win, as long as the price is less than the maximum amount he is willing to pay. The winning bidder pays, in essence, a price just above the maximum amount that the second highest bidder was willing to pay. The selling price may be considerably below the maximum amount the winning bidder would have paid. This type of auction, frequently used to sell everything from antiques to racehorses, is probably the most familiar to the general public. It is also

---

1. In addition, one could hold successive auctions for the different subcategories, perhaps on successive days. While this would increase the administrative burden for the government, it would allow bidders to adjust their bids, based on their success in the previous auctions. In any event, a smoothly functioning secondary market would still be desirable.

the method used most commonly by the US Bureau of Land Management and the US Forest Service to allocate timber cutting rights on federal lands.

In a descending price or "Dutch" auction, the auctioneer starts with a high price and gradually lowers the price until a bidder offers to buy at the quoted price. The bidders in a Dutch auction do not receive information during the auction process on how much rival bidders are prepared to bid. Each bidder wants to obtain the item, but does not want to pay any more than necessary to outbid opponents. The bidder may not bid immediately when the quoted price reaches the maximum amount he would be willing to pay if he expects other bidders to enter at lower quoted prices. If the bidder knew for certain what others would bid, the best strategy would be to bid at a price just above the next highest bidder. The point at which a bidder enters a Dutch auction depends upon his own willingness to pay for the item and his expectations as to what others will bid.

The auction that will yield the higher revenue for the seller is not immediately clear. On the one hand, one might expect higher revenue from the Dutch auction because in the ascending price auction the successful bidder only need bid up to the maximum amount the second highest bidder is willing to pay. On the other hand, the bidding in a Dutch auction depends upon each firm's expectations of what others will bid, and there is an incentive to depress bids to avoid paying any more than actually necessary. If all participants shade their bids in this way, the revenue from the auction could actually be lower.

Sealed bid auctions are similar to oral Dutch auctions in that bidders do not obtain any information on what rivals are bidding during the auction process. Each bidder wants to win the auction, but does not want to pay any more than necessary. This provides the same incentive as in the Dutch auction to lower bids below the maximum amount each bidder would be willing to pay, if he thinks he can win at a lower price.

One method of eliminating such bid shaving in a single-item sealed bid auction would be to award the item to the highest bidder, but at the price offered by the second highest bidder, thus simulating the English auction. Each bidder then has the incentive to bid the maximum amount he would be willing to pay, knowing that the bid he submits will not determine the amount he pays, but only whether he wins the auction. The worst that can happen to a bidder is that he will end up paying close to the maximum amount that he was willing to pay, if there was another bid close to his.

If a large number of items are offered, bids could be accepted starting with the highest, down through the last successful bid, with the price for all successful bids determined by the lowest successful bid. Alternatively, the price could be set at the highest rejected bid. This would be the multiunit equivalent of pricing a single item at the second highest bid. Since the prices offered determine only who wins and not what they pay, all bidders would have an incentive to bid the maximum amount they were willing to pay knowing that the final price will be lower. This system should provide unbiased information on the value of the items to bidders, which would be important in import quota auctions, because bids would give better estimates of the size of the quota rents.[2]

An alternative method of setting prices when more than one of the same item is being sold would be to charge each successful bidder the full amount of his bid, as in the Treasury auctions. This would raise more revenue from each bidder who bids more than the last bid accepted, but it would encourage all bidders to lower their bids to just above the bids they expect from rivals. Total revenue may actually be less under a discriminatory system than a uniform pricing system.[3]

We know of no examples of a sealed bid auction with the price set at the level of the highest rejected bid, however. Australia uses the last accepted price, while New Zealand uses a pay-what-you-bid system, as does the US government in most of its auctions. A discriminatory pricing system would not be appropriate in this context because it would violate the most-favored-nation principle, which is at the heart of the multilateral trading system as codified in the General Agreement on Tariffs and Trade (GATT). In practice, as bidders become more knowledgeable, there is likely to be very little difference between the last accepted and first rejected bids. The government may want to maximize revenue by using the higher clearing price.

Bidders could specify the amount of quota they want (subject to any antimonopoly limitations on the amount for which they can bid) and the price they offer. Bids would be accepted starting with the highest, until the quota is exhausted. All successful bidders would pay a uniform clearing price, either the lowest accepted or highest rejected bid. For example, suppose 100

---

2. The secondary market would also provide ongoing, updated information to the government and the markets, although at an additional cost for gathering the data.

3. See Smith (1966) and Bolten (1973) for analysis of the effects of discriminatory pricing on revenue in the Treasury auctions.

units of quota are available for auction. The authorities receive the following sealed bids by the deadline, ranked from highest to lowest:

Bid A	20 units at $5.00 per unit
Bid B	35 units at $4.50 per unit
Bid C	10 units at $4.25 per unit
Bid D	35 units at $3.00 per unit
Bid E	15 units at $2.50 per unit

Bidders A through D would receive the quota allotments they bid for. All these successful bidders would pay either $2.50 or $3.00 per unit for the quota, depending on which method of bid acceptance was chosen. This example was constructed so that bids A through D exactly equaled the amount of quota available. Of course, this is unlikely to happen in practice. If bid D had been 40 units, then bidder D would be offered 35 units at $2.50 or $3.00. Similarly, if there were more than one bidder at the clearing price, the quota could be prorated among them. In either case, the remainder could be so small that it would not be an economical shipment size; in that event, the bidders should be allowed to refrain from purchasing the remainder, and the quota should be added to the following quarter's quota pool or offered for sale in the secondary market.[4]

All bidders should be required to submit a deposit of at least 20 percent with their bid (the amount used in New Zealand and in the US mineral lease auctions), and successful bidders should pay the balance promptly, perhaps within two weeks of notification that they have won. Substantial deposits and prompt payment are common features of US government auctions in other areas. These requirements should discourage bidders from bidding cavalierly and from not picking up the license if they are successful. Frontloaded payments may discourage inefficient bidders, but efficient firms should have no problem raising the necessary capital.

Type of Bid

As noted in chapter 2, quotas can be denominated in volume terms or in value terms. Quotas expressed in volume terms that are given to importers

---

4. A shipment so small as to be uneconomical would also be too small to significantly affect the final price to consumers.

without charge, or for which a dollar fee is charged, will bias imports toward higher valued items. All of the quotas that have affected US trade have been denominated in volume terms, and in all probability any future quotas will be denominated in volume terms as well. Converting quotas that are currently given away to an auction system would cause no shift in the composition of imports if the bids are solicited in terms of a dollar bid for licenses to import a given volume. The bias toward higher valued items that already exists in the quota system would be perpetuated under the auction system, so no radical shift in the composition of imports by type would be expected.

If new import quotas are imposed on products previously not subject to quantitative restriction, auctioning the volume quotas by dollar bid could be expected to elicit upgrading of imports. Whether upgrading is viewed as a problem would depend upon the nature of the product, the structure of the industry, and the reason why the quantitative restriction was imposed in the first place. If the product under quota is more or less standardized, such as sugar or crude petroleum, upgrading is not likely to be a significant problem. If all firms in the industry produce a range of products from low valued to high valued, the protection provided by decreased imports of low-valued items should provide them with benefits, even if they lose sales in the high-value range. However, if firms concentrate on producing particular goods, and if the purpose of the quantitative restriction is to protect the industry in general, firms at the upper end of the market may not be protected by the quota if the composition of imports shifts toward products with which they are directly competitive.

If upgrading does interfere with the objective of the quota, it could be discouraged or prevented in two ways. First, upgrading could be discouraged by stipulating that bids for the quotas be in ad valorem terms, as in the Australian system. Firms could bid the rate of duty, over and above existing tariffs, that they would be willing to pay to import a given amount. The same rate of duty would apply to all imports within the quota, so there would be no incentive toward higher valued items.

Although ad valorem bids have the advantage of reducing the upgrading phenomenon, they complicate payment for the quotas. The actual payment due the government cannot be determined until the import quota license is actually used and the value of the imported goods is established. It would be possible to require a deposit at the time of the auction equal to the expected duty to be paid based on average import values in a previous period. The amount of deposit could be recorded, with extra payments due or a refund provided, after the goods are actually imported. This would not be difficult to handle, but it does involve extra bookkeeping. The value of the quota in a secondary market would then depend upon the contracted duty rate implicit in the license and the deposit already paid.

An alternative, but undesirable, method of dealing with upgrading is to divide the quota into subquotas for different products. This limits upgrading, at least between the specified categories, but introduces rigidities because the composition of imports cannot change in response to shifts in consumer demand or costs among the subcategories. As such, it freezes the composition of imports in an arbitrary way.

If upgrading were likely to be a major problem, ad valorem bids might be more appropriate. We would generally prefer to use dollar per unit bids, however, in light of the administrative problems associated with the ad valorem approach, especially for those cases where upgrading would not be a problem.

Participation in the Auctions

Who should be allowed to bid for and hold licenses? At a minimum, firms or individuals participating in the auctions would have to be creditworthy. For example, the Treasury Department requires government security dealers to have minimum capital 1.2 times their measured market risk (*Washington Post*, 12 June 1987). The government would also have to ensure that the participants were under the jurisdiction of US law, to prevent evasion of any legal penalties for misuse of the quotas. It would thus be reasonable to require auction participants to demonstrate creditworthiness, probably by submitting a deposit, and to be residents of the United States or companies incorporated in the United States. This would include US subsidiaries of foreign companies.

Beyond these minimum provisions, restricting access to the auctions would not be desirable. Any attempt to limit participation to, for example, importers of record or firms established before the auction quotas were initiated would reduce competition among the bidders, prevent potential new entrants into the import market, possibly lower the bids, and increase the risk of monopolization or collusion in importing. It is precisely the competition among traders and potential traders that would drive up the bids to the level of the expected excess profits from importing and thus transfer the quota rents to the government.

Frequency of Auctions

The main disadvantage of very frequent auctions is the cost. Publicizing the auction, obtaining and sorting bids, and announcing the results require real resources in the form of staff, office equipment, and computer time. The costs incurred by the government will be higher the more frequent the auctions.

On the other hand, frequent auctions allow importers to take into account the most recent information in formulating their bids. If importers had to bid at the beginning of 1987 for quotas to import in 1992, they would be more likely to overbid or underbid than if they had the opportunity to observe demand conditions, cost conditions, and exchange rate patterns closer to the actual period for which the quotas were valid. Frequent auctions would provide more accurate information on the size of the quota rents, as changing market conditions affect the restrictiveness of the quota.

Frequent auctions also allow bidders who are unsuccessful in one auction, and who may be unable to obtain licenses in the secondary market, to bid again fairly soon in another. The knowledge that another auction will take place soon would reduce the pressure for "panic bidding," particularly when the auction system is first initiated. Given this trade-off between cost and convenience, quarterly auctions appear to be a reasonable compromise.

Duration of Licenses

International trade can involve relatively long order-delivery lags. To avoid disrupting commercial relations any more than necessary to enforce the quota limitation, the quota license would have to be valid for long enough to allow reasonable time to order goods, produce them, and ship them. This would avoid imposing additional risk on traders by forcing them to order goods before knowing whether they will be successful in obtaining quota licenses in the auction or in the secondary market. Exactly how long a period of time would be reasonable would depend upon the nature of the restricted product.

Items designed and made to order with long production lags, such as large electrical generators, would clearly require longer quota license periods than relatively standardized commodities like sugar or bar steel.

On the other hand, licenses with long durations allow (but do not necessarily encourage) surges of imports. If licenses are issued that are valid for all of 1987, nothing prevents the entire annual amount from entering the country on the first of January. This "lumping" of imports can disrupt the market for a product.[5]

Are such surges likely? If the good can be stored, there are economic incentives against marketing the entire year's quota during some subperiod. Why should importers import and sell the full year's quota at one point in time at distress prices when they hold a quota ticket that guarantees them the ability to import at any time during the year? First-come-first-served methods of administering quotas would encourage a stampede to the border at the beginning of the quota period, but there is no reason to believe that holders of auctioned quota licenses would behave in this way. Imports may bunch up toward the end of a quota period if importers must use the licenses by a particular date, but this phenomenon would be lessened by frequent auctions so that an entire year's worth of licenses would not all expire on December 31 each year. Given that there is no identifiable incentive for surges under auction quotas, relatively long periods of duration for licenses are beneficial because they would reduce risk and avoid disrupting established relationships between importers and their suppliers.

Quotas have usually set upper limits for imports on an annual basis. An annual basis for quota licenses would seem a reasonable norm, with shorter or longer durations if surges actually became a problem or if longer order-delivery lags required longer licenses to maintain normal commercial relations.

Combining quarterly auctions with licenses valid for one year would provide a possible starting point for design of an auction system. Staggering the expiration dates would discourage unusually large quantities of imports in periods when licenses are due to expire. Firms could manage their license holdings to use licenses first that would be the earliest to expire and to exchange licenses in the secondary market for ones of longer duration if their shipments were unexpectedly delayed.

A hypothetical example of how staggered quota auctions might work is

---

5. Of course, such surges can also occur with licenses of shorter duration, but the quantity, and therefore the disruption, would be less.

FIGURE 8.1.   **Hypothetical staggered quota auction**

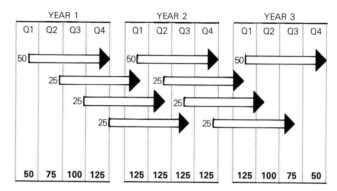

illustrated in figure 8.1. This example assumes a target level of imports of 100 units per year. The numbers in the chart indicate the volume of imports covered by licenses issued in that quarter; the arrows indicate the duration of validity for those licenses. Given the longer duration of the licenses than gaps between auctions, it seems reasonable to auction a larger proportion of the licenses toward the beginning of the auction period.

A system of this type is not immune to bunching of imports in a particular quarter. For example, the maximum possible quantity of imports that could come in during the first quarter of year two would be 110, but that would occur only if none of the licenses issued during the last three quarters of the previous year were used previously and all of the licenses issued in that quarter were used immediately—a very extreme and unusual case. If surges proved to be a problem in actual practice, the duration of the licenses could be shortened to nine months or six months.

If it is necessary to shorten the period of validity of licenses, it would be possible to auction quotas further in advance of their period of validity. This would give importers time to order and arrange for delivery of goods after they knew for certain that they had been able to obtain the quota licenses necessary. For example, quota licenses valid from January through June 1989 could be auctioned in June 1988. This would give importers the needed advance knowledge of what they would be able to import, while shortening the period of validity of the licenses to prevent bunching. The disadvantage is that bidders would have to predict market conditions further in advance to formulate their bids.

Transferability of Licenses

Many of the concerns raised by opponents of auction quotas could be addressed by allowing a secondary market in quota tickets to operate freely. If firms find that they are not successful in the actual auction, they have a possibility of obtaining licenses in the secondary market. The existence of the secondary market in conjunction with frequent auctions would help to reduce the risk of panic bidding, particularly during the first few auctions. Allowing firms to exchange tickets that expire at different times would eliminate some of the problems of timing. A secondary market also would allow firms to correct mistakes or adjust to unexpected changes in market conditions. For example, if a firm's shipments are delayed, it could arrange to exchange licenses expiring soon for licenses expiring later.

Prohibiting transfers among firms could lead to unfilled quota if a firm finds that it cannot profitably import and cannot transfer the licenses to another firm. Because fewer goods would enter the market, prices would rise. Moreover, the unfilled quota might be misinterpreted to mean that the quota was not binding.

The main disadvantage of allowing a secondary market is the possibility that firms could evade antimonopoly limitations by acquiring more quota in the secondary market. Various safeguards against monopolization of importing were discussed in chapter 4. In most cases in the United States, monopolization of markets should not be a concern. Where appropriate, however, limits could be set on the total amount of quota any single firm could use in a given quota period. This level could be defined as a set proportion of available quota and should be high enough to maintain flexibility to respond to changing market conditions, perhaps 35 percent (as in the Treasury auctions).[6]

On balance, the convenience and efficiency gains from allowing a secondary market in licenses far outweigh the potential problem of monopolization. The costs to the country as a whole of having just one importer or collusion among a few importers arise from shortshipping. Regulations or procedures that ensure that all of the licenses issued are used if the quota is binding should prevent the accumulation and exploitation of monopoly power.

---

6. The objective of such provisions would be to prevent an auction from leading to a monopolized market. If a single firm already accounted for more than the specified level of imports, forcing it to cut back would not be appropriate. If the market were already that concentrated, a tariff would be preferable to a quota in any case.

Transition Measures

Concerns about uncertainty and potential market disruption under an auction quota system could be further mitigated by including some transition features. It would be possible to offer a portion of the quota tickets, perhaps 50 percent, on a first-refusal basis to importers based on their share of imports in a representative period. Importers receiving such tickets would still have to pay for them, at the price set in the auction for the remainder. Although preferable from an economic efficiency standpoint, it would not be necessary to phase out the historical setaside as long as a large enough portion was auctioned and the secondary market was functioning smoothly so that new entrants and more efficient firms had the opportunity to acquire additional quota.

In addition, a small business setaside might be included, either as a transition measure or as a permanent feature of the quota auction. Such a setaside could be modeled after that used in Treasury securities auctions, which allow noncompetitive bidders to receive the full allotment of licenses they bid for at the price set in the competitive auction. The setaside should be limited to no more than 15 percent of the quota pool.

Summary

Our proposal incorporates the elements that, in general, we believe would most effectively and simply achieve the objectives of an auction quota system. It is very important, however, that any implementing regulations preserve the flexibility to adjust the specifics as necessary to accommodate differences among the affected industries and products. The specific recommendations are summarized below:

Type of auction: sealed bid, uniform clearing price.

Type of bid: dollar per unit bids, unless upgrading is a concern, in which case ad valorem bids might be preferable.

Participation: US citizens, companies, and foreign subsidiaries incorporated in the United States that have demonstrated creditworthiness.

Frequency of auctions: quarterly.

Duration of licenses: one year.

Transferability: freely transferable licenses, although it may be desirable in some cases to set an upper limit on the amount that can be imported under quota by any single firm, perhaps 35 percent. The Commodity Futures Trading Commission could serve as a watchdog agency to prevent abuses in the secondary market.

Transition measures: initial 50 percent allocation on first-refusal basis to historical importers at the auction clearing price; small bidder setaside for noncompetitive bids up to 15 percent of the quota.

9 International Implications

A decision by the United States to auction import quotas would have important implications for both US bilateral and multilateral trade relations and for the world trading system as a whole. The first section of this chapter examines how the use of auction quotas would affect US obligations under the General Agreement on Tariffs and Trade (GATT). We then explore the implications for the Multi-Fiber Arrangement (MFA) and US bilateral restraint arrangements if the United States institutes auctions in sectors currently subject to quantitative trade restraints. We then turn, more generally, to how auction quotas would affect the US policy of pursuing "voluntary" export restraints (VERs). The chapter concludes by exploring how auction quotas could contribute to the reform of the MFA and of the GATT safeguards system in the new Uruguay Round of trade negotiations.

Auction Quotas and the GATT

GATT rules strongly favor the use of tariffs instead of quotas. GATT Article XI calls for the general elimination of quantitative restrictions (QRs) except under certain prescribed conditions, such as to alleviate supply shortages or to enforce domestic farm price support programs. GATT also permits the imposition of QRs in several other situations: for balance of payments reasons under GATT Articles XII and XVIII; for escape clause or general "safeguards" to provide temporary relief from import competition under GATT Article XIX; for national security reasons under GATT Article XXI; and for other cases where the trade-restricting country has received a waiver under GATT Article XXV.[1]

---

1. For example, because of a "temporary" GATT waiver granted in 1955, US quotas on dairy products, peanuts, and cotton—imposed under the authority of section 22 of the Agricultural Adjustment Act of 1933—do not constitute violations of US obligations under GATT Articles II and XI.

125

When QRs are permitted, however, GATT Article XIII requires that such restrictions be applied in a nondiscriminatory manner so as to provide "a distribution of trade in such product approaching as closely as possible the shares which the various [exporters] might be expected to obtain in the absence of such restrictions." In essence, the GATT only sanctions the imposition of quotas if they are applied in a way that has the least distortive effect on trade flows.

Would the introduction of auction quotas violate GATT obligations? In his testimony before the House Ways and Means Trade Subcommittee in April 1986, US Trade Representative Clayton K. Yeutter argued that several GATT problems could arise if the United States auctioned import entitlements (Yeutter 1986, pp. 10–11). In particular, he cited the Article VIII prohibition against import fees for fiscal purposes, the impairment of tariff bindings, and possible conflicts with the GATT Code on Import Licensing. In addition to these issues, concerns also were raised during congressional debate in 1986 about whether auctions would impair the most-favored-nation (MFN) rights accorded to GATT signatories under the escape clause and other provisions of the GATT. These issues will be addressed in turn.

IS THE AUCTION PREMIUM AN IMPORT FEE?

GATT Article VIII:1(a) prohibits the imposition of import fees except those required to cover the costs of customs services, which are specifically permitted under Article II:2(c).[2] In other words, the fee must "approximate [the] cost of services rendered" and should not be used to provide "indirect protection to domestic products." GATT rules explicitly bar the use of import fees to raise revenues for other purposes.[3]

---

2. In 1986, the United States instituted a special customs fee of 0.22 percent on almost all dutiable imports to raise revenues to cover the costs of the US Customs Service. The fee is scheduled to decline to 0.17 percent for fiscal 1988–89. This measure has provoked a GATT challenge by the European Community and Canada, which have charged that the United States has violated Article VIII because the revenue raised allegedly would exceed the cost of the US Customs Service.

3. Under the terms of the Framework Agreement negotiated in the Tokyo Round, however, countries may impose import surcharges for balance of payments purposes, subject to the conditions of GATT Articles XII and XVIII. Such measures often have been used in the past without explicit GATT authorization (General Agreement on Tariffs and Trade 1980, pp. 205–9).

Whether there is a violation of Article VIII depends on how one characterizes the auction process. Those who consider the auction premium to be an illegal import fee argue that importers would have to pay for import licenses that they previously received for free or were not required to have. They consider such payment an additional barrier to importing. Others argue that the auction premium is not a fee "for services rendered" and thus Article VIII does not apply.

As we have seen in prior chapters, the auction premium does not affect the cost of the restricted good to consumers; that price is set by the underlying quota whether the quota rights are sold or given away. The total payment by importers (cost of the export good plus the auction premium) cannot exceed the payment received from consumers. Since consumers will pay only so much for a restricted good, the cost of the auction premium must come out of the windfall profits or quota rents received by exporters or importers. In most cases, importers would be able to pass the cost of the auction premium back to exporters, who would have to cut their quota-inflated prices and thereby forgo some quota rents. In a few cases (for example, US dairy quotas), importers would lose some quota rents.

In either case, the auction process would not raise the level of protection of a quota; it merely would make the cost of protection more transparent and redistribute the quota rents. The auction premium itself varies depending on market conditions for the product subject to the quota and reflects the underlying restrictiveness of the quota: from nonrestrictive (zero premium) to highly restrictive (say, more than 50 percent premium). As such, the premium is part of the cost of the underlying quota and is not an additional import charge.

To be considered an import fee, the auction premium must represent an *additional* charge that increases protection in the importing market above the level set by the underlying quota. This can occur only if one sets a minimum bid in an auction that exceeds the quota rents and thus increases the degree of restrictiveness above the level of the quota itself. In such a case, the minimum bid would increase protection and thus constitute a GATT-illegal import fee.

The Australian and New Zealand auctions were introduced in part to determine the underlying cost of import restraints. Neither country has been formally charged with any GATT violation stemming from their auction quota system. As a practical matter, such a complaint is unlikely since the system is intended to implement an import liberalization program.

DO AUCTION PREMIA IMPAIR TARIFF BINDINGS?

GATT Article II:1(b), provides for the binding of maximum tariff rates on products where concessions have been made in trade negotiations. However, the price of the auctioned quota tickets, although it may be described in ad valorem terms and gives an indication of the tariff *equivalent* impact of the quota, is not a tariff. As described in chapters 2 and 4, the shift from VERs (or other forms of QRs) to auction quotas should have no impact on the final price of the imported products. There is no additional trade restraint, and hence no additional tariff could be imputed under the new regime.

If tariffs are bound and the quota auction is used to provide a basis for subsequently converting existing quotas to their tariff-rate equivalents, the eventual conversion to higher tariffs could raise the new duty above the level bound in the GATT schedules. In such cases, auctions would lead to a violation of GATT tariff bindings. As prescribed in the GATT, however, there is a simple remedy for potential tariff problems. Tariff bindings can be restructured in the context of Article XXVIII negotiations—similar to those held as a consequence of efforts to harmonize customs nomenclature—in return for compensation for any adverse trade effects. Normally, such procedures are used for long-run restructuring of tariff schedules, but they could be adapted to apply to retariffication schemes.

Would such actions lead to claims for compensation? Such claims could arise because the exporter will be deprived of the quota rents by the importing country. We therefore believe that any conversion of existing VERs to auction quotas should be negotiated with the exporting countries, as noted later in the chapter. In most instances, however, compensation might be avoided if the importing country simultaneously adopted a phase-out of the entire quota regime—thereby enhancing the prospect for increased sales volume by the exporting countries (see chapter 10).

WOULD AUCTION QUOTAS VIOLATE THE GATT LICENSING CODE?

The GATT Agreement on Import Licensing Procedures negotiated during the Tokyo Round provides that "licensing procedures...shall not have trade restrictive effects on imports additional to those caused by the imposition of the restriction." The code calls for transparency of licensing procedures and for nondiscriminatory access to licenses (although licenses can be country specific instead of global). Code provisions also seek market access assurances for new suppliers and "special consideration" for imports from developing countries.

Auction procedures and implementing regulations can be designed to ensure that all the requirements of the GATT Licensing Code are satisfied. As noted earlier, auctions do not increase the restrictiveness of quotas; they merely make the costs of such restrictions more transparent (and shift the rents). The bidding procedure itself encourages the distribution of quota to the most competitive suppliers. Thus, auctions promote trade from competitive new suppliers who otherwise might be barred from the import market by quotas allocated on a historical share basis. In sum, auctions would promote the objectives of the GATT Licensing Code.

DO AUCTIONS IMPAIR THE GATT RIGHTS OF EXPORTING COUNTRIES?

By their nature, safeguards actions undermine the balance of concessions between GATT members. Article XIX permits affected countries to seek compensation for, or to retaliate against, such measures in order to redress the imbalance caused by the new trade restrictions. As long as Article XIX provisions are followed, however, safeguards measures do not violate GATT obligations because Article XIX allows the importing country to suspend its GATT obligations regarding the affected trade, including the obligation to maintain bound concessions. As such, auction quotas imposed under escape clause or safeguards procedures do not violate GATT obligations, although they would generate claims for compensation for affected exporting countries.[4]

A few questions still remain regarding the legal status under the GATT if existing quotas—which were not applied pursuant to Article XIX—are converted to auction quotas. First, GATT rules exhort countries not to discriminate among suppliers when imposing quotas.[5] Article XIII requires

---

4. The conversion of existing QRs under Article XIX to auction quotas could cause a problem, however, if affected exporting countries could claim that their ability to capture the quota rents was part of their compensation for the quota; auctioning could impair that implicit agreement and thus lead to new compensation claims. The issue of compensation also could arise in the conversion of VERs to auction quotas if the restrictions were brought under GATT discipline.
5. Nonetheless, discrimination is often the practice, especially in the form of VERs and other gray area measures not subject to GATT discipline. The conversion of such measures to auction quotas will be discussed below.

that the quota set by the importing country not distort normal trade patterns that would occur in the absence of trade controls. Some consider this provision to mandate quota allocations based on historical market share. But such a system does not take into account changing market conditions and discriminates against new entrants. By contrast, an auction of *global* quotas would permit imports from the most efficient foreign suppliers—the ones most likely to ship under free market conditions as well. Even if the auction involved country-specific quotas, the effect would be no more discriminatory than the previously allocated quota itself.

Auctions of global quotas are preferable to the country-specific quotas that the United States maintains under almost all its current import restraint programs. As noted in chapter 2, auctions of global quotas are the least distortive means of administering a quantitative restraint and thus provide the best means of protecting MFN rights. Maintenance of country-specific quotas when auctions are instituted is less desirable because the discrimination imposed by the quota—by excluding sourcing from suppliers in other countries—would be maintained.

Although global quotas are preferable to country-specific quotas on efficiency and other grounds, we do not advocate the conversion to truly global quotas in some existing cases because that would increase the scope and coverage of the trade restraints to countries that are currently uncovered. In such cases, it would be desirable to pursue a phase-out of country quotas in favor of "global" quotas for *covered* countries only; such a solution would be less discriminatory than the existing restraints.

Second, concerns have been raised that the conversion of existing quotas not subject to GATT rules to auctioned import quotas would violate the GATT "standstill" agreement. The declaration of Punta del Este that launched the Uruguay Round in September 1986 contained inter alia a commitment by trade ministers not to impose "any trade restrictive or distorting measure inconsistent with the provisions of the General Agreement or the Instruments negotiated within the framework of GATT or under its auspices."[6] In so doing, ministers sought to stem new protection and provide a baseline for liberalization in the new trade round.

The conversion of extra-GATT restrictions into auctioned import quotas would bring the stray sheep back into the GATT flock. It would consequently

---

6. *GATT Focus* (October 1986), p. 3.

result in an increase of restrictions that were GATT-illegal because the quotas would not apply to all countries and thus would violate the GATT's MFN principle. This does not mean, however, that the standstill would be breached. Such measures were always "inconsistent" with the provisions and the spirit of GATT rules, even though they did not fall within its legal purview. The conversion to auctioned import quotas would not impose new protectionist measures (as long as quotas were not extended to previously uncovered countries or products); they would merely allow GATT members to better monitor and pressure for the liberalization of existing restraints. Conversion of extra-GATT restrictions to auction quotas would therefore reinforce the objectives of the standstill.

In sum, the use of auction quotas would not create significant GATT problems. In most instances, auctions would comport with GATT rules. Indeed, there are several reasons why auction quotas could spur the liberalization of existing trade barriers, limit the trade-distorting effect of prospective new measures, and thus promote GATT objectives.

First, making protection more transparent should increase pressure to unravel the restrictions from domestic consumers who are paying the price of the protection, foreign exporters who would lose quota rents, and interests in third countries who might be affected by trade diversion. Indeed, to achieve such greater transparency, the seven GATT "Wisemen"—convened in 1984 to review GATT and the world trading system—proposed a protectionism "balance sheet" in its reform proposals issued in 1985 (Leutwiler et al. 1985, p. 35).

Second, auctions could lead importing countries to rationalize or simplify the administration of import controls. In the case of textiles and apparel, this could lead to conversion to global quotas for covered countries and quotas on broader categories of goods (as originally intended under the MFA).

Third, if auction proceeds are dedicated in part to adjustment, they could reduce pressure for protection by the affected industry in the future and thus ensure that safeguard measures are degressive and phased out over time. The use of auction proceeds and the linkage to trade adjustment assistance will be examined in more detail later in this chapter and in the final chapter.

Fourth, it could become harder to negotiate backroom deals via extra-GATT measures such as VERs if quota allocations were required to be determined by auction. Exporting countries would be less willing to accept quantitative restraints if they do not receive quota rents as implicit compensation for the trade restraints. As a result, they may respond to new US import quotas imposed in lieu of VERs by demanding explicit compensation or by retaliating against US exports to their markets.[7]

Less reliance on implicit "hush money" and greater scope for retaliation may be good for the GATT system. The proliferation of quotas—indeed, the growth of the system of managed trade—has been supported by the use of VERs in large part due to the provision of implicit compensation through the allocation of quota rents. Both the exporting country(ies) and the protected domestic industry benefit from VERs at the expense of domestic consumers. Instead of being a discipline against the imposition of new restraints, this type of compensation actually provides an incentive for established exporters to accede to, and perpetuate, managed trade. Affected third countries, especially prospective new entrants, have no ready access to complaint procedures to defend their rights in the GATT.

Retaliation or compensation in other sectors is, by contrast, an important discipline for the negotiated balance of concessions in the GATT. When the imposition of trade restraints upsets that balance, GATT rules call for redress. The preferred method is to offset new protection by liberalization in other areas. Alternatively, the GATT provides for retaliation, either unilaterally (in response to an Article XIX action) or with multilateral authorization (in response to the nullification or impairment of GATT rights).

The main concern about retaliation is that *by its nature* it is trade restricting. Moreover, such action could set in motion a tit-for-tat response that could unravel existing trade reforms. The memory of the "beggar-thy-neighbor" policies of the early 1930s is instructive of the dangers of retaliation run amok.

The threat of a repeat of the 1930s debacle has provided some discipline to government reactions in the postwar period. Examples of out-of-control retaliation have been few. Even the infamous "chicken war" between the United States and the European Community (EC) was settled in 1963 after an initial round of retaliation that affected only $26 million of European exports to the United States. More recently, and despite loud threats of

---

7. In congressional testimony in April 1986, Ambassador Yeutter argued that the greater difficulty in negotiating VERs would be a *drawback* of an auction system. At the time, he was busily engaged in renegotiating VERs on textiles and apparel with key suppliers in the context of the renewal of the MFA. Given the results of those negotiations, one may question whether such "flexibility" is not counterproductive. See Yeutter (1986, pp. 10–11).

retaliation and counter-retaliation in the context of the dispute over the Spanish accession to the EC, the United States and the EC opted at the last minute for a negotiated settlement in lieu of a trade war that could have damaged both economic and political relations.

But retaliation has not gone out of style. The US sanctions against Japan in April 1987 in the semiconductor dispute is the most recent example; in addition, Canada was quick to retaliate against US levies on cedar shingles and shakes in 1986, as was the EC in 1984 against US specialty steel quotas, and China in 1983 against new US textile restrictions. In each case, the retaliation was a measured reaction to the imposition of new trade restraints. More importantly, retaliation demonstrated to industries in both exporting and importing countries that trade obligations would be monitored and that rights under trade agreements would be protected.[8]

Auction Quotas and US Restrictions

As noted in chapter 3, the United States maintains an extensive network of import quotas and VERs that restrict large volumes of trade in textiles and apparel, steel, machine tools, dairy products, sugar, and several other products (Hufbauer, Berliner, and Elliott 1986). This section will examine what the implications would be for US trade relations with affected exporting countries if the United States unilaterally converted its allocated quotas, including VERs, into auction quotas.

Textiles and apparel. Under the authority of section 1102 of the Trade Agreements Act of 1979, the United States could convert the bilateral textile restraints negotiated under the MFA framework into auctioned import quotas. If such action led to the abrogation of those agreements and the subsequent collapse of the MFA, however, it would eliminate the current legal authority under section 204 of the Agricultural Act of 1956 to negotiate VERs, thus rendering the auction issue moot. That authority allows the President to negotiate VERs on products covered by an international agreement which regulates a significant share of world trade in those products.

A unilateral conversion would violate the terms of the bilateral agreements,

8. See Destler and Odell (1987). Most of the examples cited earlier involve OECD countries. Resort to retaliatory measures by developing countries may be more limited, unless they participate in joint actions with other countries.

which call for the exporting country to administer the trade restraints. It could lead to calls for compensation from the affected exporting countries and cause some countries to question the viability of the MFA regime itself. The intensity of complaints probably would depend on whether auctions involve country-specific or global quotas and whether auctions were part of a credible phase-down of US controls.

Furthermore, such a violation could result in a breakdown of talks in the new Uruguay Round and thus severely damage the international trading system. Developing countries understandably would object to a unilateral action that affected a significant share of their manufactured exports, and even more so unless accompanied by a willingness by the United States to negotiate the liberalization of textile and apparel quotas in the MFA context. A negotiated reform in the MFA to permit auction quotas would be preferable to unilateral action by the United States. These issues are discussed in more detail later in this chapter in the section on MFA reform.

Steel quotas. The current VERs negotiated since 1982 with most major suppliers of steel to the US market allow exporting countries to allocate the quota to their suppliers and thus enable them to capture the quota rents. The agreements also contain a provision reserving the GATT rights of each exporting country in the event changes are made in the nature of the trade restraints. The unilateral conversion to US auction quotas would violate the bilateral steel agreements and would likely lead to demands that the United States offer compensation to affected exporting countries or accept retaliation by foreign suppliers, especially the European Community. If the VERs were abrogated, new legislative authority would be needed to auction US import quotas on steel because the current authority in the Trade and Tariff Act of 1984 applies only to quotas imposed to enforce an international agreement.

Machine tools. The President has authority under section 232 to impose import quotas on machine tools. These quotas could be auctioned only if new authority was enacted since section 232 measures are not covered by section 1102 auction authority. Such a step would violate the terms of the VERs with Japan and Taiwan; their reaction would depend on the restrictiveness of the quota and on whether the auctions were for a global or country-specific quota. Furthermore, if import quotas are imposed, the EC has threatened to initiate a GATT challenge against the national security rationale invoked by the United States to justify its machine tool restrictions.[9]

---

9. The EC charged that the machine tool restrictions violate both GATT Article XI and the

Dairy products. Import quotas for dairy products are allocated by the United States to US importers based for the most part on historical market share, and they are excluded from the auction authority of section 1102. Nonetheless, if new authority was provided to permit the government to auction the dairy quota, there still would be a loud and vociferous foreign reaction.

First, exporting countries probably would object to a conversion to auctions of global quotas because they would not want to lose their guaranteed market access (unless they were competitive enough to believe they could win more quota in an auction). Second, while auctions would not violate GATT rights per se because of the 1955 GATT waiver for section 22 quotas, they could impair specific product concessions on cheese made at the conclusion of the Tokyo Round in 1979. Here again, both concerns could be assuaged if the conversion to auction quotas was negotiated in return for a commitment to liberalize the quota levels.

Sugar. Sugar quotas are allocated annually by country based on historical performance. Currently, exporting countries issue certificates of eligibility that they receive from the US Secretary of Agriculture for their shipments to the United States, and thereby they capture the quota rents.[10] In this case, auctions would not violate existing agreements. However, a switch to auctions and a recapture of some of the rents could create concerns about "reverse foreign aid." That issue is discussed later in this chapter with regard to MFA reform, but will become moot shortly unless the sugar program is revised to forestall the impending imposition of a total import embargo.

"Voluntary" Export Restraints

In recent years, the United States has negotiated voluntary export restraint agreements for a number of products (for example, autos, steel, machine tools) in lieu of imposing trade controls at the US border. Such agreements make it easier to impose protectionist measures for several reasons.

● The exporting country applies the controls. US legal procedures are

---

GATT standstill commitment undertaken at Punta del Este in September 1986. See Bureau of National Affairs, *International Trade Reporter*, 7 January 1987, p. 12.

10. Such rents are often regarded as implicit foreign aid for exporting countries. The United States has rewarded "friends" with extra allocations and punished "foes" with quota reductions.

avoided, lessening the prospect of countervailing antiprotectionist pressures. Thus, VERs represent "out of court" settlements of trade disputes.

• In most instances, VERs have not been subject to GATT discipline. These measures fall in a "gray area" between what is legal and illegal under the GATT. The cost of the controls is hidden, and there is no requirement to notify the GATT of such measures. As a result, the interests of third countries who might be affected by trade diversion or by the price effects resulting from the restrictions are not taken into account.[11]

• Exporters are allocated a share of the quota rents as implicit compensation for their acceptance of trade restraints. As long as their market share is not substantially eroded by unrestrained suppliers not subject to the VER regime, they have an incentive to maintain the controls and less cause for seeking other compensation or for pursuing retaliation under GATT.

• Unlike tariffs, VERs mask the cost of protection to consumers in the importing country.

The disadvantages of VERs are important in economic terms, but this may make them more compelling from a political perspective. The ability to negotiate VERs increases the tendency toward managed trade because VERs lessen the pressure for adjustment to competitive market conditions by the import-competing industry. While exporters that comply with the VER regime usually accept a decline in volume in trade, they are better off even in volume terms than they would have been with unilateral quotas, because they receive preferences in the setting of the quota levels, and most of the windfall profits generated by these quotas. Unrestrained suppliers fall into an implicit basket category; if they try to increase their market share, they are quickly pressured into the VER regime.

Both the exporters that hold quota rights and the protected industry have an incentive to maintain protection to the disadvantage of consumers in the importing country. Since both the exporting and import-competing industry benefit from a share of the quota rents, and neither is under pressure to adjust to competitive market conditions, VERs contain the seed of their own self-perpetuation.[12] Moreover, the controls lead to trade diversion to unprotected

---

11. Bilateral VERs concluded under the MFA framework are subject to surveillance by the Textiles Surveillance Body of the MFA, which in turn reports to the GATT Textiles Committee.

12. In theory, exporters do face competition from suppliers in countries not subject to the VER;

import markets, and affected third countries can do little to protect their trading interests because there is no recourse to GATT dispute procedures.

In addition, VERs have been used to extend controls over imports subject to unfair trade disputes. Provisions of the US countervailing and antidumping duty laws—consistent with the GATT codes in these areas—allow investigations to be suspended if the complaint is resolved via a negotiated arrangement acceptable to the domestic industry. As with the US-EC steel dispute, the suspension agreement often is a VER.

Such agreements have three perverse effects. First, the VER usually covers a broader range of products than involved in the original complaint (i.e., both fairly and unfairly traded goods) to gain the agreement of the petitioning industry. Second, a QR is imposed instead of a tariff (i.e., a countervailing or antidumping *duty*). Third, industries pursue unfair trade disputes instead of escape clause cases because the recourse to suspension agreements affords them more negotiating flexibility to obtain more protection, to impose quotas instead of tariffs, and to avoid the requirements of section 201 actions (for example, degressive and time-limited protection). As such, VERs have contributed to the misuse of unfair trade statutes and the disuse of the escape clause.

By their nature, VERs are hard to monitor; they are "voluntary," often private understandings between two consenting adults. Since both the governments and the industries in the affected countries prefer VERs for the "advantages" noted, governments are likely to continue to resort to VERs instead of tariffs or auction quotas unless some discipline against their use is imposed both domestically and in the GATT.

What could be done? The most direct solution would be to get major countries to agree not to resort to VERs in the future and then to secure that commitment in GATT during the Uruguay Round. Such an approach would protect MFN rights of GATT members and facilitate reforms to strengthen the GATT safeguards system. For those reasons, the GATT "Wisemen" recommended the elimination of all so-called "gray area measures."[13]

An outright ban on the use of VERs could be best incorporated in reforms

---

but VERs now usually cover the significant foreign suppliers of the product (with the exception of Canada and the European Community in textiles and apparel).

13. The "Wisemen" also called for the abolition of intraindustry arrangements, which are not relevant in the US context because of antitrust laws but could be covered in a multilateral agreement (Leutwiler et al. 1985, p. 38).

of the GATT safeguards system that are under negotiation in the Uruguay Round. The agreement should apply to all future measures and provide that all existing VERs be converted to tariffs or auction quotas under the new GATT rules within a short transition period.

Would a ban on the use of VERs lead to the imposition of more restrictive import quotas? Some argue that VERs substitute for tighter unilateral action by the importing country and affect the trade of fewer countries than would GATT-consistent safeguard actions. To be sure, VERs do restrain trade less than do measures *threatened* by the Congress. On the second point, however, recent experience has shown that VERs have had to be extended to almost all suppliers to prevent noncovered countries from taking advantage of the export restraints of others. As such, VERs have become the vehicle to globalize trade restraints.[14] The lack of the VER option would make the imposition of restrictions more difficult because formal procedures under US trade law would have to be followed. Opposition to the trade controls could then arise in response to the potential cost of the protection and the threat of foreign retaliation against US exports.

New legislation could go a long way toward deterring the United States from engaging in such arrangements. US antitrust laws currently *encourage* foreign firms to collude in a government-ordained export cartel. Under the sovereign compulsion doctrine, such firms have been exempt from US antitrust prosecution and thus able to participate in export restraint agreements without fear of antitrust prosecution. Such immunity should be revoked for companies involved in cartel arrangements that implement bilateral trade restraint agreements (including VERs and intraindustry arrangements) by amending the Sherman Act and by directing the US Customs Service not to cooperate in the enforcement of foreign export restraints. Proposals to this effect have already been put forward by scholars at the GATT and the Brookings Institution, and they merit strong consideration (Tumlir 1985, pp. 48–50; Lawrence and Litan 1986, p. 102).

As a practical matter, however, it is difficult to proscribe truly "voluntary" VERs.[15] A less desirable alternative may need to be considered. Instead of

---

14. While this is not yet the case in textiles and apparel, US industry is pressing Congress to extend the coverage of US controls through legislation sponsored by Congressman Ed Jenkins (D-Ga.).

15. For example, the United States asked Japan in 1985 to stop restraining auto exports to the US market, but the Japanese continue to do so "voluntarily"—albeit at a higher volume level than in earlier periods.

an outright ban on the use of VERs, the coverage of code rules could be extended to VERs as well as other safeguards-type measures. This approach was pursued in the unsuccessful attempt in the Tokyo Round to craft a safeguards code; it also seems to have been adopted by the Uruguay Round negotiators.

The possible inclusion of VERs in a new safeguards code raises a problem with MFN rules. GATT Article XIX requires that safeguard actions be applied in a nondiscriminatory manner. Some countries take this to mean that all exporters should be treated alike; others consider the selective application of quotas to a few suppliers to be permissible since, in their view, Article XIX also suspends the MFN requirement of Article I. VERs apply restrictions selectively to "problem" suppliers. If countries agreed to include VERs in the code coverage, they also would be condoning the non-MFN or selective application of safeguard measures.

Given the MFN problem, a ban on VERs should be the preferred negotiating approach. But if this issue threatens to torpedo the current talks as it did the Tokyo Round draft safeguards code, an agreement could alternatively provide for comprehensive notification, consultation, and dispute settlement procedures, including the right to compensation or to pursue retaliation if the VER adversely affects the trade interests of another country. The use of VERs should be conditioned upon the joint notification of the terms of the trade restraint by all the parties to the agreement and should meet the same injury and causation standards that apply to the imposition of other safeguard measures.

In the parlance of trade negotiations, this would require consensual selectivity. Although this would "legitimize" non-MFN import restraints, it also would provide greater transparency of such measures and a means to link them to industry adjustment and liberalization schedules. While such an approach clearly is second best to an outright ban on VERs, it does significantly improve the existing situation and therefore should be considered as a fall-back option.

Linkage to GATT Negotiations

The use of auction quotas could have important implications for negotiations in two key areas of the Uruguay Round. In textiles and apparel, the use of auction quotas could provide the means to implement a phase-out of the

Multi-Fiber Arrangement. With regard to GATT rules, the linkage of auctions to adjustment programs could provide the missing link needed to reach agreement on a new safeguards code. Both these linkages are detailed below.

MFA REFORM

The MFA sets up a VER system of trade restraints. Given the way the quotas are administered, the exporting country receives the quota rents created by those restrictions, thereby providing an implicit form of compensation for the MFA restraints. The use of auction quotas would shift the administration of trade controls to the importing country and could result in the loss of some or all of those rents, depending on market conditions and on whether country quotas are maintained. The conversion of MFA export restraints to auctioned import quotas clearly would violate the terms of *existing* agreements and thus could disrupt the MFA IV regime. Alternatively, auctions could be introduced in the context of a negotiated reform of the MFA, which could take place during the Uruguay Round.

How would exporting countries react to the introduction of auction quotas for textile and apparel trade? For exporting countries, the current value of quota rights depends on whether one regards the import quota as perpetual or degressive. The former enhances the value of the quota to current holders and fortifies their opposition to a system of auctioning. The latter, however, decreases the value of the quota right and increases potential export opportunities; thus, a shift to auctions could be welcomed if it supported degressive protection.

For competitive countries, the long-term prospect of import liberalization should compensate for the short-term loss of revenue. For noncompetitive countries (including many current holders of MFA quota rights), the prospect of import liberalization means a loss of market share to other foreign suppliers. Such countries would object to quota auctions unless other means were found to compensate them for their lost quota rents and exports.[16] The most logical

---

16. Many argue that compensation is not warranted since these industries emerged because of the quotas, not in spite of them. As a practical matter, however, such countries will object to MFA reforms unless compensated for the trade effects that will occur as a result of the reforms. Compensation would thus serve to pay off the companies that have invested in textiles and apparel in response to the quotas. The lesson is clear: it is costly to establish quotas, to maintain them over time, and to dismantle them as well.

avenue for such compensation would be in the context of the overall bargain in the multilateral trade negotiations. A contractual deal in the Uruguay Round would ensure that developing-country suppliers would receive tangible trade benefits in return for their acquiescence to auction quotas and a gradual phase-out of MFA restrictions.

Restraints on textile and apparel trade have been in place for several decades and will be hard to unravel. Indeed, political pressures in the OECD area have led over the past decade to a tightening of loopholes in MFA rules and coverage. Each renegotiation of the MFA has led to the introduction of new restrictive provisions, such as the "reasonable departures clause" and "antisurge provisions," and broader product coverage (for example, for new fibers). The distortion in production and trade patterns that has built up over decades of protection has created new vested interests that will resist reform in the MFA system. As such, any liberalization in the MFA regime will have to provide incentives for adjustment and a lengthy adjustment period.

Auctions could be quite useful in implementing both a transition from country-specific to global quotas and a liberalization schedule. Such a system could be introduced unilaterally, but in light of the international ramifications cited earlier, it would best be initiated pursuant to a multilateral agreement to phase-out the MFA regime.

To implement an auction system, the United States and other developed-country signatories to the MFA would need to establish a benchmark for their total imports of MFA products based on the average volume-level of the last two years of MFA IV. This benchmark would set the global quota level for MFA suppliers. The global quota would be the sum of the country-specific quotas for each product category; all suppliers not subject to MFA agreements would remain free of quantitative restrictions on their exports.

Each year the global quota for each importing country would be expanded by x percent; at the same time, the national quota of each exporting country would be reduced by y percent. The unallocated quota rights (i.e., the x percent increase in the aggregate level, plus y percent of the existing national quotas) would then be auctioned off by the importing country to the highest bidder. Over a period of time, national quotas would be reduced to zero. At the same time, global quotas would be expanded to the point where they either no longer restricted trade flows (in other words, when the supply of quota rights reached a level where the price of the rights approached zero) or where a fixed adjustment period agreed to in advance (say 10 to 15 years) dictated the abolition of the quotas.

This system of auction quotas gradually would shift the sourcing of imports to the most efficient suppliers. Inefficient developing-country exporters, currently protected by MFA quotas, and possibly Japan, would lose market share as their allocated quotas were assigned to the auction pool. Since they would, in essence, be conceding this loss in the negotiation of the terms of the MFA phase-out, these countries could count the loss of their protected textile and apparel markets as part of their contribution to the overall Uruguay Round package (as would the United States and other importing countries in the OECD for the quota liberalization) for which they would receive concessions elsewhere.

Global quotas for developing-country suppliers and Japan should lessen the unpredictability of import volumes that now occur in the United States and other OECD countries. Liberalization of the quotas would be gradual but automatic, affording both exporters and domestic industry the opportunity for long-term planning and adjustment.

Such a scheme may be open to criticism because it entails, in essence, "reverse" foreign aid by taking rents away from developing-country suppliers and putting them in the US Treasury. Many developing countries undoubtedly will object to changing MFA export restraints into quotas auctioned by the importing country because of the reflow of funds. There are several rebuttals. First, in most cases the rents are not going to the neediest developing countries but rather to the newly industrializing countries (NICs) that do not necessarily need such windfall transfers. In fact, several of them currently are running large current account surpluses (Balassa and Williamson 1987). Second, the beneficiaries of the rents in those countries are often not those most in need of foreign aid; indeed, the MFA system inhibits the potential redistribution of income to poorer people in poorer countries, a redistribution that could occur if importers could source from any supplier. Third, those NICs that stand to lose the quota rents are the countries most likely to benefit from new export opportunities in the OECD area that will emerge from adjustment by protected industries and from trade liberalizing agreements in the Uruguay Round.

Concerns about the "reverse" foreign aid aspects of the scheme are understandable. But aid given in support of an inefficient industry does neither the donor nor the recipient much good over time. The "artificial" growth of that industry attracts investment funds away from other projects and thus digs the developing country into a deeper hole. Instead of covert aid through implicit trade compensation, it would be better to give the developing countries increased market access for other exports and to channel financial resources through institutions such as the World Bank or the International Monetary Fund. We recognize the political constraints to increased funding for development in the Gramm-Rudman-Hollings era. However, if the United States agreed to a general capital increase in the World Bank that required no paid-in capital, there would be no budgetary cost. The World Bank is designed to finance development, and it is the most appropriate channel for development assistance.

GATT SAFEGUARDS CODE

GATT members face two key problems in their efforts to negotiate a new safeguards code. First, incentives are needed to induce countries to impose trade restrictions pursuant to GATT Article XIX instead of through VERs. Second, countries need some assurance that safeguard measures will be degressive and phased out over a prescribed time period. The solution to both issues depends on the availability of a viable adjustment program.

How would a system of auctioned quotas improve prospects for a multilateral accord on safeguards?

Auctions would benefit the international system in three ways. First, protection would be more transparent. Its impact on affected countries thus would be more readily discernible.

Second, auctions would discourage, although not completely eliminate, the use of VERs. One reason for VERs is to hide the resource transfer abroad. With greater transparency of restrictions and the capturing of that resource transfer by the importing country as a result of the auctions, exporting countries would have less incentive to agree to export restraints. GATT members could reinforce this trend further by seeking agreement barring the use of VERs, as noted earlier.

Third, auction revenues could be used to finance trade adjustment programs. Such programs could have two benefits: they could offer a viable alternative to protection; and they could complement trade controls, thus enabling restrictions to be phased out more quickly and reducing the need for extensions of the period of protection.[17] A new safeguards code should require that

---

17. In most cases, the revenues generated during the lifetime of the quota should be more than sufficient to fund an effective adjustment program for the protected industry. Alternatively,

adjustment programs be followed and that protection be degressive. These requirements would make it easier to gain agreement on a safeguards code; countries would be more willing to phase out protection if comparable commitments were made by other importing countries to liberalize their restrictions—thereby reducing the threat of trade diversion. In this sense, multilateral commitments to pursue adjustment programs would both reinforce a GATT accord on safeguards and make it easier to persuade domestic industries to pursue adjustment programs.

This means that a GATT code would be somewhat different from the one conceived during the Tokyo Round. Its focus would be on adjustment. Adjustment provides the best assurance that safeguard measures will be temporary and degressive and will not recur in the future. Over time, this is the best compensation for exporters affected by safeguard measures. The GATT code could waive provisions on compensation and retaliation if adjustment programs were being pursued (Hufbauer and Schott 1985; Jackson 1987). This, in turn, would remove a major impediment to the invocation of Article XIX, namely the potential compensation bill or threat of retaliation.

What role would the GATT have in adjustment programs? In essence, the GATT role should be similar to that played by the IMF in the negotiation and subsequent surveillance of stabilization programs or debt agreements. The GATT Secretariat should conduct ex post reviews of each safeguards action to ensure that code rules and adjustment plans are being followed. Each country should determine how best to pursue adjustment programs. The GATT code, however, could set minimum guidelines for adjustment programs to ensure that the safeguard measures are degressive and time limited, that they foster appropriate adjustment (including downsizing when necessary), and that they contain adequate sources of financing. Beyond these basics, each country should be free to construct a program most appropriate to its particular situation.

The safeguards code should provide for monitoring of the progress of national programs by the GATT Secretariat or by the committee of code signatories. If adjustment programs are not being pursued or are not being implemented effectively, the waiver of compensatory and retaliatory rights should be lifted.

---

auction revenues could be used to fund all trade adjustment assistance programs, not just those covering the industries that generate the funds. For other issues raised by such funding, see Hufbauer and Rosen (1986); and Hufbauer, Berliner, and Elliott (1986).

Summary

Auction quotas would have important implications for US trade relations. They could help promote long overdue liberalization of entrenched QRs and bolster the GATT system as well. They would not create significant problems with US obligations under the GATT; indeed, their use could help stem the erosion in GATT discipline caused by the increasing resort to ''gray area'' measures.

However, the unilateral imposition of auction quotas could provoke GATT disputes and foster demands that the United States compensate the affected exporting countries or face the threat of retaliation against US exports. In the most important cases, steel and textiles and apparel, bilateral agreements would be violated. If those agreements were subsequently abrogated by either party, new US legislation would be necessary to impose and auction import quotas. Unless such action was coupled with firm commitments by the United States to liberalize its longstanding quotas, the unilateral imposition of auction quotas in these cases could seriously compromise the ability of the United States to conclude new multilateral trade agreements.

Auction quotas could also play an important role in two key areas of the new Uruguay Round. In the context of MFA reform, auction quotas could be used as a means of facilitating the transition from the special protection regime back to trade governed by GATT rules. Similarly, auctions could improve the GATT safeguards system by increasing the transparency of QRs, discouraging the use of VERs, and generating revenues to fund adjustment programs to enable restrictions to be phased out more quickly. A further improvement would be the outright ban on the use of VERs.

10 Conclusions and Policy Recommendations

In our view, free trade is almost always superior to protection. If import barriers of some type must be employed, tariffs are preferable to quantitative restrictions (QRs). But QRs are widely used today by the United States and most other countries and will continue to be used in the future. Indeed, their use has been growing rapidly, at least in the United States, over the past ten years.

Hence, the method of implementing QRs is extremely important for trade policy. The issue concerning auction quotas is whether they should be employed by the United States and other importing countries when a prior decision is made to use quantitative restraints to limit imports. Auctions could be used in any new resort to QRs and to replace "voluntary" export restraints (VERs) and other quotas that are now implemented via allocation.

As pointed out in chapter 1, there are four methods of carrying out quantitative import controls: by allocation (including first-come-first-served) or by sale, by the exporting country or by the importing country (see table 1.1). These different techniques can have significantly different economic effects on the countries involved and on key groups—producers, exporters, consumers, importers, retailers, and others—within each country, as described in chapters 2 and 4. Many of these effects differ from those generated by tariffs and other types of trade restrictions; however, this study is limited to a comparison of different types of quantitative restrictions and addresses the differences between QRs and nonquantitative restraints only briefly.

One key issue in comparing the different quota regimes is the division of the windfall profits, or scarcity rents, generated by the quotas themselves. As discussed in chapter 2, such windfall profits are likely to go to exporters or producers abroad when the exporting country implements the quotas or when there are only a few firms exporting or producing the restrained goods. The importers are likely to receive the rents if the importing country allocates quotas to them or if there are only a few importing firms. Within countries, the private sector will acquire the rents if the quotas are administratively

147

allocated ("given away") by the government, whereas the government can probably capture the bulk of this premium if it auctions the quotas.

The Case for Auction Quotas

As indicated in chapter 1, there are five reasons for using auction quotas instead of allocated quotas. First, *auction quotas are much more transparent than allocated quotas.* This is because the higher consumer costs of imports generated by the quota system are usually explicitly revealed in the price of the quota ticket. There would be routine public announcement of the prices paid for the tickets after each auction, as with other government auctions (such as for oil leases and Treasury bills), and the outcome would presumably be published widely.

We regard this as an important virtue because it would maximize the use of market mechanisms and price signals within a basically restrictive system, revealing the degree of protection to all parties.[1] In particular, the price of the quota ticket will help indicate the consumer cost of the restriction and thus contribute to revealing one important impact of quantitative import restraints that is largely hidden under all other regimes. In a democracy, the voters and their representatives need to be as well informed as possible about any program of this type. One result should be a better balancing of the politics of trade policy since the position of consumer groups and other antiprotectionist forces should be strengthened by the greater transparency of the costs of protection.[2]

It is sometimes argued that the lack of transparency of existing import regimes, particularly those carried out via VERs, is beneficial. One view is that consumer costs are overstated and thus should not be given substantial weight. If that is true, of course, the price of the tickets should be very low.[3] With such an outcome, the contention would be demonstrated and those espousing it should welcome the auctions.

---

1. See Blinder (1987). Wide dispersal of the auction results would also contribute to "learning" in the bidding process and thereby to reducing uncertainty among bidders.

2. See Destler and Odell (1987).

3. This assumes a high degree of competition in the importing and retailing industries, so that bidders cannot collude to obtain the tickets at a price that understates the price increase to consumers. As indicated in ch. 4, we believe this to be the case in the industries considered in this study.

The main argument against transparency, and thus in favor of allocating rather than auctioning quotas, is that avoiding the glare of publicity provides the government with greater flexibility in applying the restraints in the first place and administering them subsequently. The US government can thus avoid the requirements of American trade law and, under the general foreign policy authority of the President, negotiate VERs with the exporting countries. Since the General Agreement on Tariffs and Trade (GATT) does not cover VERs, the US government can also avoid the strictures of the international trading rules, including the obligation to pay compensation or accept retaliation.

In our view, this notion has one serious analytical flaw and three important policy perversities. The analytical flaw is that VERs do encompass compensation by the United States to the exporting country, in the form of the transfer of the scarcity rents generated by the quantitative restriction itself. The only issue is one of distribution. With VERs, the benefits of compensation go directly to the exporting industry affected by the restraints. Alternatively, if compensation takes the form of reduced trade restrictions in other sectors, the benefits go to other industries abroad who would gain from increased exports.[4] Or, if the final outcome is retaliation rather than compensation, the "benefits" go to import-competing industries abroad. It can be argued that intraindustry compensation under VERs is more equitable than the alternative forms of compensation, and thus perhaps more politically acceptable both at home and abroad, but the use of VERs certainly does not obviate paying such costs.

The first policy perversity is that this intraindustry compensation has the practical effect of enhancing the profits of the foreign firms that are, by definition, the main competitors of the protected American industry. For example, Japanese automobile companies garnered perhaps $2 billion in additional annual profits when the auto VER was most effective (in 1984). America's willingness to transfer these huge amounts to its major competitors abroad runs directly counter to the goal of improving the country's competitive position in the world economy.

The second, and closely related, policy perversity is that this transfer of quota benefits to companies abroad can create vested interests for maintaining

---

4. In this case, there would be no net increase in trade restraints. An additional policy perversity of VERs is that in some cases they may prevent trade liberalization that would offset the initial restriction via the QR.

the protective regime in exporting as well as importing countries. This is certainly true for countries that know they would lose market shares under free trade. It is even true for those that may lose export volume but prefer the certainty provided by the quota regime along with the windfall profits that it transfers to them.

Many textile exporting countries have been quite willing to continue the Multi-Fiber Arrangement (MFA), for reasons described in chapter 9, and have indeed reacted quite negatively to its possible dissolution. The European Community (EC) actually proposed the steel VER in 1982, even though it probably produced tighter restrictions on trade than the pending actions under the unfair trade statutes preempted by the VER. At least some of the Japanese auto companies have appeared quite content to maintain that particular VER. Export restraint arrangements thus promote an unholy alliance between exporting and import-competing firms that espouses continued protection, rendering liberalization much more difficult to achieve.

The third policy perversity is that the lack of transparency inherent in VERs, and even in quotas allocated within the importing country, makes it easier to apply and preserve such restrictions by hiding their costs and the substantial transfers of revenues that are often involved. The "payment" of compensation within the affected sectors, as just described, adds to this outcome by avoiding adverse effects on third parties—who would then be likely to seek removal of the restrictions much more vigorously (or, if they were aware of the ultimate effect on them, to oppose imposition of the restrictions in the first place). As noted in chapters 1 and 3, the great majority of recent American QRs has been implemented via VERs—and most of the auto, steel, and textile and apparel restraints were adopted without those industries ever qualifying for import relief under the "escape clause" or other trade statutes.[5]

The argument for allocating quotas is thus an extension of the basic case for trade protection—as a less visible method of supporting industries than direct governmental subsidies or other forms of assistance. For the reasons noted, allocation carries this case to an extreme degree. By contrast, auctioning would reveal the costs of protection much more clearly and consequently

---

5. Indeed, the auto VER was adopted after the US International Trade Commission (USITC) rejected its injury petition. The steel industry qualified for antidumping and countervailing duties, but the QRs were imposed pursuant to a suspension agreement whose coverage was broader than the original petitions. See ch. 3.

would alter the dynamics of the trade policy process. It should thus help to deter the adoption of new quantitative restrictions and the maintenance of existing QRs beyond the period justified to permit adjustment by an injured industry. We regard this as an important benefit of the approach.

This leads us to the second reason for auctioning: *it can help provide a transition from quantitative restrictions to tariffs*. Tariffs are usually the preferred technique for implementing import relief. One difficulty in adopting tariffs, however, particularly for an industry that has experienced quantitative controls for some time, is the inherent uncertainty in setting their levels to achieve the desired degree of protection. For reasons cited in chapter 4, the price of quota tickets sold at auction can provide at least an approximation of that level and hence pave the way for a conversion of quotas to tariffs.

Indeed, the desire to achieve such conversion was a major motivation cited for the adoption of auctioning by Australia and New Zealand in the early 1980s. Their quota systems had become so extensive that immediate conversion would have been extremely difficult. To date, as indicated in chapter 7, both countries seem well on course—New Zealand, perhaps ahead of schedule—in using auctions to facilitate retariffication.

The United States does not have many quantitative restrictions that have lasted so long that direct, immediate conversion to tariffs would be impossible. However, the two largest import regimes—for textiles and apparel and for steel—do meet those criteria to an important extent.[6] An interim step to auctioning could thus facilitate any movement toward relying solely on tariffs to achieve the desired import relief.

The concept of retariffication has been espoused in some quarters because it would enhance the role of the market in determining trade flows, even when unusual protection is granted.[7] It could also become an element in the negotiation of a new safeguards code in the Uruguay Round of negotiations, and provide a solution for currently protected sectors if quotas were converted

---

6. In addition to unusually high tariffs of 12 percent and 22.5 percent, respectively, parts of the textile and apparel industry have been protected by quantitative restraints for 30 years, all of it (in principle) for almost 15 years. The steel industry has been protected by one technique or another for all but three of the past 18 years, with quantitative restrictions being the dominant means. See Cline (1987); and Hufbauer, Berliner, and Elliott (1986), respectively. The sugar and dairy controls have also existed for many years, but tariffs alone would not be an appropriate means for their implementation because the basic objective of these trade regimes is to protect domestic price supports.

7. See Hufbauer and Schott (1985); and Lawrence and Litan (1986).

to tariffs that were subsequently reduced. In such a scenario, quota auctioning could play a useful facilitating role.

A related consideration is that the preference for quotas instead of tariffs might decline if quotas were required to be implemented via auctioning, or if auctioning became the preferred vehicle even if not made mandatory. This is because the auctions would achieve greater transparency and, as just noted, would avoid the creation of international coalitions for protection. Moreover, importers would be more likely to resist import relief measures if all rents went to the government, instead of their getting at least a share (as occurs especially when the quotas are allocated directly to them, as in the dairy case). Hence, the appeal of QRs might be substantially reduced if auction quotas were increasingly used to carry them out, and the dynamics of trade policy determination might be shifted toward tariffs as a result.

Third, *auction quotas generally are consistent with the international rules of the GATT,* whereas many of the devices with which we are comparing them, notably VERs, are at best "gray area" measures outside the spirit (if not necessarily the letter) of the international trading rules. As demonstrated in chapter 9, charges that auctioning would be inconsistent with the GATT— that it would constitute a premium "import fee," impair tariff bindings, or violate the licensing code—do not stand up to close analysis. Neither Australia nor New Zealand has ever been charged with GATT violations because of their adoption of auction quota regimes. Indeed, auctions would probably represent the *best* method for implementing the mandate of GATT Article XIII regarding quota allocation: to seek "a distribution of trade in such product approaching as closely as possible the shares which the various contracting parties might be expected to obtain in the absence of such restrictions."

The most-favored-nation (MFN) rule of the GATT would be satisfied most effectively, of course, if the quotas were auctioned on a global rather than country-specific basis. In the case of voluntary export restraints, such as the MFA and steel arrangements, MFN requirements could only be satisfied by extending quota coverage to countries that are now outside the framework of controls. However, we would not want a shift to auctions for existing restraint cases to increase the scope of protection; indeed, such a shift at present would violate the standstill commitment barring new trade controls that was adopted in conjunction with the launching of the Uruguay Round.

If existing VERs are converted to auction quotas, they should be "globalized" across the existing universe of covered countries. In fact, the dynamics of an auction system would inevitably push in this very desirable direction. For such conversion cases, however, discriminatory treatment would remain, although such discrimination would be no worse than under the current regime.

Moreover, the overall trade policy benefits of the shift would weigh against the likelihood of legal challenges to it arising on these grounds. We have already noted that auctioning would substantially increase the transparency of trade controls and could represent a step toward retariffication. The revenues generated by auctioning could provide additional financing for positive adjustment programs, and thus enhance the prospects for degressivity and subsequent elimination of import restraints. Compared with VERs and other allocated quotas, auction quotas could promote some of the basic objectives of the GATT and help liberalize the trading system as a whole. But this discrimination issue adds to the case (as developed later) for achieving any shift to auctions for these sectors through international negotiation with the affected countries rather than through unilateral action by the United States.

The fourth advantage of auction quotas over those that are allocated by the exporting countries, at least from the standpoint of the importing country but perhaps more broadly as well, is the *redistribution of the quota rents from the exporting to the importing country*. As indicated in chapter 2, most of the windfall profits under VERs tend to go to the exporting country. If the exporting industries in those countries are reasonably competitive, replacing the VERs with quotas administered by the importing country will tend to enable it to capture the bulk of the rents. If the importing country implements the quotas via auction, the government rather than importers will seize most of those rents. Issues of both international and internal distribution arise in determining which technique to utilize.

A previous study at the Institute estimated that conversion of the QRs in place in 1984 to auction quotas would have generated about $9 billion of new resources for the government (Hufbauer, Berliner, and Elliott, 1986). The authors assumed that all imports are covered by the quota, that all of the quota rents go to the exporting countries, and that all of the rents would shift to the US government once quotas were auctioned. As indicated in chapter 4, the latter two assumptions are unlikely to be fully realized in practice. Furthermore, we do not advocate extending coverage under VERs to all suppliers. Finally, it might not be worthwhile or desirable to convert to auction quotas in some of the smaller cases. Recent changes affecting some of the larger restraint programs—notably, automobiles from Japan and perhaps steel because of exchange rate changes—suggest that some of the revenues might no longer be available.

Nevertheless, substantial revenue gains would appear to be possible. A shift to auctioning for textiles and apparel alone could capture about $3 billion. Another $1.3 billion would probably accrue from converting the steel quotas and just under $1 billion might be obtained from the agricultural quotas, notably sugar and dairy, and quotas on smaller industrial products such as machine tools and specialty steel (see chapter 4). The Congressional Budget Office, in its letter of 26 February 1987 to Chairman William H. Gray, III (D-Pa.) of the House Budget Committee, has similarly estimated that auction quotas could generate revenues of $3.7 billion in 1987, $3.9 billion in 1988, and $4.7 billion in 1989 (exempting, as we do, autos and meat).[8]

We would suggest that these trade-generated funds be earmarked to fund effective programs of trade adjustment assistance for both firms and workers. For example, they could fully finance the administration's current proposal to spend about $1 billion on the Worker Retraining Adjustment Program (WRAP)—a program that would help workers adjust to dislocation from all sources, including trade. A particularly useful industry adjustment program might be devised for the steel industry, which has announced its intention to cut capacity sharply but needs government help to finance the unfunded pension benefits of workers who would therefore be prematurely laid off. Even with such expenditures, however, $2 to $3 billion dollars could be obtained to reduce the budget deficit. And if programs like WRAP and the pension liabilities of the steel industry would be financed by the government in any case, much or all of the revenues generated by a shift to auction quotas would represent a net benefit for the federal budget.

In any event, it is clear that the government of an importing country could employ auction quotas, including substituting them for existing VERs and

---

8. The Congressional Budget Office (1987) analysis differs from earlier Institute estimates on the two major programs, textiles and apparel and steel. On textiles, the CBO rightly excludes any US capture of rents resulting from the substantial share of trade (about 40 percent, mainly from Europe and other uncovered countries) that is not now subject to restraint. Hence, there is a difference between the transfer to foreign countries (about $4 billion) and the quota rents that the United States could capture by adopting an auction system with the coverage we propose (about $3 billion). On steel, the CBO argues that the depreciation of the dollar against the yen and European currencies has reduced the impact of the VER and hence the amount of rents.

import quotas, to increase its revenues. As noted earlier, no GATT rules would be violated because the auction premium is properly viewed as part of the cost of the restriction itself rather than as an additional import fee. Use of the auction technique for any *new* quantitative restrictions, despite their denying the newly created rents to exporting countries, would simply fall under the usual procedures of Article XIX of the GATT—which would require compensation to those countries or an acceptance of retaliation from them. We regard this as a benefit because it might cause the importing country to consider the cost of its action more carefully before moving to restraint.

Converting existing VERs to import quotas (whether auctioned or allocated) would presumably also bring them under the GATT and thus, as with new restraints, enable the exporting countries to demand more traditional forms of compensation (or to retaliate). For such products as textiles and apparel and steel, moreover, such a shift would eliminate the de facto compensation now granted to exporting countries. Hence, the importing country could augment its revenues only at the cost of risking losses to other sectors of its economy via offsetting adjustments in unrelated trade flows.

The risk would probably depend in large part on the extent to which the revenues garnered by the shift in the rents were used to meet the adjustment problems of the protected industries. Our study of past adjustment efforts suggests that, in most cases, this will require downsizing of the industry in question. Instances of "phoenix cases" in either this country or abroad are few.[9] But whether the industry is seeking to restore its previous competitive level or downsize, there are three key requirements: providing a degressive schedule of protection over the life of the controls, setting a fixed date for their termination, and providing governmental assistance as needed to facilitate the adjustment and reduce its human costs to those involved. The first two requirements are already included in section 201 of the Trade Act of 1974, but they can be evaded by the use of voluntary export restraint arrangements— another reason to condemn this frequent practice.

This trilogy of domestic desiderata meshes precisely with the international obligations that the United States would probably have to accept to win international agreement on shifting the administration of existing VERs from the exporting countries to domestic auctioning. As noted, the exporters derive substantial benefits from the current system. All of these arrangements have

---

9. See Hufbauer and Rosen (1986); and Hufbauer, Berliner, and Elliott (1986).

been codified in bilateral or multilateral agreements. Hence, the United States could not unilaterally convert the existing VERs to auctions without incurring significant costs—demands for new forms of compensation, risks of retaliation and new trade wars, and severe disruption of overall trade policy (including the prospects for the Uruguay Round that the United States has rightly worked so hard to move forward).

However, the concerns of the exporting countries should be assuaged by the three considerations already advocated: a firm schedule for reducing the degree of protection over time; a firm termination date for the entire protective regime; and—to make these first two requirements viable—dedication to positive industry adjustment of a substantial portion of the scarcity rents transferred back to the United States via the auctions. Such a program would indicate credibly to the exporters that their loss of rents would be offset by increased market access for their exports.

This would reverse the implicit bargain that underpins the current export restraint regimes. Under VERs, the United States limits the volume of exporters' sales and, in return, gives them the windfall profits generated by the controls. Under auction quotas, the United States would capture the rents but would expand the volume of sales available for exporters. Such a shift would be extremely healthy for both our domestic economy and for international trade policy.

To implement such an approach, the Congress could direct the administration as follows: (1) implement any new QRs via auctioning; and (2) negotiate with the United States' trading partners a conversion of most of the existing VERs to auction quotas over the coming years, with the three conditions cited earlier applying to each case. (Automobiles and meat should be excluded from conversion for reasons specific to the current state of those arrangements as described below.) The administration could then bring each conversion agreement back to the Congress for approval under the familiar fast-track procedures. This process would assure the domestic industries and the foreign suppliers that the import controls would be phased down and eliminated. They then could plan their strategies accordingly.

Such a program would make a major contribution to US and international trade policy. By banning the use of export restraint arrangements by the country that pioneered their development, it would at a stroke take the lead toward eliminating the most pervasive of the "gray area" restraint measures that have undermined the trading system and blocked successful negotiation of a new GATT safeguards code. Such a code would, in turn, provide meaningful international regulation of import barriers to supplement Article XIX of the GATT and would help ensure that industries in other importing countries would also pursue positive adjustment rather than receive perpetual protection—thereby avoiding the risk of trade diversion to the United States. By enshrining assured degressivity and elimination of these current import controls, and by providing a source of substantial self-financing for positive adjustment instead, such a US initiative would convert the safeguards code into an adjustment code. (To ensure implementation of the commitments, it would be desirable to create an Adjustment Surveillance Committee that could monitor national programs under the code.) This initiative would breathe new life into the basic principles of trade liberalization of the GATT and provide major impetus to the Uruguay Round.

There is another reason why international negotiation of the conversion of existing VERs to auction quotas would be in the interest of the United States. The United States would almost certainly insist that other importing countries join it in liberalizing trade restraints, at least for sectors such as textiles and apparel and steel where such restraint is widespread. In the absence of similar commitments from other importers, the United States could liberalize alone only at the risk of becoming the primary target of exporting countries as its restraints were phased down and eliminated. It would be up to the other importers whether they wanted to join the United States in adopting auction quotas or otherwise alter their import regimes, in order to support domestic adjustment programs for the affected industries. At least the key importers (notably the EC), however, would have to participate for the entire scheme to be workable.

In the case of a shift to auctioning from quotas already administered by the United States itself but allocated domestically, fewer international issues would arise. The main consideration is whether it is more efficient to let the rents continue to accrue to the private sector, including the protected firms (if they are also importing) that need to adjust, or to transfer them to the government for adjustment purposes. The record of American firms in using the time and resources afforded by protection is mixed; some have clearly frittered away the opportunity, while others have downsized effectively and been able to forgo future protection (Hufbauer and Rosen 1986). Decisions in such instances would essentially have to be made on a case-by-case basis.

The fifth factor that favors use of auction quotas, instead of VERs or allocated quotas, centers on equity: *why should the US government give away such valuable economic rights* rather than sell them and use the proceeds for the general welfare? As indicated in chapter 5, standard practice in the United States is to charge the private sector when valuable economic assets are transferred—oil leases, timber and other natural resource rights, and the like. In most cases, the government seeks to set the price as close as possible to market levels, frequently by auction.

There have been a few exceptions to this pattern, such as landing rights at airports. However, proposals are now being made to use auctions or charge "user fees" in most of these cases as well.[10] Hence, giving away rights to import under quantitative restraint arrangements, which carry substantial economic benefits, would seem to be an anomaly.

Another lesson from our review of US government transfers of economic benefits to the private sector in nontrade policy areas is that there are several cases where the resulting revenues are earmarked for related programs. Some of the oil industry's earnings from offshore leases, for example, are allocated to environmental defense purposes and fishermen's benefits. The most famous case of earmarked revenues is, of course, the Highway Trust Fund. Users of the national highway system pay a gasoline tax that is then used to improve the roads themselves. Our proposal for earmarking the revenues from auction quotas (or tariffs from new import relief cases) to support trade adjustment assistance thus has several relevant precedents (see appendix C).

An international equity question should also be considered. The transfer to foreign exporters of scarcity rents under most QR regimes represents a kind of "foreign aid" to the exporting countries. Yet much of this "aid" is transferred to wealthy countries, such as Japan and those in the European Community. Moreover, as a matter of process, the Congress jealously guards its authority to allocate American foreign assistance but permits the sizable amounts transferred under most VERs to be determined wholly by the trade negotiators.[11] A shift to auctions would end this anomalous extension of

---

10. American Airlines President Robert L. Crandall recently called on the government to use auctions to allocate landing slots as a means of reducing overcrowding at airports (*Washington Post*, 24 June 1987).

11. The only exception was the Sugar Act of 1948, which expired in 1974. In this act, Congress allocated quotas by country precisely because it saw the allocation as foreign aid. (The allocation of country quotas under the current sugar QR is normally determined by the administration, although Congress can legislate changes as in its recent shift of quota from South Africa to the Philippines.) The surprise is that it does not apply the same principle to the other VER cases.

unappropriated and arbitrarily allocated ''foreign aid'' and provide substantial funding for assistance through normal channels if that were desired.[12]

These considerations support the use of auction quotas rather than allocated quotas in cases where quantitative trade restrictions are desirable or inevitable. None of the factors counsel the use of quantitative restrictions in preference to tariffs, or the use of import controls at all. But they do argue for auctioning in lieu of allocating, especially when the allocation is to foreign countries rather than to domestic economic agents.

The Case Against Auction Quotas

There are several substantial criticisms of auctioning, however, as listed in chapter 1, and we must assess their validity and importance before attempting to draw up a balance sheet on the basic idea. Some of the doubts raised about auction quotas were discussed in the previous section. One is that auctions would violate the GATT. As we suggested earlier and in chapter 9, this is not the case. Indeed, auction quotas are more consistent with GATT than the VERs with which we are largely comparing them.

We found more truth in the related concern that auction quotas would violate explicit or implicit agreements that determine the division of rents under some of the current VERs, notably in textiles and apparel and steel, and would thus require new forms of compensation (or retaliation) if such existing arrangements were supplanted by US auctions. Some of the exporting countries might be persuaded to forgo such compensation or retaliation, however, if the revenues shifted to the United States were used to foster positive industry adjustment and thus enable the import restrictions themselves to be phased down and out. And because of the concerns about VERs that repeatedly emerged throughout this study, we have little sympathy for the view that relying on auctions instead of VERs would reduce the flexibility of American trade policy.

Another objection that can be dismissed quickly is that auction quotas would add to the severity of protection and thus inter alia raise consumer

---

12. Lawrence and Litan (1986) have advocated recycling to the exporting countries all of the rents obtained by the United States through a shift to auctions, at least at the outset of the new regime. Their goal in adopting auctions is primarily to quantify the tariff equivalent of the quotas to pave the way for retariffication.

costs. As demonstrated in chapter 2, the restrictive impact of a QR is determined by the level of the quota itself. The method of implementing the quota should have no further restrictive effect. Hence, auction quotas would increase consumer costs only if they somehow resulted in underutilization of the quota, compared with allocated quotas. This could occur only if the auctions were monopolized by firms that sought to restrain the level of imports even further, a development that can easily be safeguarded against, as we will later explain. Indeed, it appears just as likely that an auction, coupled with a secondary market, could increase quota usage compared with allocated systems and thus help counter any potential monopoly problems.

There remain, however, six arguments against auction quotas, each of which will be discussed in turn:

(1) They would severely disrupt trade flows by disturbing commercial patterns and by generating constant uncertainty among importers and retailers as to whether they could obtain adequate quota to meet their needs.

(2) Their implementation would create an "administrative nightmare" for government.

(3) They would represent "reverse foreign aid," taking the rents away from needy countries abroad and perhaps jeopardizing the market shares of relatively uncompetitive suppliers.

(4) They would capture very little revenue for the United States because the exporting countries could take effective countermeasures to retain their rents.

(5) To the contrary, their success in generating such revenues would "hook" the government on them, especially in a period of budget stress, and thus foster additional import controls (or, at least, additional use of quantitative restrictions).

(6) Finally, and perhaps most seriously, US domestic politics could produce an auction system that would simply seek to maximize the budget take and protective effect while ignoring all adjustment, trade, foreign policy, and other considerations.

The fear of *trade disruption* is a practical concern based on the uncertainties inherent in any significant shift in the method of conducting US trade policy. It was raised primarily by some importers and retailers when the issue was debated in the Congress in 1986 and early 1987 (Milosh 1987; Mangione 1987; and Tompkins 1987), although other representatives of those same sectors have indicated support for the idea.

The main policy issue is whether firms that have relied heavily on imports should be assured of continuing to do so, given the possibility that they could be outbid in the auctions. A second issue is the risk that smaller (and perhaps newer) bidders could be shut out by bigger firms, including producer-importers. A third concern is that these bigger firms could even "corner" the market for quota tickets and deliberately leave part of the quota unutilized to drive up prices and increase their profits.

In addressing these concerns, it is important to note the uncertainty prevalent in the existing quota systems—particularly those conducted via VERs.[13] The total level of allowable imports is set through negotiations with foreign suppliers, supplemented in the case of textiles and apparel by periodic "calls" for further tightening of particular categories and the addition of new countries to the control network. The analytical issue is whether the shift in method of implementation to auctions would, on balance, have a disruptive impact.

Such analysis must distinguish between the transition to a new regime (either in the commencement of import controls for a new product or via a shift from another technique of implementation) and the steady state once auctions are in place. Like any change, a transition to auctions could cause some disruption. Companies might bid too low to obtain quota or too high to make a profit. Trade channels might be reordered as a result of the bidding process.

However, some of this "trade disruption," while understandably upsetting for the firms involved, would manifest a healthy shift in the distribution of quotas to a market approach. The more efficient importers and retailers could bid higher and obtain the quotas. Less efficient importing firms, like less efficient exporting firms (and countries), tend to be protected by quotas allocated on a historical basis and thus should be pressured to become more efficient. There is no basis for assuring current importers that they can perpetually receive 100 percent of their previous level of imports, as requested in testimony before the House Ways and Means Committee in February

---

13. USITC Chairwoman Paula Stern commented in the 1985 footwear case that an import license auction might actually reduce uncertainty and costs for importers by precluding the buildup of excess inventories in US Customs Service warehouses. See ch. 6.

1987, any more than import-competing firms should be guaranteed an unchanged market share for their output (Mangione 1987; Tompkins 1987).

In addition, some of the likely features of an auction scheme would prove beneficial to importers by expanding their flexibility and range of choices. As described in chapter 4 and recommended later in this chapter, the benefits of auctioning can be maximized by replacing country-by-country and category-by-category coverage with globalization both geographically (at least for all countries previously covered by the controls) and with respect to products. Such globalization would greatly enhance the opportunities for importers and retailers, as well as ultimate consumers, to limit the cost of the quota regime.

In addition, the details of an auction system could be tailored in ways that would limit the risks of trade disruption, at least on a transitional basis. Australia and New Zealand have done so, as described in chapter 7. Indeed, New Zealand avoided some of Australia's initial mistakes in this regard by observing its results. The United States could use the experiences of both to do even better, and it could draw as well on lessons derived from its own history of auctions in nontrade areas (chapter 5).

First, a substantial share of the auction tickets could be offered on a first-refusal basis to current importers on the basis of their historical market shares. They would have to pay for the tickets, at whatever price emerged from the actual auction of the remainder. But this technique would ensure that they would not be "shut out" of the market. Depending on the share provided on this basis, they would probably be protected against any significant cutback—and, of course, they could bid for more in the auction.

Such a "historical setaside," by ensuring that most or all current importers remained in the trade, would simultaneously protect against any one or several bidders cornering the market (as would application of the standard antitrust laws and procedures). Fifty percent of the tickets could be allocated in this way at the outset, or one could even start at 75 percent in the first year and then phase down to 50 percent in the second year and 25 percent in the third.[14]

A second safeguard would be a small bidder setaside. As in Treasury securities auctions, where "noncompetitive" (i.e., small) bidders receive the full amount of their bids at whatever price emerges from the actual auctions

---

14. The latter option was suggested by Chairman Sam Gibbons (D-Fla.) of the Trade Subcommittee in informal conversation.

among the large participants, small importers could get all they want "off the top," perhaps subject to a ceiling of 15 percent of the quota pool.

Third, an active secondary market in quota tickets should exist from the outset. Any American, including American agents of exporting countries and companies, would be eligible to bid. If some bidders found they had bought excess tickets, they could sell that excess in the secondary market. Any bidder who came up short would then have an immediate and ongoing opportunity to make up his shortfall. Unlike Australia and New Zealand, with their limited markets, the US market for most quota products is probably large enough to ensure a fairly resilient secondary market and thereby provide a safety valve against most market disruption problems.

Another argument against auction quotas is that they would require a sharp *increase in administrative costs* and bureaucratic involvement. This is extremely dubious; the General Accounting Office (GAO) in its 1986 report "saw no reason to expect any substantial difference" between auctions and other forms of administering QRs (Comptroller General 1986, p. 19). New Zealand runs its entire auction system with six officials and a computer and thus saves considerable administrative cost compared with its previous allocation technique. It is hard to imagine that administering auction quotas for textiles and apparel would be more complicated, and labor-intensive, than negotiating and administering bilateral restraint agreements with more than 40 countries and for more than 100 product categories. The recommended conversion of QRs to auction quotas could raise about $5 billion in additional revenue annually—obviously far more than even the most extreme estimate of how much the system would cost to administer.

Under an auction quota system, US Customs Service officials would have to ensure that importers of controlled products possessed valid tickets, just as they must now determine that country quotas (and often category-by-country quotas) have not been exceeded. Some surveillance would be needed of the actual bidding process, but the Treasury and Federal Reserve System handle a large volume of government financial auctions with very few personnel (see chapter 5). Monitoring the secondary markets would also be required, but it could be added to the portfolio of the Commodity Futures Trading Commission with little additional cost.

Those concerned about *"reverse foreign aid"* view the transfer of rents from developing countries to the United States, via a shift from VERs to auction quotas, as a cost of the scheme. This concern also extends to any loss of market share (and associated investment) to poorer developing countries that might result from a globalization of quotas—permitting larger market shares for more efficient suppliers—under the auction approach.

Yet most of the rents now generated under some VERs, such as those for steel and automobiles, accrue to industrial rather than developing countries—including countries (such as Japan) where per capita incomes, at current exchange rates, exceed those of the United States. Even under VERs that cover developing countries, such as those instituted under the MFA, an important share of the rents goes to more advanced and more competitive countries such as Hong Kong and other higher income developing countries in East Asia and Latin America—not the poorest countries that are the main recipients of foreign aid. Moreover, it is not clear that transferring quota rents to the particular beneficiaries thereof in developing countries—such as export quota brokers in Hong Kong and elsewhere—represents a progressive redistribution of world income.

The question of reducing the market shares of particular developing countries by shifting from country to global quotas, under an auction scheme, is more straightforward. First, much of the shift would be from one group of developing countries to another—from the less efficient to the more efficient. In some cases, this could provide a progressive redistribution of income to poorer countries from those with higher incomes. More broadly, the basic purpose of globalizing quotas—to permit greater market access for more efficient suppliers—would clearly serve the fundamental development objectives of the United States and most other countries. The shift to global quotas could be phased in if it were necessary to cushion the impact on less competitive producers.

A basic goal of the entire auction quota approach is, of course, to facilitate a reduction and eventual elimination of import controls for the industries in question, via greater transparency and explicit linkage to positive adjustment. Developing countries should thus gain increased market access over time, as long as they are sufficiently competitive to take advantage of the growing opportunity. These volume gains for most developing countries should more than offset any losses of rents from the initial shift to auctions (Balassa and Michalopoulos 1985). We would view the idea as promoting "trade not aid," and thus eminently desirable from a developmental standpoint.

In response to the claim that auction quotas would raise revenues, some argue that *the exporting countries could take effective countermeasures to retain the rents.*[15] According to this thesis, the United States would be unable

---

15. Exporting countries have also demonstrated an ability to counter the revenue effects of new

to generate self-financing for new adjustment efforts so the trade policy benefits of the scheme as well as any hopes for overall budget reduction would prove chimerical.

As the analysis in chapter 4 demonstrated, the government of the country auctioning the quota licenses would be able to obtain the quota rents through an auction *if* (1) the exporting and importing industries in the sector in question were reasonably competitive, and (2) if the governments of the exporting countries refrained from imposing additional restrictions of their own. The government of the importing country could thus be frustrated in its effort to capture the rents only if the trading entities in one or both countries were highly concentrated, or its trading partners retaliated with export taxes.

Unfortunately, relatively little empirical work has been done on export and import industries so we cannot know how concentrated they may be in the countries and products that are relevant to the debate on auction quotas. Some of the relevant industries, however, are clearly quite competitive: over 500 importers brought dairy products into the United States under license in 1986, about 160 importers of steel were recorded in 1984, over 35 importers handled sugar shipments in the early 1980s, and over 40,000 importers of apparel products were recorded by Customs in 1986 (Christie 1986; USITC 1982, 1984). Further research is needed on this key topic, and efforts to uncover the relevant data would be of great help in promoting informed policy consideration. We feel reasonably confident, however, that oligopoly situations are sufficiently rare in the industries under consideration that this factor will not undermine our basic conclusions.

Yet even for exporting countries in relatively competitive industries, it would be possible to foster (or even mandate) a consolidation of the firms involved in order to create a monopoly or oligopoly situation and thereby permit an effective counterattack. For example, an export marketing board could be created for many agricultural products. Market sharing arrangements by exporting firms have been encouraged by exporting-country governments in the past as a means of limiting exports under VERs. Although these restraint arrangements could also occur under auction quotas, they would not be necessary to implement the restrictions.

---

tariffs by instituting export duties of their own. Brazil responded to a number of American countervailing duty cases in this way during the 1970s, and Canada recently applied a 15 percent tax on its lumber exports to the United States—presumably as ''compensation,'' with explicit American approval—rather than accept a countervailing duty at the same level.

The United States could avoid, or respond to, such an effort by the exporting country to retain (or, in a new case, seize) the rents by globalizing the quotas themselves. In such a framework, the exporting countries would have to organize as a group to increase their selling prices, and they would have to include potentially new exporting countries as well. Exporters might be able to do so in a sector where one or two countries dominated the market (for example, Japan's domination to date in automobiles). It would be quite unlikely in a sector with many supplying countries, such as textiles and apparel or steel. It might also be possible to obtain agreement from the exporters not to take measures that would frustrate the shift of the rents. This agreement could be part of an internationally negotiated conversion of existing VERs to auctions that included a commitment by the importing countries to use their new revenues to liberalize and eventually eliminate the entire quota system.

A fifth criticism of *auction quotas* is that they *would be so successful in augmenting the government revenues of the importing countries that those countries would become "hooked" on the policy*. Quotas would never be phased down, let alone eliminated. New quotas, in fact, would be adopted to add further to the totals. This argument is diametrically opposed to the previous point, namely, that the importing country would be unable to capture much, if any, new revenue. But it is expressed by some of the most acute observers of trade policy and must be taken seriously, especially at a time of such budget pressure as the late 1980s.[16]

The issue is whether US trade policy could be driven by revenue considerations, as is the case in some developing countries (and was the case in the United States and other industrial countries in their early years before they had income taxes and other major sources of revenues). Historically,

---

16. Chairman Sam Gibbons (D-Fla.) of the Trade Subcommittee of Ways and Means and Congressman William Frenzel (R-Minn.), the ranking minority member of the subcommittee, have indicated this concern on several occasions (US Congress, House, Committee on Ways and Means, Subcommittee on Trade 1987). A related point is that establishment of the auctioning technique could make QRs preferable to tariffs when import relief was called for, reversing the preference that we have expressed repeatedly for tariffs. The argument is that the government and those seeking adjustment assistance would then receive revenues from the import controls and so would be less resistant to the usual industry preference for QRs than is now the case when revenues are obtainable only via tariffs. We doubt that this consideration is very important, however, mainly because of the points made in the chapter about the general "hooked on revenue" case. Moreover, we believe that government officials would lose their traditional interest in QRs if they could no longer benefit from the "negotiating flexibility" of VERs.

the answer is negative. The United States cut its tariffs by about 90 percent over the past 50 years, with little or no concern for the potential loss in revenues. Indeed, revenue effects have been ignored in the debate over reducing duties in the series of postwar trading "rounds," and tariff revenues have, in fact, risen sharply (from $3.2 billion in 1929 and a low of $1.2 billion in 1949 to $11 billion in 1985, all in 1980 dollars). This increase is due to the enormous rise in the volume of trade resulting in part from the reduction in tariff rates.[17]

Conversely, some of the most important quantitative import restrictions employed by the United States have persisted for extensive periods without providing any revenues for the US government. Some textile and apparel controls have been in place for over 30 years. Steel restraints have persisted for about 20 years with only two short interruptions. Sugar quotas have existed for most of the past 50 years; dairy quotas for almost 35 years. The failure of these programs to generate revenue has not shortened their life spans.

In the only contemporary experiences with auction quotas, in Australia and New Zealand, the technique is being used as part of a phase-down of protection. Despite the devotion of considerable budgetary resources to the adjustment program of the covered industries, the expansion of quota limits continues.

The best defense against this "opiate" effect, as it is termed by some members of the Congress, is to specify in the basic authorizing legislation that (1) a considerable portion of the revenues be earmarked for industry adjustment rather than go into general revenues; (2) the protection itself be strictly limited in time and degressive over its life span; and (3) that these same principles be enshrined in international agreements that would, in turn, be approved by the Congress as well. As already indicated, these first two steps would also help to obviate major trade policy problems and could thus contribute to foreign acceptance of the new system.

Interest has recently been expressed in some congressional quarters in using trade policy to acquire budget revenues via an import surcharge.[18] There is, of course, an enormous difference between a new surcharge and

---

17. *Economic Report of the President* (1974); US Department of Commerce (1976 and 1987a); and International Monetary Fund, various issues.

18. Every 1 percent import surcharge would generate about $2 billion in budgetary revenues, according to the Congressional Budget Office (1987).

the idea developed in this study for converting existing allocated quotas to auction quotas: the former would represent a substantial layer of new protection, whereas the latter would "simply" change the nature of implementing an existing level of protection. (This problem also applies, although with less quantitative impact, to the proposals for a low-rate tariff on all imports to finance adjustment assistance as included in the House version of the Budget Reconciliation Act in 1986 and in HR 3 and the trade bill [S 490] passed by the Senate in July 1987.) If political pressure to raise revenues via trade were to become irresistible, auction quotas could also be viewed—even by those who did not favor them in general—as a less objectionable alternative.

The final concern about auction quotas, closely related to the previous point, is that *the political processes in the United States could produce an auction quota scheme that, in practice, contained many of the undesirable elements enumerated here but failed to include its offsetting virtues.* For example, the scheme could seek to seize a maximum amount of rents for budget purposes by mandating an immediate conversion of all QRs to auction, but exclude any earmarking of funds for adjustment purposes or any phase-down of protection. We call this the "Chinese menu" problem because it would reflect a selection of items from the different components offered with no effort to construct an integrated whole in terms of trade policy or broader American and global interests.

There is no definitive answer to this problem, and it must be viewed as a serious risk. The risk may be particularly acute at the present time, with convergent pressures to "do something" about both the trade and budget deficits. The primary answer is for the trade leadership of the Congress and the administration to insist that any package in this area be held together so that the result will promote overall US trade and economic interests as well as addressing concerns about the budget and those of the protected industries.

For example, the administration could embrace auctioning as a means of making import restrictions more transparent and market oriented, in keeping with its strong belief in free enterprise and opposition to government intervention, but veto the approach if it were not firmly linked to positive industry adjustment and phase-down including eventual elimination of the QRs themselves. American trade negotiators could incorporate these desirable features into new international agreements that would then stand or fall (in subsequent submission to the Congress) in their totality. Constant attention would have to be devoted to this complex of issues, however, to ensure that desirable objectives were not subverted in actual implementation of the approach.

Issues for Decision

Under proper circumstances, auction quotas could be a useful instrument for implementing quantitative import restraints when it becomes necessary or desirable to restrict trade in that manner. In devising and implementing an auction quota scheme, five policy questions would have to be answered. After listing these questions, we will note the alternative policy packages that have been considered in the past and could be envisaged now. Finally, we will propose a specific approach, addressing the key administrative as well as policy issues, which attempts to maximize the advantages and minimize the disadvantages enumerated so far in this chapter.

If the United States were to decide that it wants to use auction quotas, it would have to resolve the following key questions:

(1) Should the auction quota scheme be utilized only for new cases of import relief that arise in the future, or should current cases of allocated quotas— automobiles, dairy products, machine tools, meat, specialty steel, carbon steel, sugar, and textiles and apparel—be converted to auctions as well? A related issue is whether any such conversions should apply only to quotas now allocated by the exporting country, which includes all but one of the major sectors now covered, or to quotas now allocated within the importing country as well (only dairy at present in the United States).

(2) Should auction quotas be mandated for use in all (only new, or old and new) cases of quantitative restraint, or should they be authorized as one option to be employed on a case-by-case basis?

(3) Should auction quotas be applied on a global basis, without distinction among product categories or individual supplying countries, or should product subcategories and country subquotas be auctioned separately? This question arises most acutely when contemplating conversion of existing arrangements that include such disaggregation, but it applies to new cases as well. Conversion of some existing cases, where some exporting countries are not covered, raises the question of whether "global" should literally mean "all countries" or only those whose exports are already restrained.

(4) Should the revenues generated by the auctions be channeled into general government revenues or allocated to adjustment:

- in whole or in part

- on an industry-by-industry basis or across the board, that is, with revenues from all auction quotas used to finance adjustment for all import-impacted industries

- with or without a mandated phase-down, and perhaps eventual elimination, of the quotas themselves?

(5) If the auction quota scheme were to include conversions from existing VERs, several additional issues arise:

- Should the importing country attempt to negotiate the conversion with the supplying countries or implement the changes unilaterally, presumably being prepared to pay new forms of compensation or accept retaliation? Should such a new approach to import relief be negotiated multilaterally, perhaps as part of the Uruguay Round?

- Should the conversion be implemented immediately or phased in, in terms of the share of the quota to be auctioned and "globalization" of the country and category quotas, per item 3?

- As noted above, does "globalization" in such cases literally mean "all countries" or only those already covered when the conversion takes place (leaving open the possibility of adding others later, if needed)?

The present US legal situation represents a minimalist approach to the issue of auction quotas. Section 1102 of the Trade Agreements Act of 1979 authorizes use of the technique, as described in chapter 6, but does not require it. Moreover, section 1102 exempts from authorization two of the leading agricultural products now under quota, meat and dairy, and it would not cover machine tools (or any other quota adopted under the national security authority of section 232 of the Trade Expansion Act).

The relevant provision of HR 3 as adopted by the House of Representatives in April 1987 expands this approach modestly. It would require the ITC to recommend auction quotas to implement any proposal it might make for "quantitative restraints" in section 201 cases, "unless the ITC finds that such auction system would lead to undesirable economic results," later defined as "monopolization of market power by either foreign suppliers or

US importers" or "serious market disruption." Moreover, the legislation listed orderly marketing arrangements (OMAs) as a separate option that could be proposed by the ITC.[19] In any event, it preserves full discretion for the administration in the choice of techniques for actually implementing QRs. The Ways and Means Committee characterized this approach as "essentially establish(ing) a presumption in favor of auctioned quotas, but does not mandate their recommendation (or their implementation by USTR [the US Trade Representative]) under all circumstances." The committee "is not yet prepared to embrace such a comprehensive scheme" as requiring auctions for all existing and future quotas (US Congress, House, Committee on Ways and Means 1987b, p. 104).

HR 3 would also create a new Supplemental Adjustment Assistant Trust Fund (SAATF) into which all revenues generated by the quota auctions, or tariffs employed in new section 201 cases, would be placed. However, separate congressional authorization and appropriation of such funds for adjustment purposes would still be required, and any excess funds in the SAATF would revert to general revenues.

The auction quota proposal included in the "discussion draft" bill (DD I) developed by the Ways and Means Subcommittee on Trade prior to its trade hearings in April 1986 adopted a somewhat more aggressive approach. It would have required the use of auctioning for all new cases of quantitative import relief generated under section 201. Similar ideas were considered in the Senate Finance Committee in 1986–87, including a provision in S 490 of 1987 to require auctions for the first three quota cases to emerge in the future under section 201 (with caveats similar to those in HR 3), and they were recommended by the General Accounting Office in its report of December 1986.

After the Trade Subcommittee's hearings in April 1986, its second "discussion draft" (DD II) carried the concept considerably further. Auctioning was mandated for all new relief cases and, within three years, for all existing cases employing quantitative restrictions. The specific questions surrounding conversion that we cited earlier were not addressed, nor were any further decisions made concerning the distribution of auction revenues between adjustment assistance and general revenues.

---

19. The Senate Committee, more logically, would require new OMAs as well as other QRs to be implemented via US auction.

If the United States decided to try to use auction quotas to maximize governmental revenues and reduce the budget deficit, an even more far-reaching package could be adopted:

● auctions for all new quantitative import controls and immediate unilateral conversion of all existing VERs and all quotas allocated domestically

● immediate globalization of the quotas to include previously unrestricted suppliers, such as Europe in textiles and Canada in both textiles and steel, in order to expand the coverage of the restraints and thus the revenue base

● no earmarking of revenues for adjustment but rather their channeling to general revenues

● no phase-down of the protection, which could reduce the revenues.

Efforts would presumably be made through diplomatic and other means to limit foreign demands for new forms of compensation. But retaliation, including the possibility of disruption of the Uruguay Round, would be accepted if necessary. Administrative techniques would be adopted to minimize domestic opposition to the shift as outlined below.

A very different, but still ambitious approach would be to adopt auction quotas primarily to pursue trade policy objectives. Movement in that direction would suggest:

● requiring auctions for all new cases where quantitative restraints were to be applied, but with indication of a strong preference for tariffs in all restraint cases

● negotiating a conversion of some existing VERS, including textiles and apparel and steel, but excluding automobiles and meat

● phasing in both the shift to auctions and movement away from country and category breakdowns toward an aggregate ceiling for all covered suppliers (as opposed to full globalization, which would bring in countries not previously restricted)

● earmarking for trade adjustment assistance as much of the new revenues as could effectively be spent for that purpose

● requiring phase-down and subsequent elimination of the quotas themselves.

A Specific Proposal

Based on the analyses in the earlier chapters and the considerations addressed in this chapter, we propose the following approach for incorporation in US trade policy and any new trade legislation. Similar strategies could be adopted by other importing countries. In fact, there would be some advantages in parallel movement in this direction by at least the major trading nations. Our proposals basically adopt the "trade policy maximization" alternative just outlined, but incorporate as well the desire to augment budgetary revenues as much as possible while still achieving trade liberalization.

First, *any new quantitative import restrictions adopted by the United States should be implemented through auction quotas*. Tariffs would be the preferred instrument for import relief when such relief is justified and essential, but any new quotas should be implemented via auction rather than allocation. The administration should follow this policy for all future cases under section 201, section 232, and section 301. The Congress should mandate such a policy in any new legislation. It should also eliminate the "suspension agreement" option in the present antidumping and countervailing duty statutes, thereby completing the barring of VERs (and paving the way for negotiating a new safeguards code in the GATT, as outlined later in the chapter).[20]

Second, *the United States should attempt to negotiate the rapid conversion of most (but not all) of the existing QRs to auction quotas*. The Congress should direct the administration to do so, subject to its approval via the fast-track procedures that have now become well established for ratification of international trade negotations. An inferior, but feasible, alternative would be for the administration to negotiate such conversions without a new legislative mandate but in close consultation with the key congressional committees—using the existing authority of section 1102 of the Trade

---

20. Under a "suspension agreement," an antidumping or countervailing duty investigation can be "suspended" (effectively terminated) if the complaint is resolved via a negotiated arrangement acceptable to the petitioning domestic industry. In practice, VERs are the device normally employed to achieve such an outcome. The current steel VER emerged from this process, as did the semiconductor agreement of 1986. We believe that the antidumping and countervailing duty laws should be administered vigorously, but that all such cases should be allowed to run their course rather than become tools for eroding the requirements of section 201 (and other broader trade statutes) to obtain industry-wide relief.

Agreements Act of 1979 to implement the auctions in those sectors where its provisions are adequate (as outlined in chapter 9).

This effort should be made on textiles and apparel, carbon and specialty steel, machine tools, sugar, and dairy products. Such conversions, especially for textiles and apparel and carbon steel, could carry substantial trade policy benefits by making the protection more transparent, by bringing these controls under the GATT system, and by providing revenues both to fund adjustment assistance (and hence facilitate a phase-down of the restrictions) and to reduce the overall budget deficit. The automobile VER should not be converted to an auction quota because it is a truly "voluntary" restraint at this time with no official US involvement (or legislative authority to restrain from its side). Moreover, only one country (Japan) is involved and it could more easily take countersteps to retain the rents. Finally, the VER may no longer be binding in light of the substantial appreciation of the yen and quota expansion. The meat VER is a uniquely on-and-off restriction, which is better handled with the current technique.

Negotiation is far preferable to unilateral conversions in order to minimize adverse trade policy effects, particularly demands for new forms of compensation and even disruption of the entire Uruguay Round, in reaction to the capture of quota rents by the United States. Such negotiations would be much more likely to succeed if the next two elements in the proposal—substantial earmarking of the new revenues to industry adjustment and firm phase-down and elimination of the quotas—were included in the package. Phase-ins of the new system and some of its features could also be helpful.

If the negotiations were to fail, the United States would have to assess the likely costs of proceeding unilaterally. Such unilateral conversion of existing VERs to auction quotas would be extremely risky in the absence of international agreement that the changes were acceptable. Some countries would presumably retaliate for unilateral US conversions in textiles and apparel and (especially) steel, claiming violation of the existing VER arrangements. Such US action might blow up the Uruguay Round.

The United States could try to minimize those effects by adopting on its own the steps already proposed—earmarking a substantial share of the revenues for adjustment and setting a fixed schedule for phase-down and elimination of those quotas. The increased transparency, GATTability, and additional resources available for adjustment would still have favorable trade policy effects. The revenue gains could still be obtained. But the outcome would be very uncertain, and negotiation is by far the more desirable course.

Third, *all revenues generated by the quota auctions* (and by increased tariffs in any new section 201, section 232, and section 301 cases) *should be placed in a Supplemental Adjustment Assistance Trust Fund* as provided in HR 3. Funds from quota auctions for all products would be used to finance adjustment assistance for all industries injured by imports, even those that did not receive import relief. By relieving the financial constraint on trade adjustment assistance (TAA), this could encourage the phase-down and elimination of existing and new trade restraints. It could also promote the use of TAA as the sole response to import problems in some industries, in lieu of import relief.

The actual amount of funds to be drawn from the SAATF would be determined, at least at the outset, by the costs of the new labor adjustment program developed by the administration (about $1 billion for FY 1988) and the needs demonstrated by each affected industry (for example, funding of uncovered pension liabilities to facilitate downsizing of the steel industry). The remainder would become general receipts of the Treasury, which would reduce the budget deficit. Our estimates envisage that converting the six recommended sectors would obtain about $5 billion when the new regime was fully in place, plus any amounts generated by new quantitative controls.

Fourth, *all auction quotas should be progressively liberalized and eliminated over a reasonable period of time.*[21] A firm requirement of this nature is essential for two reasons: to avoid the domestic problem of becoming hooked on the auction revenues for budgetary purposes, and to convince the exporting countries that they would achieve greater market access as a quid pro quo for giving up their quota rents, thus minimizing the risk of demands for new forms of compensation or retaliation. The maximum periods of protection should be retained at five years for any new cases, as at present under the escape clause, and set at a longer period for existing cases if necessary. It is particularly important to set firm dates for ending the quota regimes because the industries involved would then know that they must adjust.

Our proposal to require the use of auctions for all future QR cases would

---

21. Exceptions are QRs under section 232 (national security), section 301 (unfair foreign trade practices), and those used to defend agricultural price support programs. Such controls should also be implemented via auction. However, they could be phased down and eliminated only if their original justifications—the relevant national security concern, foreign trade practices, or price supports—were declining or eliminated as well.

automatically achieve this outcome in most future instances by effectively barring the creation of new VERs and thus channeling most petitions for import relief to section 201—whose relief programs currently have to be terminated after five years (with the possibility of one three-year extension). It would be more difficult politically to win agreement on a similar phase-down and elimination of import relief for industries that have "enjoyed" protection for extended periods, such as textiles and apparel (30 years for most of it) and sugar (over 50 years, with two brief interruptions). Because of these extended durations of protection, one could argue that these industries, some of which never passed the normal qualifying tests of section 201, have had at least an adequate period to restore their competitiveness. However, we suggest giving them twice as long to phase out the controls as industries receiving new relief—with an absolutely firm timetable for doing so to provide the necessary inducements for them to adopt the adjustment measures that are required. The history of trade liberalization within the European Community and specific sector cases shows that, under such pressure, they can do so quite effectively.

The crucial domestic political issue is likely to be whether the sharply increased adjustment funding will be seen as an adequate quid pro quo for mandating (finally) an end to import controls for these industries. Over a 15-year transition period to free trade, new estimates for textiles and apparel suggest that the resultant loss of employment would be less than the traditional attrition rate in the industry (assuming no new entrants). Hence, the adjustment funds would be used primarily to smooth the transition for workers and to help downsize the industry gradually, and this should be feasible if the purpose is to "protect people rather than positions."[22]

If the United States were willing to adopt firm phase-down and elimination commitments as suggested here, it should place such an offer on the table in the Uruguay Round as a basis for a new safeguards/adjustment code. This would maximize the likelihood that the exporting countries would accept the trade-off suggested earlier, forgoing demands for new forms of compensation. Moreover, acceptance of similar commitments by other importing countries would ensure that the United States did not become a "dumping ground"

---

22. Cline (1987) estimates that normal attrition in the textile and apparel industries would reduce employment in those industries over the next 15 years by 42.8 percent and 50.5 percent, respectively, if there were no new entrants. Elimination of the import quotas over this period would result in an estimated reduction of 26.2 percent and 29.7 percent, respectively.

for trade diverted from other national markets. Finally, placing the whole package in the context of an international negotiation in which the United States and its trading partners committed themselves to multilateral liberalization, it would become much harder to unravel domestically—better ensuring full implementation of the original pledge.

Fifth, *the auction quotas should group all restricted suppliers together, and all covered product categories as broadly as possible,* rather than be constructed on a country-by-country and/or category-by-category basis. This would not require completely "global" quotas because some countries (Europe for textiles and apparel, Canada for textiles and apparel and steel, and a few smaller suppliers of steel and machine tools) are not included in the current restraint regimes. We would not want to extend quotas to previously uncovered countries and thereby increase the protective effect of the controls.

However, treating all covered countries together is important for three reasons. It would help enhance the basic transparency and cost-minimizing purposes of the auction approach by permitting imports from the cheapest source. It would minimize the risk of losing the rents back to the exporting countries because they would then have to collude to mark up their export prices accordingly. It would also represent a healthy shift to "trade not aid" for developing-country exporters under the restraint regimes, rewarding those who were most efficient, and it could increase their market shares rather than those who happened to hold quotas because of a historical base and might no longer be able to compete effectively in the market under consideration. (The mandated phase-down and elimination of the total quota system would, of course, substantially enhance export possibilities for all covered countries.)

It is also important to cover product categories together as broadly as possible ("broadbanding") rather than provide quotas for each individual item, as indicated by the Australian experience. This, too, will maximize the transparency and efficiency objectives of auctioning the quotas by facilitating shifts among restricted products as the patterns of demand and international production change. Some categorization may remain essential, but the ranges should be as broad as possible.

Sixth, *the transition periods for converting existing VERs to auction quotas and for "globalizing" the quotas (as just defined) should be very short—* perhaps a maximum of three years, shorter if possible. It is highly desirable to achieve the trade policy and revenue benefits of the new scheme as quickly as possible. The United States could legitimately seek to obtain these gains quickly in return for committing itself to positive adjustment, including rapid phase-down and assured elimination of the restraints themselves. All new restraints implemented via auction quotas should cover all restricted suppliers together, and all covered product categories as broadly as possible, from the outset.

Seventh, and finally, *the administrative techniques for implementing the auction quotas should be designed to minimize disruption* without undermining the basic advantages of the system, as described in detail in chapter 8. Some changes in trade patterns are inevitable for importers and retailers, as well as for exporters, as the scheme achieves its objective of more efficient commerce (within a quota framework). The reallocation of rents could affect some domestic parties adversely, even as the main impact is to shift the bulk of those premia from exporting countries to the US government. There might well be some dislocations surrounding the first few auctions, until the parties involved became familiar with the new system.

Such transitional problems should subsequently settle down as the procedures become understood and accepted. Nevertheless, the system should make every effort to minimize uncertainties and unnecessary trade distortions, and we believe the following elements, drawn largely from our studies of the auction quota systems in Australia and New Zealand (chapter 7) and the US auctions of other types of valuable economic assets (chapter 5), would help do so.

All residents of the United States, including agents of foreign exporters and others, would be eligible to bid.[23] The auctions would be conducted by sealed bid, by an agency of the US government—probably the Treasury Department (with its experience in auctioning Treasury securities and its jurisdiction over the Customs Service).[24] Auctions could be held quarterly. This would permit changes in market conditions to be reflected promptly in the bidding process and would increase the information flow to facilitate submission of "accurate" bids. The licenses should generally be valid for one year, adjusted upward or downward if necessary for any particular market.

One key to minimize discontinuity in the process is to set aside a significant

---

23. Foreign nationals would not be allowed to bid directly because they can sometimes escape US legal jurisdiction and thus make it more difficult to police the system.

24. The GAO recommends Treasury management of any new system of auction quotas (Comptroller General 1986, p. 18).

proportion of the new quotas, perhaps as much as 50 percent, for existing importers on the basis of their market shares over a recent historical period on a first-refusal basis. These importers would have to pay for their quotas, like those who bid for the auctioned share, at a price determined by the result of the bidding process. But any fear of being shut out of the process would be obviated, and panic buying should be totally or largely eliminated.

This "base plus tender" system is used successfully in Australia and New Zealand. Over time, the share of the "base" could be steadily reduced, if doing so turned out to be feasible (because fears of being shut out were substantially reduced) and desirable (because auctioning a greater share of total quota would increase the advantages of the system). As long as a significant share of the quotas was auctioned, however, the basic advantages of the system should be achieved.

It would also be possible to create a "small business setaside" to permit entry of new importers who might be unable to obtain quota otherwise, as has been done in some US government auctions. They, too, would have to pay for their quota tickets, by analogy with "noncompetitive" bidders in the auctions for Treasury securities who are assured of receiving the full (but small) amount that they seek at a price determined by the outcome of the bidding among the larger participants.

In addition, it would be essential to permit, and facilitate if necessary, an active secondary market in quota tickets. Firms that bought too many tickets could then dispose of them at the market price, and firms that failed to acquire enough tickets would have an ongoing opportunity to supplement their original acquisition.

Some fears have been expressed that large firms, particularly producer-importers who could average the cost of their quota tickets over a large base, could corner the market—denying quota to their competition, perhaps deliberately leaving quotas unused and thereby driving up the price of the product to consumers. It would appear, however, that the importing industries in most of the relevant sectors are quite competitive so that such oligopoly positions are unlikely to occur in practice. If several major firms were to attempt to collude for such a purpose, they would, of course, risk prosecution under the antitrust laws. Moreover, the 50 percent setaside for historical importers—assuming it would be utilized to a substantial degree—would mitigate the risk of market control. The Commodity Futures Trading Commission should be assigned to monitor the new market to avoid all illegal practices, and the Securities and Exchange Commission should require that profits and losses incurred by firms in the market be specified in their corporate reports so that any irregularities could be detected.

Conclusion

In summarizing this set of proposals, we stress the interrelationships among them:

• Both the trade policy and budgetary goals of auctions are maximized by converting most existing QRs to auction quotas, as well as using the technique for implementing any new quantitative import restrictions, and by minimizing the phase-in time both for the auctions themselves and for their "globalization."

• Conversion of existing QRs could trigger adverse international repercussions, however, because of the transfer of the windfall profits from the exporters to the United States. Limiting such effects on the United States would require devoting a substantial part of the resulting revenues to adjustment and specifying a firm timetable for phasing down and eliminating the controls so that the change would be in the interest of the affected exporting countries as well.

• Implementation of the auction approach through successful international negotiations that commit the United States to these central features of the approach—particularly if explicitly approved by the Congress under the fast-track procedures—will thus sharply reduce and, it is hoped, eliminate both the potential costs of the scheme and the risk that key elements in the package (notably the phase-down and eventual elimination of the QRs themselves) will unravel in US domestic politics.

• Currently protected industries must receive significant assistance funds and longer phase-down periods if their support is to be obtained or overridden by broader considerations.

• The proposed administrative arrangements, or some equivalents, should limit domestic opposition to the entire scheme and thus permit its benefits to be achieved.

This is our answer to the "Chinese menu" problem, the last of the objections to auction quotas cited earlier. Obviously, no one can ensure that the package will be held together through the course of the political process. Minor deviations can be tolerated. But a substantial truncation of the trade liberalization commitments, for example, could make the scheme unacceptable and would foster opposition—including from us—to its enactment.

If the approach can be held together as outlined, institution of auction quotas and the related changes in trade policy could make an important contribution. By providing substantial self-financing for adjustment, they may represent a way to finally phase down, and eventually eliminate, some of the most durable sectors of "special protection" in the United States. In turn, this could play a critical role in promoting a successful outcome for the Uruguay Round and thereby restore momentum toward liberalization of the international trading system. Moreover, the related banning of VERs could position the United States to take the lead in achieving a meaningful GATT safeguards code, and the creation of a new source of funding for trade adjustment would enable the United States (and other countries) to turn that effort into a meaningful adjustment code.

Finally, auction quotas could make a modest contribution to dealing with two of the premier public policy issues in America today—restoring the nation's competitiveness and reducing the budget deficit. Import controls seldom if ever improve the United States' competitive position in any case, but implementing them via VERs clearly undermines the competitiveness of American firms by enabling their main rivals abroad to seize the scarcity rents generated by the quota regimes and thus increase their profits sharply. Moreover, a shift to auction quotas would provide a source of funding to promote positive adjustment of American industries hurt by imports, thus enhancing their competitiveness rather than simply insulating them behind protective walls.

Some of the revenues generated by a shift to auction quotas could also be used to reduce the budget deficit, a problem at the root of much of the global economic problem as well. Its resolution is central to correcting the huge American trade imbalance without an excessive plunge of the dollar or a sharp rise in American interest rates with a resulting risk of world recession and renewed debt explosion in the Third World (Marris 1985). Much more extensive measures obviously need to be taken by the United States to control its budget deficit, but a shift to auction quotas could help. If such a shift were to aid in preventing the adoption of an import surcharge, it would also represent a constructive rather than destructive use of trade policy to that end.

As we noted at the outset, auction quotas are a third-best option. Free trade is almost always the preferred path for trade policy. When restrictions must be adopted, tariffs are usually better. But if quantitative import controls must be used, auction quotas, applied properly and within a consistent framework of associated measures, are better than the alternatives frequently employed and deserve serious consideration.

Appendix A   Import Quota Auctions: An Analytical Approach and Discussion of Issues

Import Quota Auctions

To analyze auction quotas, it is useful to think of the activities of importing and exporting as industries consisting of profit-maximizing firms. This clarifies the incentives provided to the individuals or firms that will be bidding for licenses and helps to identify explicitly who is "domestic" and who is "foreign" in discussions of the distribution of rents. In some markets, no separately identifiable exporters or importers may exist, as when a firm markets its own products abroad, but the activity of transferring the good abroad, along with any costs incurred by this activity or constraints imposed upon it, can be considered separately.

In the context of this framework, a traded good would go through three exchanges: from the producer in the exporting country to "exporters"; from exporters to "importers"; and from importers to final consumers in the importing country. Exporters buy domestically and sell abroad; importers buy abroad and sell to final consumers in the importing country.

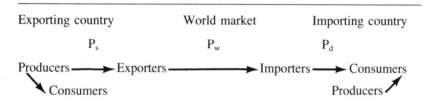

These three exchanges will take place at three identifiable prices: the "supply price" (P_s), which the producer charges and exporters pay; the "world market price" (P_w), at which exporters and importers trade; and the "domestic price" (P_d), which importers charge and final consumers pay. The distribution of any windfall profits from the quota will be determined by the equilibrium prices in these three markets, which, in turn, will be determined by the market structure and the type of constraints imposed upon the market participants. Each of these markets will be in equilibrium only when, at the price charged, the quantity the suppliers are willing and able to supply equals the quantity the buyers are willing and able to purchase.

Our main concern is the question of import quota auctions, so the first market to consider is that between importers and domestic consumers. Assume that the importers are acting so as to maximize their profits from importing. Profits (π_m) can be calculated by subtracting from sales revenue the amount paid exporters for the goods, the cost of shipping the goods, any import duties paid, and the cost of import permits.

$$\pi_m = P_d M - P_w M - C(M) - t_m P_w M - q_m M,$$

where the Ps are prices as defined above, M is the quantity of imports, t_m is the (ad valorem) tariff rate, q_m is the cost of an import permit per unit imported, and C(M) is the cost of shipping, which is a presumably increasing function of M.

On the buyers' side of this market, there is a consumer demand curve for the imported good. In the extreme case in which the imported product and the domestically produced product are identical in all respects (homogeneous), the demand curve faced by importers can be derived as the horizontal distance between the domestic demand and supply curves. If the imported good is a substitute for the domestically produced good, there will be a consumer demand curve for the imported product that will shift if there is any change in the price of the domestically produced substitute. For simplicity, we treat the case of identical home and import goods unless specified otherwise. The analysis could be adapted to the imperfect substitute case by taking into account the shift in the import demand curve when home prices change.

The equilibrium price in the market between importers and domestic consumers will depend upon the market structure and the constraints imposed upon buyers and sellers. Consumers are generally not organized, so the most reasonable way to treat their behavior is to assume that, given a price, they will purchase the amount indicated by the demand curve. We do not treat the case of a single buyer (monopsony) or the case of a few buyers because these market structures do not seem to be relevant for most imported goods. On the other hand, a monopoly importer is a relevant type of market structure to consider because such practices as exclusive franchises may create monopoly importers, and, more importantly, a system of import quotas itself could create a monopoly importer. We will discuss the determination of equilibrium price and therefore the distribution of "windfall gains" from quantitative restrictions for both the competitive and monopoly importer cases.

The exporting industry can be treated in a similar way. Exporters purchase from domestic producers and sell to importers. Their profits are revenue from sales ($P_w X$) less the cost of the goods ($P_s X$), any export taxes paid ($t_x P_s X$), fees for export permits ($q_x X$), and costs of doing business ($C[X]$):

$$\pi_x = P_w X - P_s X - C(X) - t_x P_s X - q_x X$$

As for importers, assume that the exporters are trying to maximize profits. The export industry may be competitive, or it may consist of a few firms or one firm. It may buy from a producing industry in the exporting country that is competitive, oligopolistic, or a monopoly.

The next section analyzes the incentives facing importers, exporters, and producers abroad under various possible market structures. Three major questions must be addressed: First, who would receive the quota rents or windfall profits from the quantitative restrictions? Second, if firms had to bid for the quota licenses, how much would they bid? And third, how might firms at home and abroad react to the auctioning of quota licenses?

The analysis in the following sections focuses on these questions and in doing so ignores many other important issues surrounding quantitative restrictions. The diversion of trade toward nonrestraining exporters when selective quotas, such as voluntary export restraints, are used is ignored by assuming that there are only two countries, one exporting and one importing. Any shift in the composition of imports by type due to the quotas (upgrading) is ignored by assuming a single homogeneous import good, and the role of uncertainty is ignored by implicitly assuming that firms know the market well enough to know the demand conditions and cost conditions, so that they can predict what domestic and foreign prices will be once a quota is imposed.

Quotas and Auction Quotas

We begin by analyzing the most common case, which assumes a competitive market structure in all sectors. We then analyze the effects of quotas and auction quotas if importing is monopolized and finally, if exporting is monopolized.

COMPETITIVE IMPORTERS AND EXPORTERS

"Competitive" implies that all producing, importing, and exporting firms take the market-determined prices as given; each is too small to influence the market price. Thus, the behavior of the competitive industry in the exporting country can be described by an industry supply curve, showing the amount the firms in the industry will be willing to supply at any price. Subtracting domestic consumer demand for the product in the exporting country will yield a supply curve facing exporters, or a "net supply" curve S_n in figure A.1. The domestic market in the exporting country will only clear if the supply price and amount traded lie on this net supply curve.

Profit-maximizing exporters take the supply price, world market price, any export tax rate, and any export permit fee as given, and thus they will maximize profits by exporting up to the point at which price equals marginal cost, or

$$P_w = P_s(1 + t_x) + q_x + MC(X),$$

where $MC(X)$ is the marginal cost of transferring the good from producers to importers. The competitive exporting industry thus has an export supply curve (S_x in figure A.1) which lies above the net supply curve by the sum of the export tax, export permit fee, and marginal cost of the exporting activity itself.

Similarly, competitive importers take the internal domestic market price, the world market price, the tariff rate, and any import permit fee as given and maximize profits by importing up to the point at which the price of the good they are supplying equals marginal cost, or

$$P_d = P_w(1 + t_m) + q_m + MC(M),$$

where $MC(M)$ is the marginal cost of transferring the good from the world market to domestic consumers. Thus, the importing industry has a supply curve to domestic consumers (S_m in figure A.1), which lies above the exporters' supply curve by the sum of the import tariff, import permit fee, and the marginal cost of the importing activity itself.

The interaction of the importers' supply curve with the consumer demand curve for the imported product will determine the equilibrium in the domestic market, which can then be traced back to the equilibrium in the world market and the market in the exporting country. Under free trade, competitive importing and exporting industries can be thought of as intermediaries who ensure a supply of the imported good to the domestic consumer at a price equal to the supply price plus costs incurred in transferring the good from the producer abroad to the final user.

If quantitative restrictions are applied, this will impose constraints upon the exporters or importers and create a new equilibrium. The way in which the three prices change will determine who along the chain will receive the quota rents.

FIGURE A.1   **Market equilibrium with competitive industries at home and abroad**

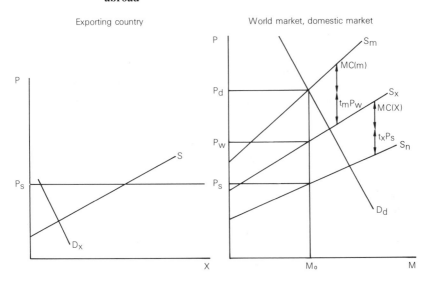

Suppose an import quota is imposed, and the permits to import are given or sold to importers. The quota will impose a constraint upon their behavior by setting an upper limit to the quantity imported. Any fee or charge for import permits also will change the importers' cost conditions. In figure A.2, an import quota of M', with a fee fixed of q_m per unit, will shift the supply curve to the domestic market, S_m, upward by q_m and make it vertical at the import quota ceiling M'. The per unit import permit fee, q_m, also changes the importers' cost conditions, if there was no import permit fee before the quota was imposed, since they must pay for the permits. The quantity that the importers are willing and able to supply at various prices cannot increase beyond the quota limit.

Consumers are not constrained directly, so the domestic market can only be in equilibrium on the demand curve. The specified import quota and fee will result in an increase in the domestic price of the good to P_d', a fall in the world price to P_w', and a fall in the supply price to P_s'. The windfall profits or quota rents must accrue to the importers who sell at P_d and buy at

FIGURE A.2   **Effect of an import quota with competitive industries**

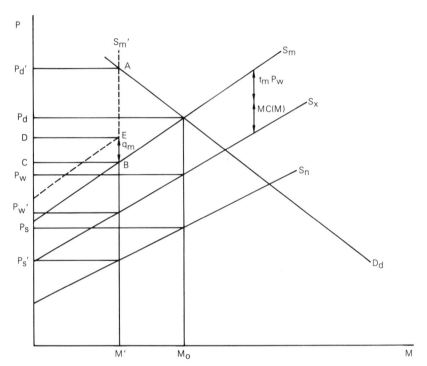

P_w. Their profits will be area $P_d'ABC$ *less* area DEBC, the amount paid to the government for the permits. Note that any increase in the permit fee (up to a maximum fee of AB) will simply shift the sloping portion of the importers' supply curve upward along the vertical section, resulting in more government revenue (and correspondingly less quota rent for importers), but it will not affect the equilibrium prices in the three markets. Another way of thinking of this is that an importer would be willing to pay up to an amount AB for the permit to import one unit because any amount less than AB leaves him with windfall profits.

If, instead of an import quota, the quantitative restriction limits the amount that the exporters are allowed to export, then the market impact and the

FIGURE A.3   **Effect of an export quota with competitive industries**

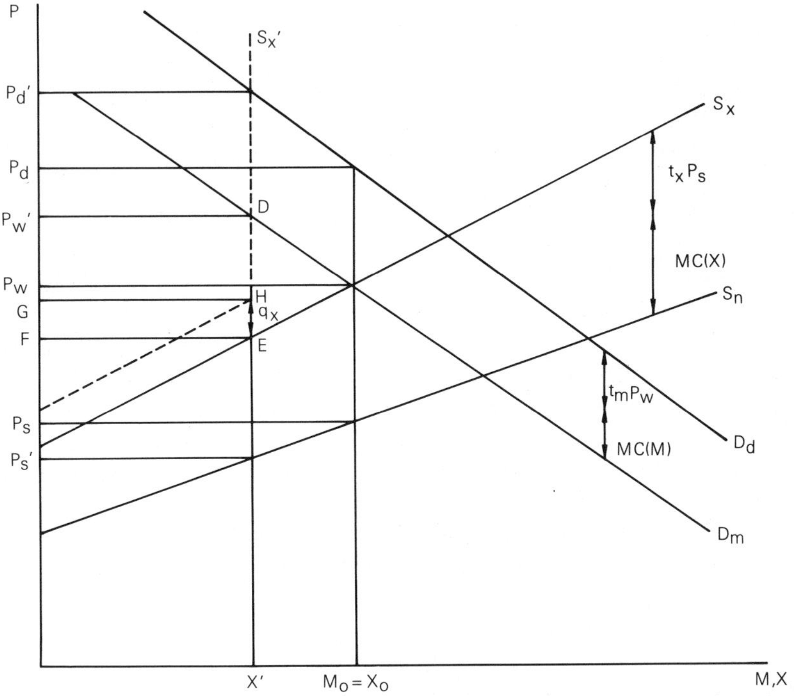

distribution of the quota rents will be quite different. The constraint will be on the amount that the exporters will be willing and able to supply to the importers. To show the impact of the export restraint, it is more convenient to work backward from consumer demand in the importing country, rather than forward from producer supply in the exporting country, as in the import quota case. It was shown earlier that unconstrained competitive importers maximize profits by importing up to the point at which the price they receive, P_d, equals the world price plus the marginal cost of importing (where cost includes all import duties and fees). We can think of the importers as demanding imports in the world market, where their demand is a derived demand, derived from consumer demand for the imported good. The importers' demand curve in the world market (D_m in figure A.3) can be derived from the final consumers' demand curve by simply subtracting marginal importing costs, tariffs, and import permit fees.

In the absence of any quantitative restrictions, the equilibrium price in the world market, P_w, will be determined by the point of intersection of the import demand and export supply curves (D_m and S_x) in figure A.3. An export restraint of X' will limit the maximum amount that exporters can supply, making the export supply curve vertical at that level of exports. The sloping portion of the export supply curve will shift upward by an amount equal to any extra charges for export permits, q_x. The export quota will increase the world market equilibrium price to P_w', the domestic price to P_d', and it will lower the supply price to P_s'. After the export restraint, exporters are selling at P_w', buying at P_s', and incurring additional costs of q_x per unit, so their windfall profits equal area $P_w'DEF$, *less* area GHEF, which accrues to the government of the exporting country. Note that an export quota limits the supply of exports and drives the world price upward, in contrast to an import quota, which limits demand, and drives the world price downward.

As the fee charged for export quota permits increases, the area representing government revenue expands upward as the sloping portion of S_x' shifts upward. Government revenue increases and the exporters' quota rents decrease, with no change in equilibrium prices as long as the export quota fee is less than or equal to DE. If the fee for an export quota permit were to exceed DE, then the sloping portion of the export supply curve would intersect the import demand curve at a lower quantity than the export quota ceiling, and the quota would not be filled. In an export quota auction, exporters with perfect knowledge would be willing to pay up to the amount DE for a permit to export one unit of the good because any payment less than DE would leave them with windfall profits.[1]

---

1. The conclusion that the quota rents will go to the importers in the case of an import quota and exporters in the case of an export quota when all markets are competitive and licenses are issued to importers and exporters, respectively, will not be changed if production in the importing country is monopolized or oligopolistic, as long as exporting and importing remain competitive. These conclusions on the distribution of the quota rents between importers and exporters also would still hold if there were third-country suppliers or if the imported good and the domestic good were imperfect substitutes, but the analysis would be somewhat different.

MONOPOLY IMPORTER

A single importing firm, or monopoly importer, may exist before the import quota is imposed or may be created by the import quota system. If the import permits are allocated to just one firm or a group of firms that begin to act collectively to maximize joint profits, or if a single firm or group of firms acting collectively successfully bids for all of the quota in a quota auction, a monopoly importer would be created by the quota system.

Consider first the case in which importing is monopolized both before and after quantitative restrictions are imposed. Unlike each individual importer in the competitive market, the single importing firm cannot take the domestic price of the imported product as given because the amount it imports will determine the equilibrium price.

Suppose that the demand for the imported product is given by D_d in figure A.4. For simplicity, assume that the world market price is given, so that the supply of exports from exporters can be represented by a flat, infinitely elastic, supply curve, S_x, at the world market price P_w. The marginal cost to the importer, MC_t, equals P_w plus any tariff charges or import permit fees, as well as the marginal cost of transferring the goods from exporters to final consumers. Again for simplicity, the marginal cost of transferring the goods is assumed constant and equal to average cost. In the absence of any quantitative restrictions, the profit-maximizing import level would be M, where marginal revenue from sales equals marginal cost; domestic price would be P_d; profits from importing would be area P_dNQR.

If imports were limited to M′ by quota, and the permits given to this importer without extra charge, profits would decline by the area of triangle UQT, the area between the marginal revenue and marginal cost curves. The quota must decrease the importer's profits because he has already chosen M as the profit-maximizing import level, so any level below that must represent lower profits.

In the monopoly importer case, the "windfall profits" from the quota are more difficult to identify than in the competitive case. Before the quota, the monopoly importer was earning higher profits because of his monopoly position. One could identify the increase in profits due to the higher price, $P_d'SVP_d$, as windfall profits from the quota, but these really serve to offset to some extent the fall in profits due to constrained volume, VNQT. After the quota, the importer still is earning some profits ($P_d'STR$) but they are smaller than before the quota was imposed.

FIGURE A.4   **Effect of a quota when importing is monopolized**

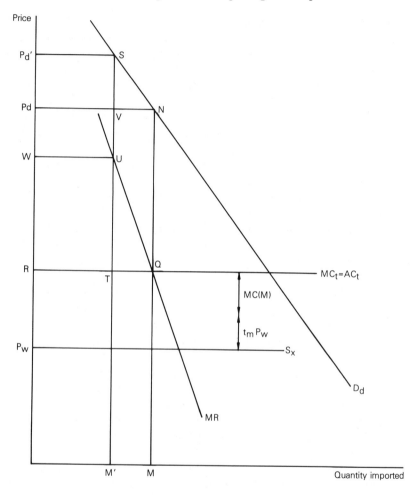

How would the monopoly importer react to fees or charges for import permits, or the auctioning of the quotas? Suppose the charges took the form of a fee per unit of quota allocated to the firm. The fee would shift the marginal cost curve upward. The marginal cost curve is the base of the rectangle representing the firm's excess profits, so charging fees for the quotas would transfer profits from the importer to the government without affecting the price at which the imported good sells in the domestic market *unless* the fee exceeded UT. A fee greater than UT would shift the marginal cost curve upward by so much that the firm would maximize profits by not filling the quota. Imports below the quota ceiling would imply higher domestic prices.

Suppose the government auctioned the quotas. The monopoly importer earns profits of $P_d'STR$ from importing M', so presumably he would be willing to pay up to that amount to obtain the quota rather than not import at all.

However, the revenue the government could expect to earn from an import quota auction would depend upon why the importer held a monopoly position. An auction implies that other individuals or firms would be allowed to bid as well, but if the importer were the only firm importing because it held an exclusive franchise, or controlled production abroad, no other firm could import even if it held the quota permits. At best all it could do would be to bargain with the monopoly importer to resell the permits to it. Under the circumstances, the monopoly importer may be the only bidder in the auction. It could obtain the quota with a minimal offer. In this case, the government may do better to impose a minimum bid or simply charge the firm for the permits. As noted earlier, an extra charge per unit imported up to UT could be imposed without changing the price to consumers. Any charge greater than UT would leave the quota unfilled.

The maximum revenue the government could expect from imposing a minimum bid per unit while still filling the quota, WUTR, is less than the government could extract from the monopoly importer by offering him an ''all or nothing'' offer. An all or nothing offer of all the quota permits for slightly less than $P_d'STR$ would be accepted because it leaves the importer with at least some profits, which it could not earn if prohibited from importing. In essence, the government would expropriate the monopoly rents as well as any windfall rents from the quota.

If importing is monopolized, an export quota, administered by giving export permits to exporters, will not necessarily transfer any quota rents or monopoly profits to the exporting country. If the export permits are widely distributed, and the import monopolist knows the supply conditions of the exporters, he knows they are willing to supply the good at the price P_w. No other importers will be attempting to outbid him, so he could exploit his monopoly position by only accepting offers of the good at that price. On the other hand, if the exporting country allocated all of the export permits to a

FIGURE A.5   **The case of an import monopoly created by a quota**

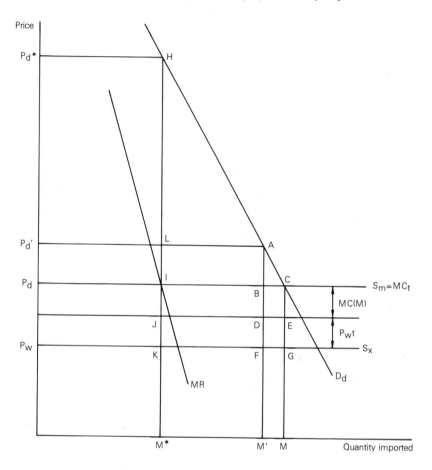

single firm or entity, this would transform the market between exporter and importer into a bilateral monopoly, and the price would have to be determined by bargaining, in which case the price is likely to be above P_w, and some of the monopoly profits are likely to be transferred to the exporting country. An export tax could ensure that some of the monopoly profits are obtained by the government of the exporting country. Any tax would add to the exporters' costs, shifting P_w, S_x, and MC_t upward, thus eating into the importer's profit rectangle.

One concern frequently expressed about auctioning quota permits is that an auction quota could create a monopoly importer where a competitive importing industry existed before. This would occur if the government sold all of the permits in one lump, or if one bidder bid successfully for all of the permits.

To investigate the consequences of creating a monopoly importer, retain the simplifying assumptions that the world market price of the good is given and that the marginal cost of importing is constant and equal to the average cost. Suppose that before the import quota is adopted the importing industry is competitive. The importers' supply curve is S_M in figure A.5. It will lie above the exporters' supply curve by the sum of import duties, import fees, and the marginal cost of importing. Without any quantitative restrictions, the equilibrium in the market would be at a price P_d and a quantity of imports M. With an import quota limiting imports to M', with quotas distributed or auctioned in such a way that importing remains competitive, the price of the product would increase to P_d'. Importers would be buying at P_w and selling at P_d', so they would be willing to pay up to the amount $P_d' - P_d$ to obtain a permit. The government could expect to earn $P_d'ABP_d$ from an import quota auction among competitive importers. The revenue earned by the government in the quota auction will be partially offset by the lost tariff revenue DEFG.

What would happen if importing did not remain competitive because one firm was given all of the quota permits or obtained them all through the auction? That firm would then become a monopolist and would maximize profits by importing only up to the quantity at which marginal revenue equals marginal cost. This profit-maximizing import level could be either above or below the quota ceiling. If it is above, the importer will fill the quota. The impact on consumers, the efficiency losses, and the impact of the quota on the domestic import-competing industry would be the same as if importing were not monopolized.

If, however, the importer's profit-maximizing import level were *below* the quota ceiling, the quota would not be filled. Prices to consumers, the efficiency losses, and the protective effect of the quota would be larger than if importing had remained competitive.

Given the cost and demand conditions shown in figure A.5, the profit-maximizing import level would be M^*. The importer would not fill the quota, and the price of the product would be driven up to P_d^*. Consumers would be worse off than with competition among the importers, and the government's target level of imports would not be achieved.

What would a firm be willing to bid to obtain this import monopoly position? The monopolistic importer's profits would be area P_d*HIP_d, so if firms could correctly forecast the gain from monopolizing the import market, they presumably would be willing to bid up to this amount to corner the market for permits. This analysis raises the possibility that an importer would be willing to bid high for the quotas in an attempt to monopolize the import market, ship less than the quota ceiling, and earn higher profits. If the government allowed this, it could possibly earn more revenue from the auction, but only by imposing a larger burden on consumers and creating greater efficiency losses from the restriction.

In figure A.5, competitive importers who correctly forecast the impact of the quota on domestic price if importing remained competitive would be willing to bid the difference between P_d' and P_d per unit of imports for the quota, or a total amount of $P_d'ABP_d$. A firm that realized the potential profitability of monopolizing import trade would be willing to bid up to P_d*HIP_d. This bid would exceed the bids by competitive firms, so in this instance an auction that allowed a single firm to bid for all of the quota without restriction would create a monopoly importer.

Note that figure A.5 depicts a special case. If the quota had set an import ceiling below $M*$, there would have been no incentive to bid to monopolize importing because the quota itself reduced imports below the profit-maximizing level. Note also that the monopoly importer can impose an extra burden on consumers (above the burden of the quota itself) only if it shortships. Safeguards could be designed to detect and prevent this abuse.

MONOPOLY EXPORTER

As in the case of the import monopoly, an export monopoly may exist before any quantitative restrictions are imposed, or it may be created when quotas are imposed and administered from the export side, either by giving export permits to one or a small number of firms, or by encouraging exporters to collaborate to divide up the quotas, which encourages them to collude on price.

The method of analysis for the export monopolist resembles that for the import monopolist and has similar conclusions. First take the case where exporting was monopolized before any quantitative restrictions and continues as a monopoly after the limitations are imposed. Figure A.6 shows the impact

FIGURE A.6   **Effect of a quota when exporting is monopolized**

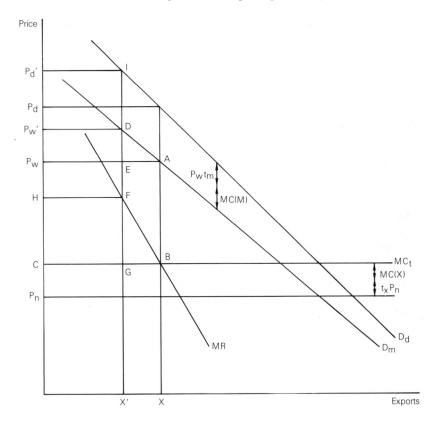

of quotas on an export monopolist. The consumer demand curve for the imported product is given by D_d, and the competitive importer's demand curve is D_m, which lies below D_d by the marginal cost of transferring the good plus import duties. For simplicity, assume that the good is available to the exporter at the given price P_n, and that the marginal cost of transferring the good to the importer is constant and equal to average cost. The total marginal cost to the exporter is MC_t.

Without quantitative restrictions, the exporter would maximize profits at export level X and price P_w. Adding the importer's costs would result in a price to consumers in the importing country of P_d. The exporter's profits would equal area P_wABC.

An export quota of X' would constrain the exporter to a volume below his profit-maximizing level, driving up the world price and final price to consumers to P_w' and P_d', respectively, but reducing the exporter's profits by the area of triangle FBG. A quantitative restriction must decrease the exporter's profits if the export market was monopolized before the restrictions were imposed because it will constrain the firm to an export level below the profit-maximizing level chosen before.

As in the case of the monopoly importer, it is difficult to identify the quota rents or windfall gain from the quota. One could identify the extra revenue $P_w'DEP_w$ from the higher price as a windfall gain, but that is not sufficient to offset the lost revenue (EABG) from lower volume.

In the case illustrated, the exporter still does earn profits of $P_w'DGC$. The government could charge up to an amount FG for the permit to export one unit without changing equilibrium prices. Any charge greater than FG would push the exporter's marginal cost curve above point F, so that profits would be maximized at an export level lower than the quota ceiling. On the other hand, if the government offered the permits to the exporter as an all or nothing proposition for a total fee of up to $P_w'DGC$, the monopoly exporter would accept the offer, as long as there were some (albeit small) profit to be made. The different impact of a lump sum charge and a charge per unit results from the way in which the two charges affect costs: the fee per unit increases marginal cost; the all-or-nothing offer increases total cost, but not marginal cost.

An import quota set at the same level as X', with the import permits distributed to importers, may or may not transfer the monopoly rents to the importing country, depending upon the way the import quota is administered. Take first the case where the permits are simply given to the importers. Their cost conditions and therefore their demand curve for imports would not change except that it would become vertical at point D. If the export monopolist realized that the importers would be willing to buy the quantity X' at any price up to P_w', he could simply set price at P_w', leaving no excess profits or windfall gain for the importers. Competition among them would ensure that the quota would still be filled. If the government were to hold an auction for the import permits, importers would bid no more than the difference between the expected domestic selling price and the full cost of the good to them. To sell the amount allowed under the quota, the export monopolist would have to sell at a price only minimally below P_w', so that importers would be willing to offer a minimal bid.

The government of the importing country could appropriate some of the remaining export monopoly profits by charging a fee for the permits or insisting upon a minimum bid. A fee for the permits would increase the importers' costs, shifting their demand curve for imports (and thus the marginal revenue curve facing the export monopolist) downward by the amount of the fee. An import permit fee equal to FG in figure A.6 would shift the exporter's marginal revenue curve to intersect the marginal cost curve at G. The exporter would still maximize profits by filling the quota, but the world price would decline by the amount of the fee, leaving domestic price unchanged at P_d'. If exporting is monopolized, the importing-country government can obtain some revenue from the import quota rights, but only by charging a fee for the quotas or insisting upon a minimum bid.

Another possible way to transfer some monopoly profits to the importing country would be to auction off or allocate all the permits in one lot, thus creating a monopoly importer. This would transform the market between importer and exporter into a bilateral monopoly where the price would be determined by bargaining. This would most likely transfer some of the profits to the importer, but the exact outcome of the bargaining process would be uncertain.

So far we have discussed an export monopoly that existed before a quota was imposed. It is often argued that VERs encourage collusion among exporters, thus potentially creating a monopoly exporter where the industry previously was competitive. It can be shown that a newly created export monopoly may not fill the export quota. The analysis is similar to that of a newly created import monopoly, treated earlier.

Suppose that, before any restrictions, all markets are competitive. The consumer demand curve for the imported product is D_d in figure A.7; the import demand curve is D_m. Suppose the good can be purchased in the exporting country at P_n, to which competitive exporters add their costs, selling in the world market at P_w. A quantity X would be traded at a world market price of P_w and a price to consumers of P_d. Suppose an export limit of X' is declared and administered by either giving the export permits to one entity or encouraging the formation of an export cartel. Given the cost and demand conditions, a single exporter would maximize profits by exporting the quantity at which marginal revenue equals marginal cost, which is X*. The quota would not be filled. World price would increase to P_w*, and the

FIGURE A.7   **The case of an export monopoly created by an export restraint**

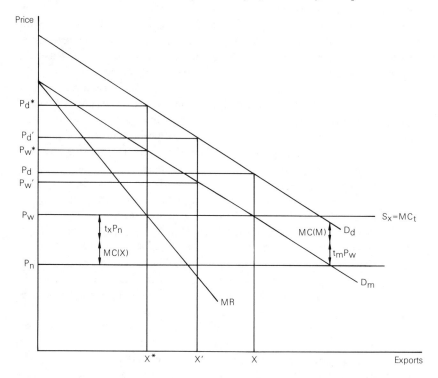

price to consumers would be driven up to P_d^*. The cost to consumers, the efficiency costs, and the protective effect of the quota will be larger if the creation of a monopoly exporter causes the quota to remain unfilled.[2]

---

2. The analysis of the case of a monopoly producer abroad would be virtually identical to the case of the monopoly exporter. As noted earlier, unconstrained competitive exporters act just as intermediaries, ensuring that the good is available in the world market at the price prevailing in the exporting country plus actual export costs. Thus, the analysis of the monopoly producer abroad would be the same as that of the monopoly exporter, except that the demand curve facing the producer would be the consumer demand curve in the importing country, less costs of importing *and* less costs of exporting. The conclusions would be identical.

Summary

Quantitative restrictions, whether they take the form of import or export quotas, increase prices to final consumers and create windfall profits. The degree to which prices increase and the distribution of the windfall profits among producers, importers, exporters, and governments depends upon the degree of industry concentration, or market structure, in the relevant industries and the method of administering the quotas.

If there are a large number of competitive producers, importers, and exporters, the windfall profits, or quota rents, are likely to remain with the recipients of quota licenses, or be captured by the government in an auction if the licenses are auctioned to the highest bidder.

If there is only a single importer, exporter, or producer abroad, or so few that there is potential for collusion among them, the quota rents are likely to accrue to the monopoly or concentrated sector, irrespective of who receives quota licenses, and the government may not be able to capture those rents through a simple auction. Minimum bids or "all-or-nothing" offers may be required, but these run the risk of further restricting trade if set too high. If either import or export monopolies are created by the quota system (by giving one firm all the permits or requiring firms to divide up the market to keep within the quota ceiling) or by auctioning (if one firm is the only successful bidder), then shortshipping may result, which would further increase prices to consumers.

Appendix B Quantitative Restraints Imposed by the United States

QUANTITATIVE RESTRAINTS IMPOSED BY THE UNITED STATES

Period in effect	Industry	QR type
1936 to 1940	Cotton textiles	VER
1937 to present (with interruptions)	Sugar	Import quota
1939 to present	Cotton, certain cotton products and cotton wastes	Import quota
1941 to 1974	Wheat and wheat flour	Import quota
October 1952 to October 1953	Shelled filberts	Import quota

How administered	Legal authority
Unilateral Japanese restraint failed to slow increasing US imports of certain cotton textiles so US selectively raised tariffs. When that also failed, US and Japanese trade associations negotiated agreement under which Japanese industry "voluntarily" restrained shipments; in return, the US industry agreed not to press for other forms of protection.	First Japanese "voluntary" restraint was unilateral; second agreement was negotiated by industries themselves, so no legal authority was necessary.
Current quotas are allocated by country annually and adjusted quarterly if necessary. Certificates of eligibility are issued by the Secretary of Agriculture to a designated official in the exporting country who then executes and issues them to the shipper or consignee for sugar shipments to the United States. The certificates must be presented at the time of entry.	Sugar Act of 1937 until 1941; Sugar Act of 1948 until 1975; authority under headnote 2 of the Tariff Schedules of the United States since 1982.
As of 1981, country quotas were in effect for short staple cotton and certain cotton wastes; global but category-specific quotas on other lengths of raw cotton and cotton products at any stage between waste and yarn. Quotas are administered on an unlicensed first-come-first-served basis by Customs. In recent years, the quotas have not been binding.	Section 22 of the Agricultural Act of 1933 (1935 amendment). Quotas grandfathered under GATT.
Allocated by country and administered by Customs on an unlicensed, first-come-first-served basis.	Section 22
A global quota was imposed on June 17, 1953, effective immediately and retroactive to October 1, 1952.	Section 22

Period in effect	Industry	QR type
1953 to present	Peanuts	Import quota
1953 to present	Dairy products, primarily cheese	Import quota
October 1954 to October 1955	Barley	Import quota
October 1954 to October 1955	Oats	Import quota
1954 to 1961	Rye, rye flour, and rye meal	Import quota
1954 to 1959	Alsike clover seed	Tariff quota

How administered	Legal authority
Annual global quota administered on unlicensed, first-come-first-served basis by Customs.	Section 22
Imports of dried buttermilk, dried skimmed whole milk, cream, butter, malted milk, and most cheeses are administered by USDA via historical, nonhistorical, and supplementary licenses divided among eligible importers on a prorated basis "under provisions of Import Regulation I, as revised and amended"; cheese quotas mostly on a country- and category-specific basis. A small quantity of other imports are administered by Customs on an unlicensed, first-come-first-served basis.	Section 22
Bulk of quota allocated to Canada with a minor quantity reserved for other suppliers.	Section 22
From December 1953 to September 1954, Canada agreed to limit its shipments. From 1954 to 1955, an import quota was imposed with the bulk allocated to Canada and a small portion for other suppliers.	Section 22
A global quota was imposed in the first year; in each of the remaining years, the vast majority was allocated to Canada with a minor quantity for other suppliers.	Section 22
Imports above the quota level were charged three times the normal tariff level.	Escape clause, at that time, section 7 of the Trade Agreements Extension Act of 1951; GATT Article XIX.

Period in effect	Industry	QR type
1956 to present	Tuna canned in water	Tariff quota
1957 to 1962	Tung nuts and tung oil	Import quota
1957 to present	Textiles and apparel	VERs
1958 to 1965	Lead and zinc	Import quota
1959 to 1967	Stainless steel flatware	Tariff quota

How administered	Legal authority
Penalty rate is twice the underquota rate.	A concession granted Japan during GATT negotiations lowered statutory tariff rate but reservation limited the lower duty to 20 percent of prior year's domestic pack; tariffs lowered in Kennedy Round to current 6 percent and 12.5 percent on under and overquota tuna, respectively.
Bulk of the quota was allocated to Argentina and Paraguay with a small quantity for other suppliers. Restrictions were placed on the quantity that could be entered in the first quarter of each quota year. The regulations were modified in May 1958 to require that imports under quota "shall have been direct shipment destined to the United States on an original through bill of lading from the country of production." The order was intended to "assure equitable treatment to supplying countries." (*Federal Register*, 2 May 1958)	Section 22
Bilateral agreements negotiated with suppliers on product-specific basis. Administered by exporting countries via export licenses allocated generally on basis of export performance.	Section 204 of the Agricultural Act of 1956 provides authority to negotiate agreements to limit imports or to impose unilateral quotas if a majority of trade in the product is covered by agreements.
Annual quota allocated by country on a quarterly basis and administered on a first-come-first-served basis.	Escape clause
Overquota imports were subject to ad valorem duties of over 50 percent plus specific duties.	Escape clause

Period in effect	Industry	QR type
1959 to 1973	Petroleum and products	Import quota
1965 to present, intermittently	Meat	VERs
1969 to 1974	Carbon steel	VERs
1982 to present	Carbon steel	VERs

How administered	Legal authority
Licenses issued to domestic refiners on the basis of the prior year's inputs. Licenses not transferable although imported oil could be traded for domestic crude as necessary.	Section 232 of the Trade Expansion Act of 1962 and prior national security statutes.
Restraint limits negotiated with foreign suppliers; administered by the exporting country.	VERs negotiated under authority of section 204 of the Agricultural Act of 1956; there is backup authority to impose quotas unilaterally under the Meat Act of 1979 (originally passed in 1964).
Agreements negotiated with European Community and Japan; administered by those countries.	Executive agreements
Agreements negotiated with 27 major suppliers; export licenses required.	Executive agreements; original agreement with EC negotiated to avoid imposition of unfair trade remedies; later agreements under President's steel program negotiated in lieu of relief under affirmative escape clause case. 1984 Trade and Tariff Act included sense of Congress resolution that steel imports be limited to 20.2 percent of US consumption; Title VIII of the act (the Steel Import Stabilization Act) gave the President authority to negotiate voluntary agreements and take whatever steps necessary to enforce them.

Period in effect	Industry	QR type
1976 to 1980	Specialty steel and alloy tool steel	OMA and import quota
1983 to 1989	Specialty steel and alloy tool steel	Import quota and VERs (also increased duties on certain products)
1977 to 1981	Nonrubber footwear	OMAs
1977 to 1982	Color televisions	OMAs
1979 to 1984	Clothespins	Import quota
1981 to present	Automobiles	VER

How administered	Legal authority
OMA negotiated with Japan; quotas imposed on a country-specific basis for other major suppliers (EC, Canada, and Sweden), a basket for other MFN-eligible suppliers, and another basket for all other suppliers. Imports were on a first-come-first-served, unlicensed basis. No more than 60 percent of the quota level was supposed to be entered during the first six months of each quota year.	Section 201 of the Trade Act of 1974, the escape clause.
Higher duties waived for countries agreeing to restrain voluntarily those specialty steel products; also import quotas waived for EC, which included specialty steel in carbon steel VER; other suppliers covered by country-specific and category-specific quotas.	Escape clause
Agreements negotiated with Taiwan and Korea; those countries allocated quota among exporters. Export visas were required for entry.	Escape clause
Agreements negotiated with Japan, later Taiwan and Korea. Export certificates required for entry.	Escape clause
Global quota subdivided into three categories based on value and administered on a first-come-first-served basis.	Escape clause
Agreement negotiated with Japan with quantitative restraint administered by Japan.	Executive agreement; negotiated after escape clause relief denied by USITC.

Period in effect	Industry	QR type
1986 to present	Machine tools	VERs and implicit quotas

VER voluntary export restraint.
OMA orderly marketing arrangement.

How administered	Legal authority
VERs negotiated with Japan and Taiwan. Switzerland and Germany refused to negotiate; they have been threatened with unilateral action if they exceed "acceptable" levels. Export licenses will be issued by Taiwan for all covered products. Japan will issue licenses for major product categories and will offer "administrative guidance" to manufacturers on exports in other categories.	Case brought under section 232 of Trade Expansion Act, which authorizes the President to limit imports for reasons of national security. Administration did not invoke this authority in negotiating restraints but indicated intention of using it to take unilateral action if imports from West Germany, Switzerland, or other uncovered suppliers exceeded recommended levels.

*Appendix C   Major US Government User Fee
Programs*

MAJOR US GOVERNMENT USER FEE PROGRAMS
Condensed from ACUS (1986), "A Survey of Federal User Fee Programs"

Agency	Service or product	1985 revenue
US Department of Agriculture (USDA), Agricultural Marketing Service	Inspections, grading, and classing services for buyers and sellers of fruits, vegetables, dairy products, meat, poultry, cotton, and tobacco.	$106 million
USDA, Food Safety and Inspection Service	Meat and poultry inspections, as required by law.	$40 million
USDA, Forest Service	Permits to remove firewood for personal use from National Forests.	$6 million (1984)
USDA, Forest Service; Department of Interior (DOI), Bureau of Land Management	Permits and leases to graze livestock on public lands.	$9 million (USDA) $15 million (Interior)

Comments	Disposition of revenues
Fees are based on the costs of providing the services, and the program is fully funded through collections; no additional appropriation is provided for these services. Overhead as well as direct costs are included.	Receipts are deposited in a trust fund, which is available for appropriation to the program. There is a separate revolving fund for cotton and tobacco fees.
Currently, fees can be charged only for overtime and holiday inspections and voluntary inspections performed by request. The administration has proposed expanding fees to all inspections at a level to recover their costs.	Fees are placed in separate funds used to pay overtime wages.
Fees are charged in areas where demand exceeds supply or where there is no direct competition with private firewood sales. In 1984, 1.1 million cords were given away, 1.5 million cords sold.	Receipts go either to the Treasury general fund or appropriate cooperative accounts, such as Brush Disposal Fund, Salvage Sale Fund, and the Reforestation and Stand Improvement Funds. 25 percent goes to states of origin.
There are three methods for calculating Forest Service fees, depending on the region. In the Northeast, a competitive bidding system is used. In the Southeast and West, different base periods and formulas are used but both are tied to ability to pay, based on livestock prices. The vast majority of grazing is in western states. The Bureau of Land Management uses the third method. In 1986, a minimum fee was set, which was at that time higher than the calculated fee from the formula. CBO recommended auctioning and estimated a competitive bidding system could double revenue.	A portion of receipts goes to the state involved. 50 percent goes back into the program for range improvement; the remainder goes to the Treasury general fund.

Agency	Service or product	1985 revenue
USDA, Forest Service; DOI, National Park Service; Department of Defense (DOD), Army Corps of Engineers	Access to recreational facilities.	$31 million (Forest Service) $11 million (Army Corps) $21 million (National Park Service)
Department of Commerce, Bureau of the Census	Economic, demographic, and social data and statistical analysis.	$90 million
DOC, National Bureau of Standards	Calibration services; production and sale of standard reference materials; and miscellaneous testing.	$15 million
DOC, National Oceanic and Atmospheric Administration	Climatic and satellite data services.	$1 million
DOC, Patent and Trademark Office	Processing patent and trademark applications.	$107 million
Commodity Futures Trading Commission	Regulation of futures trading, including market surveillance, enforcement, registration, and audits.	$1 million

Comments	Disposition of revenues
Fees in recreational areas are usually limited to areas where they already exist and often have not been increased in many years. The Forest Service also issues permits to lease ski resorts, summer homes, and other privately run recreational facilities and concessions. It also charges user fees at some sites for entry and for camping at all. The Army Corps of Engineers is allowed to charge for certain campsites, while the National Park Service charges for all camp sites and entrance at some 62 parks.	Forest Service receipts are divided among affected states, special funds, such as the Land and Water Conservation Fund, and general Treasury revenues. All National Park Service fees go into general revenues as of fiscal year 1987, while Corps of Engineers collections are returned to the sites that collected them for operations and maintenance costs.
Regular, "off-the-shelf" reports are sold for fixed fees, while fees for other special projects are based on overhead and production costs.	Receipts either deposited in a trust fund or used to reimburse regular appropriations that initially bear the cost of reimbursable projects.
Fees based on actual costs of providing services; only recently this was revised to allow NBS to charge replacement costs for materials purchased for projects.	Receipts deposited in the Working Capital Fund, which funds NBS services for other government agencies and the public.
Photographs, negatives, and computer tapes are sold at prices derived from the actual costs of archiving, retrieving, and reproducing the data.	Fees deposited in revolving fund used to satisfy contractor expenses and other obligations associated with these services.
This office alone has nearly 200 user fees to cover costs of processing patent and trademark applications, including photocopying.	Collections are credited to a reimbursable account that reduces appropriations.
Fees are based on the cost of providing the service.	Treasury general fund.

Agency	Service or product	1985 revenue
Library of Congress, Copyright Office	Copyright protection.	$14 million
Federal Communications Commission	Construction permits and operating licenses for television and radio stations, licenses for interstate and international common carriers and private radio services.	$30 million (estimated for FY 1988)
DOD, Army Corps of Engineers	Construction, maintenance, and operation of the inland waterways system, including 25,000 miles of improved channels, locks, and dams.	$40 million
Federal Energy Regulatory Commission	Regulation of interstate natural gas, hydroelectric, oil pipeline and electricity services.	$43 million
Department of Energy (DOE)	Nuclear waste disposal.	$1,800 million
DOE, Power Marketing	Hydroelectric power.	$3,525 million

Comments	Disposition of revenues
This office is operated on a self-sustaining basis through the collection of fees and the value of materials deposited and transferred to the Library of Congress.	Revenues are deposited in a Treasury account that is available to offset Copyright Office appropriations.
For legal reasons, the FCC was unable to charge user fees for several years until April 1987. The reasons were related to the way the fees were calculated, not to the validity of the fees themselves.	Treasury general fund.
Tax on fuels used by shallow draft vessels implemented after more than 50 years with no charge for use of the inland waterways.	Revenues go into Inland Waterways Trust Fund, from which funds must be specifically appropriated and must be used for construction.
FERC charges fees for services that have identifiable beneficiaries, based on the cost of providing those services. The majority of collections come from annual charges to licensed hydroelectric projects.	Proprietary receipts are deposited in a special Treasury account that is used to offset FERC appropriations.
Special fund created for nuclear waste disposal; funded from tax on nuclear energy production.	Revenues go into the Nuclear Waste Disposal Fund account with the bulk being held for use when disposal becomes necessary.
There are 123 hydroelectric projects built by the Army Corps of Engineers and run by five Power Marketing Administrations, which sell the electricity produced therefrom.	Revenues are deposited in general revenues of the Treasury, except for the Bonneville Power Administration, which operates directly out of revenues from energy sales.

Agency	Service or product	1985 revenue
DOE	Uranium enrichment.	$1,350 million (1986)
Environmental Protection Agency	Review of petitions to modify pesticide tolerance levels.	$1 million (1986)
Department of Health and Human Services, Food and Drug Administration (and other affected agencies)	Processing of Freedom of Information Act requests.	$0.4 million (FDA only in 1986)
DOI, Office of Surface Mining, Reclamation and Enforcement	Issuance of permits for surface and underground coal mining, whether on federal, state, Indian, or privately owned land.	n.a.

Comments	Disposition of revenues
Fees set to cover all costs, including capital, and at a level that does not disadvantage private sector firms.	Revenues go into a special Treasury fund used to offset appropriations; excess funds are returned to the general fund.
Petitioners must pay the full costs of processing the petition, unless they demonstrate hardship or public benefit.	Revenues dedicated to the Pesticide Tolerance Revolving Fund, funds from which are permanently appropriated to this program.
FDA receives the second highest volume of FOIA requests (after the Pentagon), most from regulated companies interested in competitors' activities. Other agencies also receive requests motivated by commercial, rather than public welfare, concerns. Therefore, the administration requested and Congress approved changes in setting fees for processing different types of requests. Document search, duplication, and review costs for FOIA requests with a commercial purpose may be recovered in full; petitioners from educational or noncommercial scientific institutions may be charged only the costs of duplication; all others with a noncommercial purpose are charged costs of document search and duplication.	Treasury general fund.
OSMRE has granted regulatory primacy to most of the states that have significant coal mining activity. In a few cases, it issues permits directly, and in those it charges a fee to cover processing and review costs. States that issue permits generally charge fees and are allowed to keep all such receipts.	Treasury general fund.

Agency	Service or product	1985 revenue
DOI, Bureau of Reclamation	Water projects providing irrigation water, drinking water, power, recreation, and flood control.	$23 million (1986)
Interstate Commerce Commission	Regulation of interstate surface transportation, including railroads, trucking, buses, water carriers, and freight forwarders and brokers.	$4 million (1986)
Department of Justice (DOJ), FBI	Fingerprinting.	$10 million
DOJ, Immigration and Naturalization Service	Inspections at airports, land borders, and sea ports of entry to administer and enforce immigration laws.	n.a.
National Aeronautic and Space Administration	Placing of satellites and wind tunnel facilities.	$595 million

Comments	Disposition of revenues
Flood control costs are not considered reimbursable; irrigation water users pay all operating and maintenance costs and repay capital costs, according to their ability to pay within 40 years; other users pay fees according to applicable reclamation laws.	Payments go into account used to offset appropriations; interest revenues go into Treasury general fund.
Fees are set to cover full costs of services provided.	Treasury general fund.
A fee based on the average cost of processing is charged for each noncriminal fingerprint.	Fees are retained within the program to reimburse expenses; the program receives no appropriation.
New fee, in effect as of December 1, 1986, is incorporated in tickets for travel from foreign locations, excluding contiguous territories and the Caribbean, and are supposed to cover costs of all inspections. New fee proposed to cover costs of alien requests for amnesty under new immigration law.	Fees deposited into Immigration User Fee Account will be used to reimburse expenses of program.
Fees cover entire cost, including overhead.	Satellite launch revenues used to directly offset cost of space flight activities; wind tunnel revenues (less than $1 million in 1985) go into Treasury general fund.

Agency	Service or product	1985 revenue
Nuclear Regulatory Commission	Nuclear energy regulation.	$86 million
Panama Canal Commission	Panama Canal passage, also pilot assistance, shuttle services, towing, anchorage, use of launches, and other related services.	$416 million
US Postal Service	Mail delivery.	$28,000 million
Small Business Administration	Production and dissemination of informational publications.	$0.1 million
Department of State	Issuance of passports and visas.	$200 million
Department of Transportation (DOT), US Coast Guard	Boater safety programs.	n.a.

Comments	Disposition of revenues
Fees charged based on average license and permit processing time; in addition, Consolidated Omnibus Budget Reconciliation Act of 1985 directed NRC to recover 33 percent of annual costs of operation so NRC instituted annual charge to be paid by all plants licensed to operate a power reactor.	Treasury general fund.
There are set fees, based on capacity, for both loaded and empty ships passing through the canal and additional fees, based on cost, for the other services.	Revenues go into Panama Canal Commission Fund at Treasury, out of which appropriations come.
None.	All receipts go into the Postal Service Fund and may be used to reimburse expenses without fiscal year limitation.
Beginning in 1987, new fees are being charged for publications previously distributed free of charge to small business clients.	Treasury general fund.
Fees based on cost of providing service.	Treasury general fund.
Although proposals have been made repeatedly by the administration to impose user fees on a variety of Coast Guard services, no such fees are currently in place. The Coast Guard does, however, receive a portion of the revenues from the motor boat fuel tax, collected through the Highway Trust Fund (see below) and transferred to the Aquatic Resources Trust Fund to be used for the boater safety program.	Collections placed in Highway Trust Fund and transferred to Aquatic Resources Trust Fund with a portion allocated to the Coast Guard.

Agency	Service or product	1985 revenue
DOT	Airport construction and improvement; FAA facilities, R&D, and a portion of operations and maintenance.	$2,840 million (from taxes) $746 million (from interest)
DOT, Federal Aviation Administration	Washington National and Dulles International Airports.	$54 million
DOT, Federal Highway Administration	Interstate highway system.	$13,363 million (FY 1986)
Department of Treasury, Customs Service	Customs inspections.	$73 million ($700 million estimated for 1987)
Treasury, US Mint	Proof coin sets, gold and silver coins, special commemorative coins.	$55 million (for proofs) $800 million (est. for gold and silver coins)

n.a.   not available.

Comments	Disposition of revenues
Excise taxes are collected on airline tickets, international tickets, shipping, jet fuel, and aviation gasoline.	All collections go into Airport and Airway Trust Fund, from which funds are appropriated according to statutory rules and formulas.
Certain fees negotiated with individual airlines and concessionaires using airport; set fees charged for landing; others for space rental and use of mobile lounges.	Treasury general fund.
Program financed out of excise taxes on gasoline, diesel, gasohol, tires, truck and trailer sales, and heavy vehicle use.	All fees collected go to Highway Trust Fund and are released through appropriations to reimburse states for work approved as a federal aid project.
Customs administered some 50 fees before receiving authority to impose new fees on entry of passengers and vehicles, dutiable mail, and customs broker permits in the Consolidated Budget Reconciliation Act of 1985. The Budget Reconciliation Act of 1986 added authority to impose an ad valorem fee on merchandise entered.	The specific users fees are to be deposited in the Treasury general fund, while revenues from the ad valorem fee will go into a dedicated account to offset Customs appropriations for salaries and other expenses incurred in conducting commercial operations.
Prices depend on metal content, production costs, and profit margins associated with each product.	All proceeds go to Coinage Profit Fund or to Suspense Fund of US Mint. Funds allocated to pay expenses, some earmarked for special uses (for example, surcharge on US Olympic coins earmarked for US Olympic Committee and Los Angeles Olympic organizing committee).

References

Administrative Council of the United States. 1986. "A Survey of Federal User Fee Programs." Arlington, Mass.: Eastern Research Group, Inc., December. Processed.

Allen, R., C. Dodge, and A. Schmitz. 1983. "Voluntary Export Restraints as Protection Policy: The US Beef Case." *American Journal of Agricultural Economics*, vol. 65: 291–96.

Amacher, Ryan C., Robert D. Tollison, and Thomas D. Willet. 1973. "Import Controls on Foreign Oil: Comment." *The American Economic Review*, vol. 63, no. 5 (December): 1031–33.

Anderson, James E. 1985a. "The Relative Inefficiency of Quotas: The Cheese Case." *The American Economic Review*, vol. 75, no. 1 (March): 178–90.

———. 1985b. "The Relative Inefficiency of Quotas: Employment Protection." Chestnut Hill, Mass.: Boston College, October. Unpublished.

———. 1986. "Quotas as Options: Optimality and Quota License Pricing Under Uncertainty." Chestnut Hill, Mass.: Boston College, March. Unpublished.

Australian Department of Industry, Technology, and Commerce. 1986a. By communication, September.

———. 1986b. *Eleventh Report on Textiles, Clothing, and Footwear.* Canberra, May.

Automotive Industry Authority. 1986. *Report on the State of the Automotive Industry, 1985.* Canberra: Australian Government Publishing Service.

Aw, B. Y., and M. J. Roberts. 1986. "Measuring Quality Change in Quota-Constrained Import Markets." *Journal of International Economics*, vol. 21: 45–60.

Balassa, Bela, and Constantine Michalopoulos. 1985. *Liberalizing World Trade.* World Bank Discussion Paper, Development Policy Issues Series. Washington, October.

Balassa, Bela, and John Williamson. 1987. *Adjusting to Success: Balance of Payments Policy in the East Asian NICs.* POLICY ANALYSES IN INTERNATIONAL ECONOMICS 17. Washington: Institute for International Economics, June.

Baldwin, Robert E. 1984. "Trade Policies in Developed Countries." In *Handbook of International Economics*, vol. 1. Edited by Ronald W. Jones and Peter B. Kenen. Amsterdam: North-Holland.

Bark, Taeho, and Jaime de Melo. 1987. "Export Quota Allocations, Export Earnings, and Market Diversification." World Bank, January. Processed.

Bergsten, C. Fred. 1975. "On the Nonequivalence of Import Quotas and Voluntary Export Restraints." In *Toward a New World Trade Policy: The Maidenhead Papers.* Edited by C. Fred Bergsten. Lexington, Mass.: Lexington Books, D. C. Heath and Co.

———. 1986. "Reforming the Escape Clause: Self-Financing Adjustment for American Firms and Workers." Statement before the House Ways and Means Subcommittee on Trade. 99th Cong., 2d sess., 15 April. Washington.

235

————. 1987. "Auction Quotas and Trade Policy: The Case for Reform." Statement before the House Ways and Means Subcommittee on Trade. 100th Cong., 1st sess., 27 February. Washington.

Bhagwati, Jagdish. 1965. "On the Equivalence of Tariffs and Quotas." In *Trade, Growth and the Balance of Payments*. Edited by Robert E. Baldwin et al. Chicago: Rand McNally.

————. 1968. "More on the Equivalence of Tariffs and Quotas." *The American Economic Review*, vol. 58, no. 1 (March): 142–47.

————. 1982. "Directly Unproductive, Profit-Seeking (DUP) Activities." *Journal of Political Economy*, vol. 90, no. 5 (October): 988–1002.

Bhagwati, Jagdish, and T. N. Srinivasan. 1980. "Revenue Seeking: A Generalization of the Theory of Tariffs." *Journal of Political Economy*, vol. 88, no. 6 (December): 1069–87.

Blinder, Alan S. 1987. "US Import Rights: Going Once, Going Twice. . ." *Business Week*, 9 March, p. 27.

Boadway, R., S. Maital, and M. Prachowny. 1973. "Optimal Tariffs, Optimal Taxes, and Public Goods." *Journal of International Economics*, vol. 2, no. 4 (November): 391–403.

Bohi, Douglas R., and Milton Russell. 1978. *Limiting Oil Imports: An Economic History and Analysis*. Baltimore, Md.: Johns Hopkins University Press.

Bolten, Steven. 1973. "Treasury Bill Auction Procedures: An Empirical Investigation." *The Journal of Finance*, vol. 28, no. 3 (June): 577–85.

Cabinet Task Force on Oil Import Control. 1970. *The Oil Import Question: A Report on the Relationship of Oil Imports to the National Security*. Washington.

Cassing, James H., and Arye L. Hillman. 1985. "Political Influence Motives and the Choice Between Tariffs and Quotas." *Journal of International Economics*, vol. 19, no. 3/4 (November): 279–90.

Caves, Richard E., and Ronald W. Jones. 1977. *World Trade and Payments*. 2d ed. New York: Little, Brown, and Co.

Caygill, David (Minister of Trade and Industry). 1987. "Import Licensing." Address to the Bureau of Importers and Exporters. Auckland, New Zealand, 7 April.

Christie, Phillip (Licensing Officer, Dairy, Livestock, and Poultry Division, US Department of Agriculture). 1986. By communication.

Cline, William R. 1987. *The Future of World Trade in Textiles and Apparel*. Washington: Institute for International Economics, September.

Comptroller General of the United States. 1970. *Opportunity for Benefits Through Increased Use of Competitive Bidding to Award Oil and Gas Leases on Federal Lands*. Washington: General Accounting Office.

————. 1974. *Economic and Foreign Policy Effects of Voluntary Restraint Agreements on Textiles and Steel*. Washington: General Accounting Office, March.

————. 1986. *International Trade: Trade Law Remedies under Floating Exchange Rates*. Washington: General Accounting Office, December.

Congressional Budget Office. 1984. *The Effects of Import Quotas on the Steel Industry*. Washington, July.

————. 1987. "Revenue Estimates for Auctioning Existing Import Quotas." Memorandum to Chairman William Gray, House Budget Committee. Washington, 28 February.

Corden, W. M. 1971. *The Theory of Protection*. London: Oxford University Press.

————. 1984. "Normative Theory of International Trade." In *Handbook of International Economics*, vol 1. Edited by Ronald W. Jones and Peter B. Kenen. Amsterdam: North-Holland.

Cox, James C., Vernon L. Smith, and James M. Walker. 1985. "Open and Sealed-Bid Auctions: Experimental Development of Sealed-Bid Auction Theory; Calibrating Controls for Risk Aversion." *The American Economic Review*, vol. 75, no. 2 (May): 160–65.

Dasgupta, Partha, and Joseph Stiglitz. 1977. "Tariffs vs. Quotas as Revenue Raising Devices under Uncertainty." *The American Economic Review*, vol. 67, no. 5 (December): 975–81.

Destler, I. M. 1986. *American Trade Politics: System Under Stress*. New York and Washington: Twentieth Century Fund and Institute for International Economics.

Destler, I. M., and John S. Odell. 1987. *The Politics of Antiprotection*. POLICY ANALYSES IN INTERNATIONAL ECONOMICS 21. Washington: Institute for International Economics, September.

Executive Office of the President. 1974. *Economic Report of the President*. Washington, February.

Falvey, R. 1979. "The Composition of Trade within Import-Restricted Product Categories." *Journal of Political Economy*, vol. 87, no. 5: 1105–14.

Federal Trade Commission. 1984. "Brief on Section 201 Investigation Regarding Imports of Carbon and Alloy Steel Before the Office of the United States Trade Representative, Trade Policy Staff Committee." Washington, 10 August.

Feenstra, Robert C. 1984. "Voluntary Export Restraint in Autos, 1980-81: Quality, Employment, and Welfare Effects." In *The Structure and Evolution of Recent US Trade Policy*. Edited by Robert E. Baldwin and Anne O. Kreuger. Chicago: University of Chicago Press.

Fowler, Mark S. 1986. "Spectrum Auctions: Proposals for FCC Management of the Airwaves." Statement before the Subcommittee on Telecommunications, Consumer Protection, and Finance of the Committee on Energy and Commerce. 99th Cong., 2d sess., 1 October. Washington.

General Agreement on Tariffs and Trade. 1980. "Declaration on Trade Measures Taken for Balance of Payments Purposes." In *Basic Instruments and Selected Documents*. Twenty-sixth supplement. Geneva.

Greenaway, David. 1983. *Trade Policy and the New Protectionism*. New York: St. Martin's Press.

Hagenstein, Perry R. 1984. "The Federal Lands Today: Uses and Limits." In *Rethinking the Federal Lands*. Edited by Sterling Brubaker. Washington: Resources for the Future.

Hamilton, Carl. 1986a. "Economic Aspects of Voluntary Export Restraints." In *Current Issues in International Trade: Theory and Policy*. Edited by David Greenaway. London: MacMillan.

———. 1986b. "An Assessment of Voluntary Restraints on Hong Kong Exports to Europe and the USA." *Economica*, vol. 53: 339–50.

———. 1986c. "The Upgrading Effect of Voluntary Export Restraints." *Weltwirtschaftliches Archiv*, vol. 122: 358–64.

———. 1986d. "ASEAN Systems for Allocation of Export Licences Under VERs" and "Import Quotas and Voluntary Export Restraints: Focusing on Exporting Countries." In *The Political Economy of Manufacturing Protection: Experiences of ASEAN and Australia*. Edited by Christopher Findlay and Ross Garnaut. Winchester, Mass.: Allen and Unwin.

———. 1986e. "Restrictiveness and International Transmission of the New Protectionism." Institute for International Economic Studies Seminar Paper No. 367. University of Stockholm.

Hansen, Robert G. 1985. "Open and Sealed-Bid Auctions: Empirical Testing of Auction Theory." *The American Economic Review*, vol. 75, no. 2 (May): 156–59.

Harris, R. 1985. "Why Voluntary Export Restraints Are Voluntary." *Canadian Journal of Economics*, vol. 18, no. 4: 799–809.

Hay, George A. 1971. "Import Controls on Foreign Oil: Tariff or Quota." *The American Economic Review*, vol. 61, no. 4 (September): 688–91.

———. 1973. "Import Controls on Foreign Oil: Reply." *The American Economic Review*, vol. 63, no. 5 (December): 1035–36.

Heuser, Heinrich. 1939. *Control of International Trade*. London: George Routledge and Sons.

Hufbauer, Gary Clyde, Diane T. Berliner, and Kimberly Ann Elliott. 1986. *Trade Protection in the United States: 31 Case Studies*. Washington: Institute for International Economics, March.

Hufbauer, Gary Clyde, and Howard Rosen. 1986. *Trade Policy for Troubled Industries*. POLICY ANALYSES IN INTERNATIONAL ECONOMICS 15. Washington: Institute for International Economics, March.

Hufbauer, Gary Clyde, and Jeffrey J. Schott. 1985. *Trading for Growth: The Next Round of Trade Negotiations*. POLICY ANALYSES IN INTERNATIONAL ECONOMICS 11. Washington: Institute for International Economics, September.

Hufbauer, Gary Clyde, and Joanna Shelton Erb. 1984. *Subsidies in International Trade*. Washington: Institute for International Economics.

Hunsberger, Warren. 1964. *Japan and the United States in World Trade*. New York: Harper and Row for the Council on Foreign Relations.

Industries Assistance Commission. 1981. *Annual Report, 1980–81*. Canberra: Australian Government Publishing Service.

———. 1986. *The Textile, Clothing, and Footwear Industries*, vol. 1. Canberra: Australian Government Publishing Service, 19 May.

International Monetary Fund. *International Financial Statistics*. Various years. Washington.

Isaac, R. Mark, and Charles R. Plott. 1981. "Price Controls and the Behavior of Auction Markets: An Experimental Examination." *The American Economic Review*, vol. 71, no. 3 (June): 448–59.

Itoh, M., and Y. Ono. 1984. "Tariffs versus Quotas Under Duopoly of Heterogeneous Goods." *Journal of International Economics*, vol. 17: 359–73.

Jackson, John H. 1987. "The Role of GATT in Monitoring Safeguards and Promoting Adjustment." In *Domestic Adjustment and International Trade*. Edited by Gary Clyde Hufbauer and Howard Rosen. Washington: Institute for International Economics, forthcoming.

Keesing, David B., and Martin Wolf. 1980. *Textile Quotas Against Developing Countries*. Thames Essay 23. London: Trade Policy Research Centre.

Kindleberger, Charles P., and Peter H. Lindert. 1978. *International Economics*. 6th ed. Homewood, Ill.: Richard D. Irwin, Inc.

Kreinen, Mordechai E. 1970. "More on the Equivalence of Tariffs and Quotas." *Kyklos*, vol. 23: 75–79.

Krishna, K. 1985. "Trade Restrictions as Facilitating Practices." Working Paper 1546. Cambridge, Mass.: National Bureau of Economic Research, January.

Krueger, Anne O. 1974. "The Political Economy of the Rent-Seeking Society." *The American Economic Review*, vol. 64, no. 3 (June): 291–303.

Krugman, Paul. 1984. "Import Protection as Export Promotion: International Competition in the Presence of Oligopoly and Economies of Scale." In *Monopolistic Competition and International Trade*. Edited by H. Kierzkowski. Oxford: Oxford University Press.

Kwerel, Evan, and Alex D. Felker. 1985. "Using Auctions to Select FCC Licensees." Office of Plans and Policy Working Paper 16. Washington: Federal Communications Commission, May.

Lawrence, Robert Z., and Robert E. Litan. 1986. *Saving Free Trade.* Washington: Brookings Institution.

Leutwiler, Fritz, et al. 1985. *Trade Policies for a Better Future: Proposals for Action.* Independent Study Group. Geneva: General Agreement on Tariffs and Trade, March.

Litan, Robert E. 1986. Statement to the House Ways and Means Subcommittee on Trade. 99th Cong., 2d sess., 15 April. Washington.

Mangione, Peter. 1987. Statement to the House Ways and Means Subcommittee on Trade. 100th Cong., 1st sess., 27 February. Washington.

Marris, Stephen. 1985. *Deficits and the Dollar: The World Economy at Risk.* POLICY ANALYSES IN INTERNATIONAL ECONOMICS 14. Washington: Institute for International Economics, December.

Maskin, Eric S., and John G. Riley. 1985. "Open and Sealed-Bid Auctions: Auction Theory with Private Values." *The American Economic Review,* vol. 75, no. 2 (May): 150–55.

McCulloch, Rachel. 1973. "When Are a Tariff and a Quota Equivalent?" *Canadian Journal of Economics,* vol. 6, no. 4 (November): 503–11.

McCulloch, Rachel, and Harry G. Johnson. 1973. "A Note on Proportionally Distributed Quotas." *The American Economic Review,* vol. 63, no. 4 (September): 726–32.

McDonald, Stephen L. 1979. *The Leasing of Federal Lands for Fossil Fuels Production.* Baltimore, Md.: Johns Hopkins University Press for Resources for the Future.

Mead, Walter J. 1967. "Natural Resource Disposal Policy: Oral Auction versus Sealed Bids." *Natural Resources Journal,* vol. 7 (April): 194–224.

Mead, Walter J., Asbjorn Moseidjord, Dennis D. Muraoka, and Philip E. Sorensen. 1985. *Offshore Lands: Oil and Gas Leasing and Conservation on the Outer Continental Shelf.* San Francisco: Pacific Institute for Public Policy Research.

Mead, Walter J., Mark Schniepp, and Richard B. Watson. 1981. "The Effectiveness of Competition and Appraisals in the Auction Markets for National Forest Timber in the Pacific Northwest." Prepared for the US Forest Service, 30 September.

Miller, Edward M. 1972. "Oral and Sealed Bidding, Efficiency versus Equity." *Natural Resources Journal,* vol. 12 (July): 330–53.

Miller, James C. 1986. Letter to Chairman John C. Danforth, Senate Committee on Commerce, Science, and Transportation. Washington, 29 January.

Milosh, Eugene J. 1987. "Auctioning of World Trade." *Journal of Commerce,* 6 February, p. 15A.

Mintz, Ilse. 1973. *US Import Quotas: Costs and Consequences.* Washington: American Enterprise Institute.

Morkre, Morris E. 1984. *Import Quotas on Textiles: The Welfare Effects of United States Restrictions on Hong Kong.* Bureau of Economics Staff Report. Washington: Federal Trade Commission, August.

Muraoka, Dennis D., and Richard B. Watson. 1985. "Economic Issues in Federal Timber Sale Procedures." In *Forestlands: Public and Private.* Edited by Robert T. Deacon and M. Bruce Johnson. Cambridge, Mass.: Ballinger Publishing Company for the Pacific Institute for Public Policy Research.

Murray, Tracy, Wilson Schmidt, and Ingo Walter. 1978. "Alternative Forms of Protection Against Market Disruption." *Kyklos,* vol. 31: 624–37.

————. 1983. "On the Equivalence of Import Quotas and Voluntary Export Restraint." *Journal of International Economics*, vol. 14: 191–94.

Nogues, Julio J., Andrzej Olechowski, and L. Alan Winters. 1986. "The Extent of Nontariff Barriers to Industrial Countries' Imports." *The World Bank Economic Review*, vol. 1, no. 1: 181–99.

Office of Management and Budget. 1986. *Major Policy Initiatives, Fiscal Year 1987*. Washington: Executive Office of the President.

————. 1987a. *Budget of the United States Government, Fiscal Year 1988*. Washington: Executive Office of the President.

————. 1987b. *Budget of the United States Government, Fiscal Year 1988: Supplement*. Washington: Executive Office of the President.

Panagariya, Arvind. 1981. "Quantitative Restrictions in International Trade Under Monopoly." *Journal of International Economics*, vol. 11, no. 1 (February): 15–31.

Pastor, Robert A. 1980. *Congress and the Politics of US Foreign Economic Policy, 1929–76*. Berkeley: University of California Press.

Pearson, Charles. 1983. *Emergency Protection in the Footwear Industry*. Thames Essay 36. London: Trade Policy Research Centre.

Pelcovits, Michael D. 1976. "Quotas versus Tariffs." *Journal of International Economics*, vol. 6, no. 4 (November): 363–70.

Pomery, J. 1984. "Uncertainty in Trade Models." In *Handbook of International Economics*, vol. 1. Edited by Ronald W. Jones and Peter B. Kenen. Amsterdam: North-Holland.

Riley, John G., and William F. Samuelson. 1981. "Optimal Auctions." *The American Economic Review*, vol. 71, no. 3 (June): 381–92.

Rodriguez, C. 1974. "The Nonequivalence of Tariffs and Quotas under Retaliation." *Journal of International Economics*, vol. 4: 295–98.

————. 1979. "The Quality of Imports and the Differential Welfare Effects of Tariffs, Quotas, and Quality Controls as Protective Devices." *Canadian Journal of Economics*, vol. 12, no. 3: 439–49.

Santoni, G. J., and T. N. Van Cott. 1980. "Import Quotas: The Quality Adjustment Problem." *Southern Economic Journal*, vol. 46, no. 4: 1206–11.

Schniepp, Mark. 1985. "The Economic Consequences of the Setaside Program in the Douglas Fir Region of the Pacific Northwest." In *Forestlands: Public and Private*. Edited by Robert T. Deacon and M. Bruce Johnson. Cambridge, Mass.: Ballinger Publishing Company for the Pacific Institute for Public Policy Research.

Sherwell, Chris. 1986. "Canberra Unveils Plan to Cut Textile Tariffs." *Financial Times*, 3 December, p. 5.

Shibata, Hirofumi. 1968. "A Note on the Equivalence of Tariffs and Quotas." *The American Economic Review*, vol. 58, no. 1 (March): 137–42.

Smith, Vernon L. 1966. "Bidding Theory and the Treasury Bill Auction: Does Price Discrimination Increase Bill Prices?" *Review of Economics and Statistics*, vol. 48, no. 2 (May): 141–46.

Stokes, Bruce. 1987. "Selling Quotas." *National Journal*, 14 February, pp. 370–73.

Sweeney, Richard J., Edward Tower, and Thomas D. Willet. 1977. "The Ranking of Alternative Tariff and Quota Policies in the Presence of Domestic Monopoly." *Journal of International Economics*, vol. 7, no. 4 (November): 349–62.

Syntec Economic Services. 1984. "The Structure of Industry Assistance in New Zealand: An Exploratory Analysis." February. Processed.

Takacs, Wendy E. 1978. "The Nonequivalence of Tariffs, Import Quotas, and Voluntary Export Restraints." *Journal of International Economics,* vol. 8, no. 4 (November): 565–73.

Tompkins, Doug. 1987. Statement to the House Ways and Means Subcommittee on Trade. 100th Cong., 1st sess., 27 February. Washington.

Tumlir, Jan. 1985. *Protectionism.* Washington: American Enterprise Institute.

US Congress. 1978. *International Sugar Stabilization Act of 1978.* Conference Report to Accompany HR 13750. 95th Cong., 2d sess., 15 October.

———. House. Committee on Interior and Insular Affairs. Subcommittee on Mines and Mining. 1968. *Mandatory Oil Import Control Program: Its Impact upon the Domestic Minerals Industry and National Security.* Hearings, 90th Cong., 2d sess., 13, 14, 16 May.

———. Committee on Ways and Means. 1975. *The Energy Crisis and Proposed Solutions.* Panel discussions, 94th Cong., 1st sess., March.

———. 1979. *Trade Agreements Act of 1979.* 96th Cong., 1st sess., 3 July.

———. 1987a. *Overview and Compilation of US Trade Statutes.* 100th Cong, 1st sess., 6 January.

———. 1987b. *Trade and International Policy Reform Act of 1987* Report to Accompany HR 3., 6 April.

———. Subcommittee on Trade. 1979. *Oil Import Policy Issues.* 2 vols. Hearings, 96th Cong., 1st sess., 16, 17 July, 10 October.

———. 1987. *Trade Reform Legislation.* Hearings, 99th Cong., 2d sess., 20–21 March; 8, 10, 11, and 15–17 April 1986.

———. Senate. Committee on Finance. 1979. *Trade Agreements Act of 1979.* 96th Cong., 1st sess., 17 July.

———. 1987. *Omnibus Trade Act of 1987.* Report to Accompany S 490. 100th Cong., 1st sess., 12 June.

US Congressional Research Service. 1979. "Economic Effects of Oil Import Quota Proposals." Prepared by Lawrence C. Kumins. Washington, 28 November.

US Department of Commerce. 1976. *Historical Statistics of the United States.* Washington.

———. 1987a. *Statistical Abstract of the United States, 1987.* Washington.

———. 1987b. *US Industrial Outlook 1987.* Washington.

US International Trade Commission. 1977. *Sugar.* Publication 804. Washington, March.

———. 1979. *Stainless Steel and Alloy Tool Steel.* Publication 968. Washington, April.

———. 1982. *Sugar.* Publication 1253. Washington, June.

———. 1984. *Carbon and Certain Alloy Steel Products.* Publication 1553. Washington, July.

———. 1985. *Nonrubber Footwear.* Publication 1717. Washington, July.

———. 1987. *Monthly Reports on the Status of the Steel Industry.* Publication 1946. Washington, February.

Walter, Ingo. 1971. "On the Equivalence of Tariffs and Quotas: A Comment." *Kyklos,* vol. 24: 111–12.

Yeutter, Clayton K. 1986. Statement to the Subcommitee on Trade, House Ways and Means Committee. 99th Cong., 2d sess., 8 April.

American Trade Politics: System Under Stress
I.M. Destler/1986

The Future of World Trade in Textiles and Apparel
William R. Cline/1987

Capital Flight and Third World Debt
Donald R. Lessard and John Williamson, editors/1987

SPECIAL REPORTS SERIES

1   **Promoting World Recovery: A Statement on Global Economics Strategy** *by Twenty-six Economists from Fourteen Countries*/December 1982

2   **Prospects for Adjustment in Argentina, Brazil, and Mexico: Responding to the Debt Crisis**
John Williamson, editor/June 1983

3   **Inflation and Indexation: Argentina, Brazil, and Israel**
John Williamson, editor/March 1985

4   **Global Economic Imbalances**
C. Fred Bergsten, editor/March 1986

5   **African Debt and Financing**
Carol Lancaster and John Williamson, editors/May 1986

FORTHCOMING

The United States as a Debtor Country
C. Fred Bergsten and Shafiqul Islam

Domestic Adjustment and International Trade
Gary Clyde Hufbauer and Howard F. Rosen, editors

Japan in the World Economy
Bela Balassa and Marcus Noland

World Economic Problems
John Williamson and Kimberly Ann Elliott, editors

Correcting the United States Trade Deficit: The Global Impact
William R. Cline and Stephen Marris

Energy Policies for the 1990s: A Global Perspective
Philip K. Verleger, Jr.

The Outlook for World Commodity Prices
Philip K. Verleger, Jr.